MW00387908

Praise for the Third Edition of *The Detroit Tigers*

"An entertaining and well-researched study. . . . A delight to hold and read. . . . Many notches above the cartloads of sports schlock being published today."
—*Library Journal*

"Detroit fans will cherish this book. . . . A very attractive volume.
—*Sporting News*

"Luxurious. . . . A fine, detailed history of the Tigers."
—Bob Burns, *Grand Rapids Press*

"We remember the summers of our youth, the sounds of the game taking us over the airwaves to Tiger Stadium and beyond. Time has marched on but because pictures can freeze time, we can go home again. Bill Anderson's book goes to the heart of Tigers history as it will to the hearts of Tigers fans."
—Ernie Harwell

"The book is a gem, the most comprehensive photographic history of the Tigers ever published."
—Lloyd Wallace, *Ludington Daily News*

"Bill Anderson, one of Michigan's premier authorities on the history of Detroit Tigers baseball, has topped his previous masterpiece on this subject with another marvelous collection of carefully selected photographs and an accurate summary history of big league baseball in the Motor City. All the great diamond heroes of Detroit's past plus more than a few lesser known Tigers players are brought to life in the pages of this book. This volume is a 'must' for the library of any fan of Tigers baseball or of the game in general."
—Marc Okkonen, author of *Baseball Uniforms of the 20th Century* and the Baseball Memories series

The Detroit Tigers

Great Lakes Books

A complete listing of the books in this series can be found online at wsupress.wayne.edu

Editors

Philip P. Mason
Wayne State University

Charles K. Hyde
Wayne State University

Advisory Editors

Jeffrey Abt
Wayne State University

Sandra Sageser Clark
Michigan Historical Center

John C. Dann
Dexter, Michigan

De Witt Dykes
Oakland University

Joe Grimm
Detroit Free Press

Richard H. Harms
Calvin College

Laurie Harris
Pleasant Ridge, Michigan

Susan Higman Larsen
Detroit Institute of Arts

Dennis Moore
Consulate General of Canada

William H. Mulligan Jr.
Murray State University

Erik C. Nordberg
Michigan Technological University

Gordon L. Olson
Grand Rapids, Michigan

Deborah Smith Pollard
University of Michigan–Dearborn

David Roberts
Toronto, Ontario

Michael O. Smith
Wayne State University

Michael D. Stafford
Cranbrook Institute of Science

Arthur M. Woodford
Harsens Island, Michigan

The Detroit
TIGERS

A PICTORIAL CELEBRATION OF THE GREATEST PLAYERS
AND MOMENTS IN TIGERS HISTORY

FOURTH EDITION

WILLIAM M. ANDERSON

WITH A FOREWORD BY DAVID DOMBROWSKI

Wayne State University Press
Detroit

Fourth edition © 2008 by Wayne State University Press,
Detroit, Michigan 48201. All rights reserved.
No part of this book may be reproduced without formal permission.
Manufactured in the United States of America.
12 11 10 09 08   5 4 3 2 1

Library of Congress Cataloging-in-Publication Data

Anderson, William M. (William Martin), 1938–
The Detroit Tigers : a pictorial celebration of the greatest players and moments in Tigers history /
William M. Anderson ; with a foreword by David Dombrowski. — 4th ed.
p. cm. — (Great Lakes books)
Includes index.
ISBN-13: 978-0-8143-3414-0 (cloth : alk. paper)
ISBN-10: 0-8143-3414-8 (cloth : alk. paper)
1. Detroit Tigers (Baseball team)—History. 2. Detroit Tigers (Baseball team)—History—Pictorial works.
I. Title.
GV875.D6A54 2008
796.357'640977434—dc22

Publication of this book was made possible through the generosity of the Ford R. Bryan Publication Fund.

Designed by Brad Norr Design
Typeset by Maya Rhodes
Composed in Caslon 540 and Futura

Contents

Foreword

A picture. A moment frozen in time captured with the push of a button. The image that results can come to life and take a person back through time. In the mind's eye, the image not only captures the moment, but it can conjure up the sounds, the smells, the sense of place, and the people who made that event so special.

On October 4, 2006, Magglio Ordonez stepped to the plate in the bottom of the ninth inning of a 3–3 tie with the Oakland Athletics in game four of the American League Championship Series. With one swing of the bat on that cold October night, he created a moment, a snapshot, that Detroit baseball fans had been waiting for since 1984. One swing of the bat resulted in a majestic home run and put the Tigers back in the World Series. One swing, frozen in time, lifted the spirits of a city and state and restored the pride of a franchise for the world to see.

When Bill Anderson contacted me and asked me to contribute the foreword to the fourth edition of *The Detroit Tigers: A Pictorial Celebration of the Greatest Players and Moments in Tigers History*, I was honored. This edition of this magnificent work includes the 1999 season, the final one played upon the hallowed grounds at the corner of Michigan and Trumbull in Tiger Stadium. It transitions into the twenty-first century and the move into Comerica Park, the new home of the Tigers in downtown Detroit.

The Detroit Tigers have a history and tradition that rivals any in professional sports. Our classic home uniform and the Old English "D" on our caps are recognized as icons of our city and our team. Star players have graced our playing fields and live on in our imagination through efforts like this fine book. The list of Tigers in the National Baseball Hall of Fame reads like a who's who of our national pastime and includes Ty Cobb, Mickey Cochrane, Sam Crawford, Charlie Gehringer, Hank Greenberg, Harry Heilmann, Hughie Jennings, Al Kaline, George Kell, Heinie Manush, and Hal Newhouser.

Our heritage includes world championships in 1935, 1945, 1968, and 1984. The American League pennant has called Detroit home in 1907, 1908, 1909, 1934, 1940, and 2006.

Detroit is a blue-collar city. In 2006, Jim Leyland implored our team to go to work each day and play nine hard innings. This new generation of Tigers heard his message loud and clear. With the same mentality this city takes to work each day, the Tigers clawed their way back to the top of the American League and are poised to remain a championship contender for years to come.

The future is bright. However, we should never forget the moments in our past that have elevated us to emotional highs, created fond memories, and brought families and friends together to rally for a common goal. Turning the pages of this book allows us to travel through the years. From Bennett Park to Navin Field, Briggs Stadium, and Tiger Stadium and now Comerica Park, we cheer for our team, for our players, the Detroit Tigers.

DAVID DOMBROWSKI

Preface to the Fourth Edition

Tradition has an inescapable influence on this franchise, and despite dramatic changes in major league baseball it continues to shape the culture of the organization. Nowhere is that dominant influence expressed more forcefully than in the team's uniform and its dedication to the Old English "D." To see this team wearing a uniform shirt resembling a softball team is unfathomable. The organization has, of course, embraced the assets of technology, yet is very difficult to conceive of an exploding scoreboard at its ballpark. Like society, baseball has become more liberal; however, the Tigers certainly have a code of conduct and have little patience for deviant behavior.

This pictorial history of the team has enjoyed a remarkable life. The first edition, published by Diamond Communications, appeared in 1991 and presented the team's history through 1990. Wayne State University Press published the second edition in 1999, extending the club's history through the 1998 season. In 2005, Easton Press issued a collector's edition of the history. In preparing the fourth edition, I am constantly reminded of the historic events that have occurred in the years since the close of the 1998 season—the final season at Tiger Stadium and the treasured memories associated with that ballpark, the opening of Comerica Park, the resurgence of a team featuring a cadre of star players, and the first no-hitter at home in more than fifty years.

The intervening years also remind us of how challenging it is to rebuild a major league ball team. Over the past fifteen years or so, the Tigers endured periods in which losing seasons were the norm; they were once even the laughingstock of baseball after nearly setting the all-time record for losses in a season. With few exceptions, teams in the current environment must invest heavily in the free-agent market to stay competitive. The Tigers learned that even generous offers could not lure quality players to an inept team. Despite the new dynamics of the game, some influences never change. Breaks even out but injuries do not. Injuries to key players can derail a great team. Connie Mack said that pitching was 85 percent of the game, and that truth has not diminished. In their remarkable 2006 season, the Tigers had the best pitching staff in baseball and remained healthy. But in 2007, with an even more potent offense, injuries undermined both the starting rotation and what had been an outstanding bullpen.

Naturally, each edition of this history adds a new chapter, and I consistently aim to refresh the face of the book with different photographs—this one introduces well over 300 new images. I spent a lot of time searching for high-quality photographs. A pictorial history could be more of the same without the great support of many individuals and organizations. There is always a shorter list of people who have played a vital role in making images available, and for this volume it includes Mel Bailey, Ray Billbrough, Dianne Chapman, Mark Cunningham, Mike Litaker, and Mark Patrick, Burton Historical Collection, Detroit Public Library; Rick Thompson, Detroit Tigers; Richard Vettese, Grand Rapids History and Special Collections, Grand Rapids Public

Library; and Lloyd Wallace and Pat Zacharias, *Detroit News.* I also owe thanks to Sharon Arend, Detroit Tigers Archives; Ryan Alexander, West Michigan Whitecaps; Mary Brace, Brace Photo; Christina Branham, Elizabeth Clemens, Walter P. Reuther Library, Wayne State University; Greg Gania, Erie Sea Wolves, *Detroit Free Press;* Jason Griffin, Toledo Mud Hens; Mark Harvey, Michigan State Archives; James Hawver, Library of Congress; Jan Lovell, *Detroit News;* Andrew Miller, National Baseball Hall of Fame; Russ Miller, Sam Nader, Oneonta Tigers; Ron Rossi, Mark Rucker, Transcendental Graphics; Jeremy Strout, Lakeland Tigers; and Neva Weidig.

I am greatly indebted to Dave Dombrowski, president, general manager, and chief executive officer of the Detroit Tigers, for writing an insightful foreword.

I am also indebted to the Wayne State University Press team that managed the copyediting, design, and production of the composition and photographs for this new edition. Collectively, Jane Hoehner, Kristin Harpster Lawrence, Jennifer Backer, and Maya Rhodes have greatly contributed to this team effort.

A spouse is a true partner in so many respects, and for a writer that supportive relationship cannot be adequately measured or recognized. Anna Marie's understanding of my passions is a great gift. Although her work here is not evident, she contributed to this edition in many helpful ways. Thank you.

WILLIAM M. ANDERSON

Recreation Park, July 4, 1887, home of the Detroits during their eight-year membership in the National League, 1881–88. The Detroits are in the field in this championship season photo. Located on Brady Street between Beaubien and Brush Streets, Recreation Park could seat 5,000 fans. (State Archives of Michigan)

1
Early Beginnings
1881–1900

The grand tradition of baseball was in its infancy in 1881 when the major league game was first played in Detroit. The rudiments of the game were the same—nine players on a team, nine innings in a game, and three outs in an inning. But there were differences, too. Teams carried only 15 players, two or three of whom were pitchers who were expected to go the distance. Hitters could call for a high or low ball, depending on their preference. And, as in sandlot baseball, players were versatile. In 1884, when Detroit was a member of the National League, George "Stump" Weidman, a pitcher, played 53 games in the outfield, one game at shortstop, another at second base, and he pitched in 26 games. The winningest pitcher in Detroit's National League history, Weidman was also a 20-game loser four successive seasons for the team.

The drive to launch a baseball enterprise in Detroit was initiated by Mayor William H. Thompson in 1880. The team was sanctioned by the National League and began play in 1881.

Baseball teams of the 1880s were fledgling and transitory. During Detroit's eight-year membership in the league, 13 different clubs came and went over a five-year span.

Characteristically, many players were known by nicknames, their given names suppressed from all but official records. Even the records and recollections on some players have faded through time. Two Detroit players, Bryant and Lowe, are known only by their last names. Lowe was a catcher with the

The 1887 world champion Detroits. *Left to right, back row:* Charlie Bennett, Dan Brouthers, Sam Thompson, Charlie Ganzel, Larry Twitchell, Charles Baldwin. *Middle row:* Jack Rowe, Charles Briody, Fred Dunlap, William Watkins, James White, Ned Hanlon, Bill Shindle, Charles Getzein. *Front row:* George Weidman, Hardy Richardson. (State Archives of Michigan)

team in 1884, and Bryant was an infielder in 1885.

When the team began, it lacked a sobriquet, being known simply as "The Detroits." Organized and managed by Frank "Banny" Bancroft, the team set up shop (in 1881) at a downtown cigar store at the corner of Woodward and Jefferson Avenues. It wasn't until 1884, however, that the business was listed in the city directory.

The nucleus of the first team was recruited from other professional teams; most of the players had major league experience. Games were played at Recreation Park, a bandbox facility with an amateurish-sounding name that featured permanent billboard fences and a grandstand likely patterned after those constructed at local fairgrounds.

The Detroits were hardly the scrapping, snarling Tigers of later years. How could they be with an ace pitcher called "Lady" Baldwin and a world championship team dethroned, in part, by overindulging in social activity?

And yet, a unique baseball culture was introduced, befitting a nineteenth-century America and a little western town of 116,000 residents. Reports of this infant major league team began appearing in the *Detroit Evening News*, a four-page daily with no Sunday edition and no sports page. The Detroits were working out against amateur teams, getting ready for their first season in the National League. They traveled to Ann Arbor to play the University of Michigan, and a team from Kalamazoo played a warm-up game in Detroit. On April 23, 1881, the *Evening News* reported that an outfielder named Reilly had run a rusty nail into his foot. A later edition related the donation of a trunk to carry the uniforms; it was hoped, of course, that the new uniforms would arrive in time for the season opener.

In 1881, the National League was made up of Boston, Buffalo, Detroit, Chicago, Cleveland, Providence, Troy, and Worchester, with the teams from

Considered a "nervy catcher" and "good-natured chap," Charlie Bennett was an early Detroit baseball hero. He was the principal catcher in Detroit's National League history. His first three seasons were his best; he hit above .300 in each. After Detroit's franchise folded in 1888, Bennett joined Boston and had his career abruptly ended with a terrible accident, requiring two leg amputations. The Tigers' first ball field was named Bennett Park in his honor. (Transcendental Graphics)

A lifetime .300 hitter, James "Deacon" White played third base during the glory years of Detroit's nineteenth-century National League history. One of the famed "Big Four" acquired from Buffalo, White hit .303 for the Detroits in its championship season. (William M. Anderson)

In those days, an entertainment business like baseball could not expect to attract ladies unless it provided restricted seating free from the rowdiness and vulgarities of the crowd. Physical improvements were soon undertaken, including the construction of a new section of grandstand to be reserved for ladies and gentlemen accompanying ladies.

On their first eastern trip, Detroit mixed in exhibition games with non-league teams.

The Detroits completed a respectable first season, finishing fourth in the standings with a winning percentage of .488 on the strength of 41 wins and 43 losses. First baseman Marty Powell was second in the league in hitting at .338, and star catcher Charlie Bennett took runner-up honors in home runs with seven, an impressive total in the dead-ball era. George Derby was a dominant pitcher, ranking among the leaders in several categories and chalking

Among nineteenth-century ballplayers, Dan Brouthers at 6' 2" was considered a big man and he swung a big stick. Brouthers played first base for the Detroits in 1886–88. During his 19-year major league career, he hit over 300 for 16 consecutive years and won the batting title five times. He joined the baseball elite in Cooperstown in 1945. (William M. Anderson)

Principally an outfielder, Jim Manning saw limited action during three seasons with Detroit, 1885–87. In 1901, he piloted the Washington franchise in the inaugural year of the American League. (William M. Anderson)

Massachusetts and New York making up half of the league.

Detroit's first major league season began with a home opener at 4 p.m. on May 2, 1881, with 1,286 in attendance. The locals played gamely and, despite a dramatic ninth-inning home run, lost to Buffalo, 6–5.

Charles "Lady" Baldwin had an incredible year in 1886. Despite pitching in an era when starting pitchers were expected to go the distance, Baldwin started 56 games, completed 55, and racked up an amazing record of 42 wins and 13 defeats. (William M. Anderson)

up 29 wins. There were many player transactions this first season as management sought a winning combination. Lost in the shuffle was pitcher Will White, who lost his only two decisions with Detroit. Discarded to Cincinnati, he won 82 games in the next two seasons.

The 1882 Detroits played .500 ball and finished closer to the top, but then began a three-year slide into the league's cellar. Led by outfielder George Wood, Detroit tied for league leadership in 1882 with 20 homers. That same year, two workhorse pitchers, Derby and Weidman, accounted for every team decision except one.

In 1883 and 1884, the team finished deep in the second division, occupying the seventh and eighth rungs. In those years, the Detroits led only in futility; 1884 produced the worst season in Detroit his-

Edward "Ned" Hanlon was a mainstay in the outfield during Detroit's eight-year history in the National League. He went on to achieve an outstanding record as a manager. During a seven-year period (1894–1900), Hanlon's teams won five pennants. One of his star players was Hugh Jennings. Hanlon's illustrious career finally earned him election to the Hall of Fame in 1996. (William M. Anderson)

tory, 28 wins and 84 losses, equating to a miserable .250 winning percentage. The 1884 squad finished seven games out of seventh place, hit a paltry .208, and its most effective pitcher compiled a 9–18 record.

The 1885 team advanced to sixth place in the standings, yet still finished 16 games below .500. Without draft picks and farm systems, nineteenth-century teams had limited sources for new talent. But Detroit management was learning. During and after the close of the 1885 season, they became aggressive and shrewd buyers of quality personnel and their purchases in a single year were astonishing.

Charlie Getzein was a star pitcher for the Detroits, averaging 19 wins a season during his tenure with the club, 1884–88. When Detroit disbanded after the 1888 season, he was acquired by Indianapolis. (William M. Anderson)

Another member of the famous "Big Four," Hardy Richardson was considered a utility man because of his versatility. Richardson had a career-high .351 batting average while playing for Detroit. (Ray Billbrough)

acquiring star outfielder Sam Thompson and Indianapolis manager William "Wattie" Watkins.

The revamped Detroits unleashed a talent-laden team, carrying its flag through two remarkable seasons in the big time. Among 11 offensive categories in 1886, Brouthers and Richardson led in six. As a team, the Detroits captured league honors in hitting (.280), home runs (54), fielding percentage (.928), and complete games pitched (122). Star hurler Charles "Lady" Baldwin pitched brilliantly, winning 42 games, but even all this failed to produce

When Buffalo disbanded, Detroit acquired its four stars, which included shortstop Jack Rowe. Rowe was primarily a catcher when he started his career but then made the switch to shortstop. He batted .286 in 11 seasons. (Courtesy of the Burton Historical Collection of the Detroit Public Library)

The big jackpot included Dan Brouthers, two-time batting champion; Jack Rowe, a .289 career hitter; Deacon White, who had six .300-plus seasons to his credit; and Hardy Richardson, who carried a .292 lifetime batting average. The "Big Four," as they were known, represented a total infield transplant as Detroit purchased these star players from a disbanding Buffalo franchise. This acquisition followed an earlier purchase of the entire Indianapolis club. Apparently Detroit bought the whole lot as a means of

When Sam Crane joined Detroit in 1885 as a player, he had already experienced two stints as a manager in the National League. In the parlance of the time, Crane was designated a substitute. (William M. Anderson)

Brimming with confidence, owner Fred Stearns challenged his St. Louis counterpart "to a series of contests for supremacy" of the baseball world. The American Association was the rival big league in 1887, and St. Louis had repeated as AA champs. The two baseball heavyweights agreed to play a 15-game marathon "World Series." The series resembled a grand tour, with games being played in Pittsburgh, Brooklyn, New York, Philadelphia, Boston,

Detroit purchased the entire Indianapolis team in order to land star outfielder Sam Thompson in 1885. Thompson, who would later be selected for the Hall of Fame, accumulated a .331 lifetime batting average. He was the big offensive gun on the 1887 Detroit championship team, hitting .372 and knocking in 166 runs. (Detroit Free Press)

a pennant as Chicago topped runner-up Detroit by two and a half games. This team won 71 percent of its games, the best ever in the organization's history in both the National and American Leagues.

Carried by the lusty hitting of Thompson and company, Detroit swept the field aside en route to a championship season in 1887. Thompson paced the league with a .372 average and led in runs batted in, slugging average, and total bases. The team led in batting with a .299 mark, runs scored, and slugging. In total bases, Thompson, Brouthers, and Richardson were first, second, and third. Manager Watkins utilized five pitchers, with Charlie "Pretzels" Getzein winning 29 games, giving him 59 victories in two campaigns. All but two of the nine All Stars selected by Spalding were members of the Detroit Baseball Club. Detroit's representatives included Charlie Bennett, Fred Dunlap, Charlie Getzein, Ned Hanlon, Hardy Richardson, Jack Rowe, and Sam Thompson. Richardson was selected as an outfielder though he split the second-base duties with Dunlap.

Looking more like a ballet dancer or magician, pitcher George "Stump" Weidman was Detroit's number one hurler in 1882 and 1883. (Courtesy of the Burton Historical Collection of the Detroit Public Library)

Charles "Fatty" Briody caught for Detroit in 1887. (Courtesy of the Burton Historical Collection of the Detroit Public Library)

Washington, Baltimore, Chicago, and, of course, Detroit and St. Louis. One day the two teams played a game in Washington, D.C., in the morning and a second in the afternoon in Baltimore. The reigning champions hosted the series opener on October 10, 1887, and beat Detroit, 6–1, but that was the last time the Browns were in command. After 11 games, Detroit had the needed eight victories and the world championship. Again typical of the era, the teams played the remaining games.

Fortune was cruel to the 1888 Detroits. They were hit with an array of prolonged injuries to key players, and plagued with internal dissension and an inability to cope with their success. Although leading the league in hitting, Detroit slumped badly in over-

all offensive production. They completed their last National League season in the second division. At 68–63, they finished 16 games off the pace of the pennant winners and barely above the .500 mark.

A combination of factors—expensive veteran players, a relatively small city that limited attendance, and the anticipation of labor strife—influenced the demise of the Detroit Baseball Club. Like Buffalo had done three years earlier, management sold off its star players and then disbanded the franchise.

Glory is a fleeting intangible. In eight short seasons, Detroit baseball had started, spurted, and dissolved.

Fred "Sure Shot" Dunlap was the regular second baseman in the 1887 lineup. He was the premier player in the Union Association League in 1884 when he batted .412. (Courtesy of the Burton Historical Collection of the Detroit Public Library)

Ty Cobb is the most dominant player in franchise history. No other Tiger player totally defined an era. Cobb is the seventh player (*left to right*) in the middle row. He joined the team during the summer of 1905. *Back row, left to right:* Bill Donovan, George Disch, Chris Lindsay, Tom Doran, Matty McIntyre, John Eubanks, George Mullin. *Middle row:* Bobby Lowe, Lew Drill, Ed Killian, Sam Crawford, Bill Armour, Jimmy Wiggs, Ty Cobb, Jimmy Barrett, Charley O'Leary. *Front row:* Frank Kitson, Jack Warner, Bill Coughlin, Germany Schaefer. (Brace Photo)

2
Detroit Unleashes a Tiger
1901–1910

After Detroit left the National League, 13 years passed before major league baseball returned to Detroit. In the interim, the city's professional teams played briefly in the old International Association and then, in 1894, Detroit aligned with baseball pioneer Ban Johnson as a charter member of the Western League. That association provided the opportunity for reentering major league baseball seven years later.

In 1900, Johnson, president of the Western League, was laying the foundation for his dreams as he changed the organization's name to American League, seeking to give it a more national perspective and appeal. The door for the opportunistic

Johnson and his visionary compatriot, Charles Comiskey, swung open when the National League chose to reduce its ranks from 12 to its original eight teams. Johnson promptly abandoned Grand Rapids in favor of the now available Cleveland site, and Charles Comiskey shifted his St. Paul team to Chicago's south side. The compression of the senior circuit also released numerous players with big league experience. Owners of aspiring American League teams quickly signed many of these available big leaguers.

Naturally, the architect of the new American League wanted to anchor his ambition in major cities and the strongest markets. Detroit's place in the grand scheme was far from secure as Johnson dumped Kansas City, Indianapolis, Minnesota, and Buffalo in preference for Philadelphia, Washington, Baltimore, and Boston. Detroit's earlier voluntary withdrawal from major league competition and its poor attendance record continued to weaken its chances for admission.

Detroit survived this turbulent time of transition to become an original member of the newly founded American League, which was seeking recognition as a full-fledged member of the major league baseball fraternity. Along with the new eastern clubs, Detroit

The Tigers' first American League pennant-winning team poses for posterity at Bennett Park, 1907. *Left to right, back row:* Ty Cobb, Ed Seiver, Claude Rossman, Wild Bill Donovan, Sam Crawford, Jerome Downs, Fred Payne, Bobby Lowe. *Middle row:* Jimmy Archer, Hugh Jennings, Charles Schmidt, Elijah Jones. *Front row:* Ed Killian, Germany Schaefer, Bill Coughlin, Davy Jones, Charlie O'Leary. (Ray Billbrough)

Ty Cobb examines the bat of hitting rival Napoleon Lajoie in 1909. Lajoie won three batting crowns before Cobb joined the Tigers. He made only one more serious bid for the honor in 1910, when Cobb won a highly disputed batting championship. (Courtesy of the Burton Historical Collection of the Detroit Public Library)

One of the early stars in Tiger history, outfielder Jimmy Barrett hit .292 in five seasons (1901–5) with Detroit. He was also among the league leaders in coaxing free passes to first base. In a stretch of four seasons in Detroit, he averaged 75 walks a year. (Courtesy of the Burton Historical Collection of the Detroit Public Library)

joined holdover teams located in Chicago, Cleveland, and Milwaukee.

Among Detroit's inheritance from its minor league association were at least nine members of its 1900 team, plus manager George "Tweedy" Stallings and the nickname Tigers. Unlike the name Tigers, which stuck, the nicknames of many other franchises changed frequently before tradition took root. Apparently credit for introducing Detroit's nickname goes to an unidentified *Detroit Free Press* writer who first referred to the team as Tigers in 1895.

Detroit's first American League team was stocked with several experienced big league players, and the competition started in 1901 with similar strengths and weaknesses. Among key personnel were William "Kid" Gleason, a former pitcher with 138 recorded wins, now converted to second base; Norman "Kid" Elberfeld, a highly regarded young shortstop; and Jimmy Barrett, who had demonstrated impressive hitting in his first two seasons with Cincinnati. Despite these bright spots, this was still an expansion club in an expansion league.

The greatest baseball photograph? Photographer Charles Conlon considered it his best shot. Ty Cobb slashes into third base to beat the tag of New York Highlander Jimmy Austin in a 1910 game. As Conlon recalled, "Ty Cobb was on second base, restless as always. I took my stand about fifteen feet from third, so I could get a good view of Cobb . . . and then Ty, edging far off second, lowered his head and came tearing like a greyhound for third base." (Courtesy of the Burton Historical Collection of the Detroit Public Library)

Sam Crawford's first year with the Tigers, 1903. *Left to right, back row:* Joe Yeager, Clements, Charles Carr. *Third row:* Ed Barrow (manager), Fred Buelow, Frank Kitson, Charles Kissinger, Doc Gessler, John Deering. *Second row:* Simon Nicholls, Heinie Smith, Sam Crawford, Mel Eason, Lillie, Kid Elberfeld. *Front row:* John Burns, Sport McAllister, Wild Bill Donovan, Jimmy Barrett, George Mullin. The first names of Clements and Lillie are unknown. (Brace Photo)

The Tigers, owned by Wayne County sheriff James Burns and Manager Stallings, played their home games at two ballparks: weekdays and Saturdays at Bennett Park and Sundays at Burns Park. The team played at Burns Park because Detroit's blue laws prohibited professional baseball on the Christian Sabbath, and Burns Park was just outside the city's western limits.

The inaugural game was packed with high drama and a fairy-tale ending as an overflow crowd of 10,000 encircled the diamond and anxious fans stood in the outfield. Trailing Milwaukee, 13–4, as they came to bat in the bottom of the ninth, "Casey" did not strike out. Rallying behind the clutch hitting of Frank Dillon, who doubled twice in the inning, Detroit scored 10 runs to win, 14–13.

Stallings led the Tigers to a respectable first-division finish, fourth in the standings, but his managerial tenure in the American League was over. His wild antics on the bench, a running feud with co-owner Burns, and an indiscreet proposal to transfer the Tigers to the National League made him a first-campaign casualty.

During this tenuous and shaky beginning, league president Johnson exercised autocratic control, ousting Burns in a clean sweep of Tiger ownership and engineering the sale of the team to insurance man Samuel F. Angus. Johnson kept his heel squarely in the middle of team management by demanding possession of 51 percent of the stock of each organization.

Frank Dwyer, former player and umpire, succeeded Stallings as Tiger field boss in 1902, in a less-than-mediocre season. Compiling the league's

Shortstop Donie Bush has just snagged a ground ball in a 1912 game at Bennett Park. Bush broke into organized baseball with Saginaw in the Southern Michigan League. He made his entry into major league baseball with the Tigers in 1908. The following season he became the regular shortstop, where he played through most of 1921. A slick fielder, Bush believed that "the hardest play the shortstop makes is fielding a slow roller that comes right at him and looks so easy." (William M. Anderson)

A .366 career hitter, Ty Cobb had amazing bat control and a mind faster than that of most of his would-be peers. Manager Hughie Jennings said of him, "You cannot harness a genius and Cobb is a genius." (Library of Congress)

worst batting average netted Detroit a seventh-place finish, 30 1/2 games behind the winner. Ed Siever's 8–11 win-loss record represented the best by an inept pitching staff.

The baseball civil war between the American and National Leagues continued to heat up in 1902, with frequent AL sorties on National League players. Johnson also strategically shifted the Baltimore franchise to New York and yearned to stake a claim in Pittsburgh. Finally, peace was restored at a meeting in Cincinnati in January 1903. The agreement was a major victory for the junior circuit, Johnson winning major league recognition for his teams, the right to remain in New York provided that he stay out of Pittsburgh, and subsequent rights to a majority of the players in contention. Throughout the later stages of the hot war, Detroit's security was

While the upstart American League challenged National League supremacy, Detroit snared its first big star in Sam Crawford. Wahoo Sam became a Tiger in 1903 and batted .308 over 15 seasons. He batted a career-high .378 in 1911. (Library of Congress)

Hugh Jennings (*left*) became the Tigers manager in 1907 and immediately led them to their first American League pennant. A member of the National Baseball Hall of Fame, he made his mark both as a player with the old Baltimore Orioles and as Tiger manager. Detroit purchased third baseman Bill Coughlin (*right*) from the financially bankrupt Washington club for $8,000, a hefty price in 1904. Although he never came close to his .301 batting average in 1902, Coughlin played regularly for the Tigers during his last four seasons in the majors. (William M. Anderson)

threatened by Johnson's ambition for a Pittsburgh base. The peace treaty ensured the Tigers' immediate future. Their stability and development, however, would determine their longer existence.

The introduction of Frank Navin during the first decade of modern baseball history laid the foundation for this highly successful Detroit franchise. Beginning as a bookkeeper and trusted assistant to owner Angus, Navin learned baseball management in the behind-the-scenes vineyard. His formal legal and business education and superior ability at poker undoubtedly influenced his systematic, calculating, and unemotional management style. "Old Poker Face" acquired increasing shares of team stock, ulti-

First baseman Frank Dillon played only one full season for Detroit but was in the starting lineup for their first game in American League history on April 24, 1901. That day he set a major league record that still stands, rapping four two-base hits. (Courtesy of the Burton Historical Collection of the Detroit Public Library)

Hard-throwing Wild Bill Donovan pitched in Detroit for 11 seasons, 1902–12. He achieved the league's best record in 1907, winning 24 and losing only four. In 1903, he started 34 games and completed every one. (William M. Anderson)

Kid Elberfeld teamed with Kid Gleason to give Detroit an exceptional keystone combination in 1901. "The Tabasco Kid" was a fiery, pint-sized shortstop who hit .310 in his first year with the Tigers. He got caught up in the intraleague wars, but ended up playing for the New York Highlanders in the American League in 1903. (Courtesy of the Burton Historical Collection of the Detroit Public Library)

Another of the original Detroit Tigers, William "Kid" Gleason brought 13 years of major league experience to the new franchise. He was the regular second baseman for Detroit during its first two seasons in the American League. A longtime baseball veteran, Gleason started as a pitcher, winning 35 games in 1890 for Philadelphia and later served as manager of the 1919 Chicago Black Sox. (Courtesy of the Burton Historical Collection of the Detroit Public Library)

mately owning half of the club and becoming president of the organization with a ballpark named Navin Field. Like many powerful leaders, Navin demonstrated contrasting behavior: frugality with the ball club yet passion for horses and gambling.

Among the tribute extracted from the National League during the baseball war were two superb players: Sam "Wahoo" Crawford and Bill Donovan, both signed by the Tigers. Named for his birthplace of Wahoo, Nebraska, Crawford was familiar with Detroit, having played for Grand Rapids in the old Western League. Contemporary baseball scribes compared his awesome power to that of Babe Ruth, contending that only a dead ball prohibited similar home run records. Like most, Donovan, too, had an inseparable nickname—he was called "Wild Bill,"

largely because he could not control his pitches when he broke into organized baseball. This pair seeded the beginning nucleus of an outstanding Detroit team.

Frank Dwyer made his exit after one season and Angus named pitcher Win Mercer to lead the team. In an unexplained twist of fate, the 28-year-old hurler took his own life during the off-season. The fourth Tiger manager in three seasons was Edward G. Barrow, who was deep in experience despite his relative youth. Though still not a .500 ball club, the Tigers advanced to fifth in the standings in 1903.

Newcomers contributed greatly, with Crawford hitting a robust .335, second best in the league, and Donovan winning 17 games. Second-year pitcher George Mullin chipped in with 19 victories. Between seasons Ban Johnson again handled the sale of the Tigers, transferring ownership from Angus to young William Hoover Yawkey. Both Navin and Barrow acquired a small interest in the team.

Barrow broke precedent, continuing as manager for the 1904 season; but his team played badly, losing 90 games, good for seventh place and a distant 32 games from the top. Pitching and hitting failed. The hitters in particular went on vacation, with the team collecting only nine home runs. Pitcher Mullin had the leading batting average with .298. Halfway through the campaign, Barrow resigned and second baseman Bobby Lowe finished up the season. Barrow went on to achieve great success with the Boston Red Sox and New York Yankees and ultimately earned selection to the Baseball Hall of Fame.

Next in the succession of managers was Bill Armour, who had recently been dropped by Cleveland. Although he managed for just one season, his year was very eventful. The 1905 Tigers climbed back into third position. Crawford regained his form and ranked among the better hitters in several categories, and the pitching was especially impressive: Ed Killian won 22, Mullin 21, and Donovan 19.

Herman "Germany" Schaefer joined the Tiger cast in 1905 and, although lacking great playing skills, he brought cohesive value to the team and became a major attraction for spectators. Blessed with original humor, Schaefer made the baseball diamond his stage—Germany's routines were legendary. His stunt of stealing bases in reverse caused a new rule

Hugh Ambrose Jennings, inspirational leader of the hard-charging Detroit Tigers, demonstrates his trademark coaching style. The ever-grinning Irishman was a master psychologist, constantly whistling and pulling grass, kicking, and yelling his famous battle cry while skillfully intertwining his signals and antics. Winning pennants in his first three seasons at the helm, Hughie Jennings served as manager for 14 years, second-longest tenure in franchise history. (William M. Anderson)

Detroit purchased outfielder Davy Jones from Minneapolis and he spent seven seasons (1906–12) with the Tigers, compiling a .270 batting average. Jones could run and was a valuable lead-off man and defensive player. (Detroit News Archives)

stretch every hit. . . . He tries to steal when the pitcher is holding the ball. If he's on second when a grounder is hit to the infield, he runs right over third and keeps on for the plate. Wait till you see him, Bill—you'll laugh your eyes out." Bush league stuff—precisely the abandon Cobb would soon use to assault his major league adversaries.

Before the season ended, the Tigers acquired Cobb and brought him up to the majors. The second dominant force of the Tigers' future was now on-board. Despite an inauspicious start, he stuck with the team and therefore posed some threat of dislodging one of the veterans. Certainly, in Cobb's opinion, Detroit had an established "old boys" fraternity that enjoyed tormenting bushers. His readiness to fight

Ed Killian pitched for all three of Hughie Jennings's pennant-winning teams from 1907 to 1909. During his seven years on the Tiger roster, Killian twice won 20 and compiled an outstanding 2.38 earned run average. (Library of Congress)

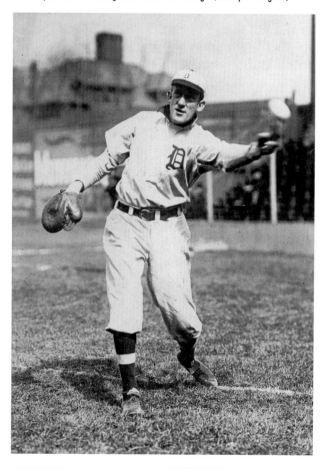

to be written prohibiting this maneuver.

Detroit's first exposure to a conspicuous kid named Tyrus Raymond Cobb occurred during spring training in Augusta, Georgia, in 1905. When owner Bill Armour visited camp, he heard of the youngster's antics from Germany Schaefer, who said, "They've got a crazy kid on this Augusta club. . . . He's the craziest ballplayer I ever saw. He tries to

Bobby Lowe, the first major league player to hit four homers in a game, was acquired by the Tigers through the urging of manager Ed Barrow. "The day I reported to the Tigers in Detroit—July 28, 1904—Barrow was fired," stated Lowe. (Barrow actually resigned.) The Tigers made him their new manager for the remainder of the season and he filled a utility player's role for the next three seasons. After his exit from the Tigers, Lowe managed Grand Rapids in the Central League. (William M. Anderson)

ceptional baseball skills. A great hitter capable of adjusting to any pitch or situation, Cobb stealthily hit to all fields, was a superb bunter, and could hit for power, and his speed allowed him to beat out many chop hits. Once on base, he was an immediate threat to score. He took big leads and attacked the gatekeepers by sliding at the last moment in a cloud of dust, hurtling steel, and a toe to tag. Playing Cobb and the Tigers also forced other teams to cope with mind games and psychological warfare, as the Georgian taunted his adversaries and confronted the opposition with cunning and trickery.

Matty McIntyre joined the Tigers in 1904, the year prior to Cobb's arrival. Despite their mutual dislike, McIntyre played in the same outfield with Cobb and was a .261 hitter for Detroit during seven seasons. (Courtesy of the Burton Historical Collection of the Detroit Public Library)

back fueled the conflict, and Cobb took up the challenge of proving his supremacy. The antagonism sparked a smoldering fire of competitiveness in young Cobb. This very intense ballplayer stayed fighting mad throughout his career.

"The Georgia Phantom" and "Tyrus the Untamed" seemed so much more fitting than his more famous nickname, "The Georgia Peach." The period from 1906 to 1920 is often called the Cobbian Era for he dominated baseball and the style of play. Cobb had so many offensive weapons in his arsenal: sudden acceleration, blazing speed, a mind as quick as his feet, supreme confidence, and mastery of ex-

Tiger owner Frank Navin checks the location of an overflow crowd on the field, circa 1908. Navin began his employment with the team in 1902 as an accountant. He gained a small ownership interest the following year and steadily increased his holdings and control of the organization. Navin was the foundation upon which the franchise took root and developed. (Detroit News Archives)

Three Tiger hurlers are being celebrated on the eve of the opening game (October 8, 1908) of the World Series with the Chicago Cubs. Star pitcher George Mullin is seated next to the driver, and Bill Donovan is directly behind him in the back seat. Rookie pitcher Edgar Willett, wearing the Derby hat, is seated next to Donovan. (Detroit News Archives)

Other than Cobb's .320 average and Mullin's pitching, things deteriorated in 1906. Detroit slipped below .500 again and sank into sixth position in a season with few leaders in anything.

The appointment of Hugh Jennings to the Tiger helm in 1907 gave the team the last element needed to be a winner. Jennings, a fine ex–major leaguer, blended the parts, and his enthusiasm and energy instilled a new Tiger spirit. Hughie personified excitement and emotion in his coaching exuberance with his famous rally cry, "E-y-a-ah!" The Tiger leader had a highly distinguishable style, yelling, whistling, pulling grass, and kicking his knee in the air while extending his arms. Aside from leading the cheers, Hughie's antics concealed a coded set of messages.

Johnson tried to block the appointment, assuming Jennings represented the worst of the Baltimore Oriole legacy of rowdiness, but Navin used the threat of owner Yawkey withdrawing his financial

Pitcher Win Mercer was 15–18 in 1902, his only year with Detroit. Following the season, he was named to replace ousted manager Frank Dwyer. On February 12, 1903, 28-year-old Mercer took his own life in a San Francisco hotel. (Courtesy of the Burton Historical Collection of the Detroit Public Library)

◀ First baseman Claude Rossman played two full seasons for the Bengals, 1907 and 1908. Participating in two World Series, he hit a fine .308. (Ray Billbrough)

▲ Although he played just six seasons in the big leagues, all with Detroit, Charles "Boss" Schmidt had the distinction of being on three World Series teams, 1907, 1908, and 1909. The burly catcher once fought the combative Ty Cobb in a long-brewing fisticuff. (Detroit News Archives)

▼ A character of characters, Herman "Germany" Schaefer forced the adoption of a new rule prohibiting a runner from stealing bases in reverse. (Schaefer would steal second, then steal first.) A gritty player, Schaefer played second base in Detroit for five seasons, 1905–9. (Ray Billbrough)

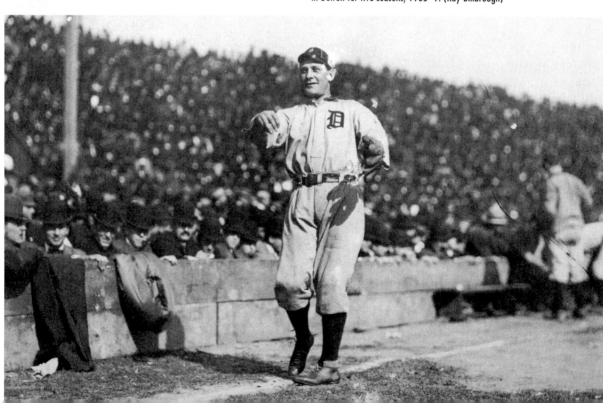

Following the most controversial batting championship in baseball history (1910), the Chalmers Company presented both Napoleon Lajoie (*left*) and Ty Cobb (the champion) with a new automobile. Trainer Harry Tuthill is seated behind the wheel. (Detroit Free Press)

Ira Thomas hit a very respectable .307 in 1908, his only season with Detroit. Thomas has just released his throw as he loosens up at Bennett Park. (William M. Anderson)

investment in the Tigers to neutralize the league president.

After Chicago led the 1907 race in the early months, Detroit and Philadelphia moved up to challenge. These two teams squared off in a battle to the wire, with the Tigers finally prevailing after outlasting Philadelphia in an extra-inning contest that Cobb called his greatest game. That year marked the beginning of Cobb's baseball reign. He won his first of 12 batting championships and dominated most other offensive measures. The 1907 Tigers manufactured runs in wholesale fashion, scoring a league-leading 696; the other teams averaged 544. Their four starting pitchers produced the best individual records for a single staff in Detroit history: Ed Killian and Donovan each won 25 games, Mullin won 21, and Ed Siever won 19.

The National League champion Chicago Cubs won 107 games in 1907 and proved to be a formidable foe in the World Series. For Detroit, the first game was the Series. They fought gamely for 12 innings, squandered a chance to win in the ninth, and ultimately settled for a tie. Jennings's crew lost the next game, 3–1, and began a losing streak that got progressively worse, dropping the finale, 2–0. In four consecutive losses, Tiger hitters generated a total of

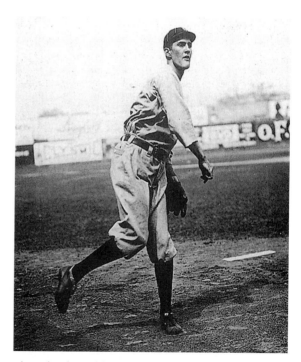

Nicknamed "Judge," Ralph Works won 23 and lost 22 during his four-year career with Detroit. He was a member of the 1909 AL championship team and compiled a sterling earned run average of 1.97 in 16 games. (William M. Anderson)

Charlie O'Leary played shortstop for the Tigers for nine years, 1904–12. During the first four years, he held down the regular job and played in each of the team's first three World Series. He and his second base partner, "Germany" Schaefer, also teamed up to perform vaudeville on stage. (William M. Anderson)

Doc Casey held down the hot corner for Detroit during the first two seasons of the American League. Though he hit for a respectable .278 over the course of his tenure, he was not retained. He had his career year in 1901 when he scored 105 runs. (William M. Anderson)

A crowd of Tiger fans gathered in front of Detroit City Hall on October 6, 1908, to watch the *Free Press* scoreboard when Detroit clinched the American League pennant by a margin of one-half game. (Library of Congress)

only three runs. With no offense and catchers who could not stop Chicago base stealers, even great pitchers could not win.

The finish was even tighter in 1908, as Detroit edged out Chicago and Cleveland in a three-horse race, the margin of victory being one-half game. Though pitching slipped, the deficit was overcome by a crushing offensive machine; the Bengals led the American League in doubles, runs, slugging, and batting average. In addition to Cobb, Sam Crawford, Matty McIntyre, and Claude Rossman were the hitters in the Tiger lineup.

With Detroit facing the Cubs for the second straight time, the Series again lasted five games. This time the Tigers managed their first and only postseason win in game three.

Detroit made it three pennants in a row in 1909; again it was a struggle to the end, as the Tigers nosed out Philadelphia in the final week. Championship teams usually make minor repairs before the next season, but the Tigers totally overhauled their infield prior to the 1909 season, adding particular strength with shortstop Donie Bush and third baseman George Moriarty. A late season 14-game winning streak positioned Detroit for a run at the flag.

Cobb and associates led in team batting for the third consecutive season, and the young star captured batting crowns in 1907, 1908, and 1909. During those three years, Cobb also led the league in runs batted in, slugging average, hits, and total bases. Dependable Mullin had a league-high 29 wins, and his teammate Ed Willett added 21 victories.

Pittsburgh displaced Chicago as the National League representative in the 1909 Series, and the Pirates and Tigers traded blows, each team winning and losing in successive games until the Series was deadlocked at three games apiece. The Bucs ended the Tigers' dream with a convincing 8–0 win in the seventh game. Big George Mullin pitched his heart out in a losing effort.

The championship run ended in 1910, when the Philadelphia Athletics overpowered the field and Detroit settled for third, 10 games down. Although Mullin won 21 and Donovan rebounded from a sub-par season with 18 wins, the Tiger pitching staff ranked next to last in earned run average.

Winning three pennants during the first nine years of the league's history was a remarkable feat; it would take the Tigers 24 years to win the next one.

Like all great hitters, Ty Cobb was a careful custodian of his bats. As part of his style, Cobb allegedly introduced the manner of wielding three bats while waiting in the on-deck circle. (Detroit News Archives)

3
Cobb Dominates Baseball
1911–1920

During one of the many rifts between Frank Navin and Ty Cobb, Navin said, "Cobb is not bigger than baseball." However, he was bigger than anyone else in baseball, dominating the game and Navin's attention. Perhaps it was unreasonable to expect that a force like Cobb, extremely competitive and intense, could conceivably be ordinary in his behavior off the field. Predictably, Cobb would rule most every measure of hitting achievement and with equal certainty be embroiled in serious altercations and hostile relationships. He was the consummate maker of headlines, first in baseball excellence and first in trouble. Although greatness is frequently

more fully recognized after death and following the passage of time, Cobb's superiority was a given during his playing career.

Tyrus the Terrible charged the opposition, threw down the gauntlet, and tried to short-circuit their nerves. Provocation and reputation resulted in numerous conflicts, including bloody brawls and death threats. Pitchers who made a practice of throwing at him were met with equal acts of aggression, as Cobb perfected the ability to drag a bunt down the first-base line, forcing the pitcher to field the ball while in the path of an angry Tiger. While running the bases, Cobb slid hard at the bag and its defender. During one particular retaliatory mission, Cobb re-

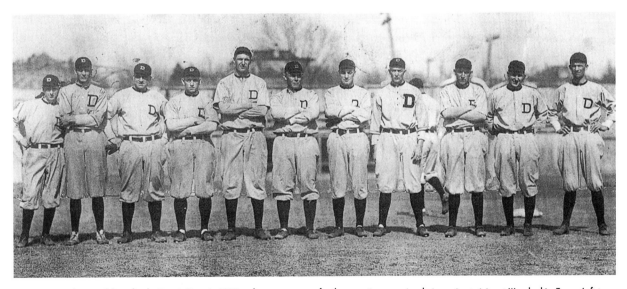

Here are 11 pitching candidates for the Detroit Tigers in 1917 as the team prepares for the upcoming campaign during spring training at Waxahachie, Texas. *Left to right:* Bernie Boland, Howard Ehmke, Harry Coveleski, George Cunningham, Bill James, Flannigan, Johnny Couch, Deacon Jones, Willie Mitchell, George Dauss, Watson. Flannigan and Watson never played for Detroit and their first names are unknown. (William M. Anderson)

Jack and Eddie Onslow were brothers and played together for Detroit in 1912, Jack's sole season with the club. Although most catchers didn't hit much in the earlier years of baseball, Jack Onslow batted a miniscule .159 in 1912. (William M. Anderson)

called, "The crash was as violent as I could make it."

Cobb detested spring training, was frequently absent without leave, and often reported only when the team began its spring tour. Navin's appeal to Cobb in February 1911 reflects how little control management had over its star player. Navin wrote: "If you will try your best to have harmony on the team this year, and will report on time, and will help Mr. Jennings in every possible way, I will show you in a very substantial way my appreciation of your service." Cobb did as he pleased and went to camp late.

The Tigers opened the 1911 season with a great start, winning their first 11 games and 21 of their first 23. Building up a substantial lead, they were front-runners through the first four months. In August, they floundered while the powerful Athletics took command. The collapse continued through September despite a phenomenal performance by Ty Cobb. In his career season, Cobb led both major leagues in hitting (.420), runs batted in (144), hits (248), slugging average (.621), stolen bases (83), and runs scored (147). Ironically, Sam Crawford also had his best season, batting .378 and finishing second or third in the league in RBIs, hits, slugging, and total bases. Still, this awesome one-two punch could not overcome the liability of a weak pitching staff, the

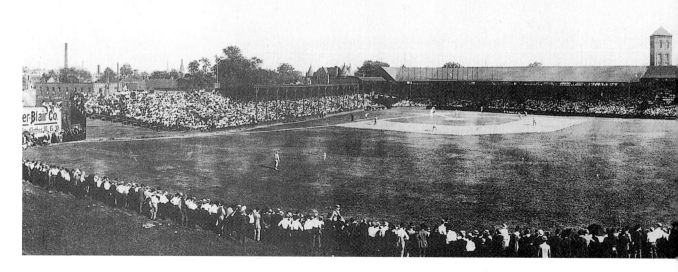

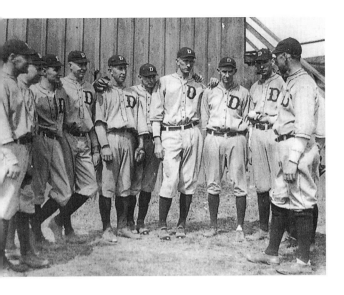

Jack Coombs (*right*) instructs his prospective pitching staff during spring training at Macon, Georgia, in March 1920. Coombs joined Tiger manager Hughie Jennings when pitching coaches were a rarity. (William M. Anderson)

though primed for a winner in 1912, the Tigers were never in the race. They finished below .500 for the first time in six years, ending a disappointing season buried in sixth position, 36 1/2 games behind Boston.

Cobb's second straight .400-plus batting average (.410) capped another spectacular individual season, although it was marred by unusual strife. On May 15, 1912, following a verbal battle with a New York fan at old Hilltop Park, Cobb went into the stands and beat up the spectator. Cobb was suspended indefinitely. Most of his teammates signed a telegram, informing league president Ban Johnson of their intention not to play again until Cobb was reinstated. Johnson responded by saying, "I am amazed at the attitude of player Cobb and his teammates. . . . An American League player who is taunted or abused by a patron has only to appeal to an umpire for protection from attacks . . . to have the objectionable party escorted from the grounds." When the umpire ordered Cobb off the field before the next game, Tiger players followed him into the dressing room and a strike began. Detroit was scheduled to play on Saturday, May 18, in Philadelphia. To avoid a threatened $5,000-per-game fine for not playing, the Tigers hurriedly assembled a pickup team of manager Hughie Jennings, his two coaches, and 12 semi-pro and college players. The Athletics showed no mercy, punishing the imposters, 24–2. The league president canceled Monday's game, and the Tigers were coaxed into returning, although each of the strikers was fined $100 and Mr. Cobb, the catalyst, drew a 10-day suspension and $50 fine.

Six consecutive batting crowns, the last two above .400, should have given Ty Cobb immense

loss of promising rookie Del Gainor to an injury, and, of course, the balanced strength of the Philadelphia A's. Detroit finished second, a distant 13 1/2 games back.

Having baseball's greatest player and a winning ball team generated increasing demand for tickets. Frank Navin initiated a temporary expansion of Bennett Park in 1911 and then, following the season, brought in the wrecking crew, reoriented home plate to its current location, and constructed a 23,000-seat facility with a concrete and steel grandstand. Al-

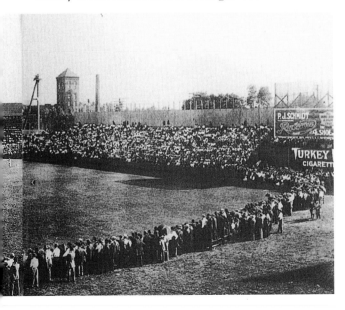

An overflow crowd rings the outfield for a May 21, 1911, game against the Philadelphia Athletics at Bennett Park. (Courtesy of the Burton Historical Collection of the Detroit Public Library)

The end of the left-field bleachers at Bennett Park can be seen on the extreme left as the fence extends around to the centerfield scoreboard and flagpole. Far from a manicured lawn, the outfield grass resembles a pasture. (Courtesy of the Burton Historical Collection of the Detroit Public Library)

bargaining power, but the man with money, Frank Navin, was a tough sell. Cobb set his sights on $15,000 a year and the overtures began. Cobb became a holdout as the parties polarized and even Congress got involved. After missing two weeks of the 1913 season, Cobb received a $3,000 raise, which was $3,000 less than he demanded.

Following his late entrance, Cobb "slumped" to

.390 in 1913 while capturing his seventh straight batting championship. Crawford's numbers fell off more dramatically. He hit .317, although he remained among the leaders in six batting categories. Ineffective pitching, the worst in the league as gauged by earned run average, ensured a losing season, but newcomer Jean Dubuc notched 16 wins to pace the staff. Another youngster, outfielder Bobby Veach, showed promise in his first full season. A sixth-place finish, with 57 losses, mirrored the previous campaign.

Navin and Jennings were revamping their team; the great pitchers of the glory years—Donovan, Ed Summers, Willett, and Mullin—were departing, leaving an all-too-obvious void. Other stalwarts, such as outfielder Davy Jones and infielder Charlie O'Leary, were also deemed over the hill.

During 1914 and 1915, the Federal League rose up to threaten the older American and National circuits. Although few players broke ranks, the Feder-

After brief and ineffective trials with Philadelphia and Cincinnati, Harry Coveleski was acquired by Detroit in 1914, and he blossomed with three straight 20-win seasons. His younger brother Stan eventually pitched his way into the Hall of Fame. (William M. Anderson)

Jackson beware, that friendly smile is probably a decoy. These two exceptional hitters, Ty Cobb (*left*) and Shoeless Joe Jackson, rank first and third, respectively, in career major league lifetime batting average. Jackson compiled a .356 lifetime average but never won a batting crown. Cobb recognized Jackson's formidable threat and admitted to playing mind games with his naive adversary. (Courtesy of the Burton Historical Collection of the Detroit Public Library)

Mighty Sam Crawford enjoyed his last hurrah in 1915, hitting .299 and leading the American League with 112 runs batted in. He would play two more seasons with Detroit but without his characteristic productivity. In one of the best seasons in Detroit history, only a talented Boston pitching staff denied the Tigers a fourth pennant. A slim two and a half games separated these teams as the Bengals won 100 games and compiled a .649 winning percentage. They dominated team and individual hitting statistics with an overwhelming leadership in runs scored. Cobb, Crawford, and Veach were the top three in runs batted in, hits, and total bases. The one-two punch of Coveleski and Dauss carried the pitching load for Detroit. Together they hurled in 96 games, won 47, and worked 613 innings, more than any other pair in baseball. Ty Cobb won his ninth consecutive batting championship and established a new season record for stolen bases with 96.

als did pull fans away and influenced escalating salaries. Detroit's Edgar Willett signed with St. Louis, but his prowess was nearly spent.

Roaring out to an early lead in 1914, the surprising Tigers stayed near the front through most of July before their fortunes reversed. Injuries to team captain George Moriarty and Cobb contributed to the downfall. One of Cobb's injuries, a broken thumb, occurred when the overheated Cobb engaged in a scrap with a butcher boy. In the final standings, Detroit finished fourth, winning 80 games and losing 73. Despite a mound corps that ranked seventh in earned run average, a fine young pitching tandem emerged: Harry Coveleski won 21 games, and George "Hooks" Dauss won 18. Cobb racked up another batting crown, his eighth in a row, and the team's batting average of .258 was second best in the league.

Pitcher Bernie Boland spent most of his career wearing a Tiger uniform. He won 67 and lost 49, 1915–20. (William M. Anderson)

Frank Navin, owner and president, enjoys a relaxed moment with his star player, Ty Cobb. Though Navin was a tough guy he had to make exceptions for this fiery and determined ball player. (Detroit News Archives)

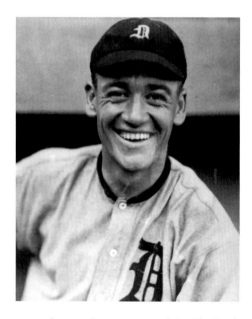

George Burns got his start with Detroit in 1914 and played first base for the next four seasons. Traded to Philadelphia after a poor season in 1917, Burns began hitting like never before. He enjoyed eight .300 or better seasons after departing the auto capital. (William M. Anderson)

Eddie Onslow played first base for Detroit in 1912 and 1913 and then jumped to the upstart Federal League. (William M. Anderson)

One of five brothers who played in the majors, infielder Jim Delehanty came to Detroit from Washington in exchange for Germany Schaefer in August 1909. A good hitter, he compiled a .306 average in three-plus seasons with the Bengals. (William M. Anderson)

Boston won again in 1916, with Detroit in the chase throughout the season. The Tigers finally fell to third, four games back, after running second most of the year. As usual, offensive productivity carried the team. The Tigers were leaders in batting and slugging averages. Tris Speaker dethroned Cobb as batting champion. The combative Georgian, however, maintained his record for trouble by angrily throwing his bat following a called third strike, and a prolonged protest led to an early shower. His bat landed in the stands, earning him a three-day cooling-off period.

Harry Heilmann played his first full season at a variety of positions en route to becoming a star fixture in the Tiger outfield.

Always committed to aggressive style, Cobb got off to a fighting start in 1917 when he tangled with New York Giant infielder Charley Herzog in a two-round bout during spring training. During a game, the two wrestled on the field following an altercation at second base. Allegedly Herzog was rescued from greater bodily harm in Cobb's room that night when other players intervened.

Based upon quality of performance, the American League was divided into three divisions of competency in 1917: Chicago, Boston, and Cleveland participated in a pennant race; Detroit, Washington, and New York vied for a first-division post; and St. Louis and Philadelphia fought to escape the cellar. The Tigers won fourth and about as many games as they lost. Cobb regained the batting championship, hitting .383, and the team had the best batting average in the league. After winning 66 games the three previous seasons, Coveleski's arm wore out. His partner, George Dauss, continued to be the mainstay of the pitching staff.

Detroit slipped further down the ladder in 1917, with a 55–71 record, to finish seventh, four games out of the cellar. The Tigers had been a great hitting

Born Jean Baptiste Arthur Dubuc but better known as "Chauncey," this right-hander pitched for the Tigers from 1912 through 1916. He twice won 17 games in a season. (Courtesy of the Burton Historical Collection of the Detroit Public Library)

After spending six years in the minors, George "Hooks" Dauss was purchased by Detroit from St. Paul in 1912. Dauss had longevity in Detroit, pitching 15 years and winning 221 games, more than any other Tiger pitcher. He won 10 or more games in 14 consecutive seasons, including three in which he won over 20. (William M. Anderson)

This sensitive young hurler never got along well with manager Ty Cobb. Howard Ehmke won 75 games for Detroit, yet the pitching-poor Tigers peddled him to Boston in 1923, where he promptly won 20 games and pitched a no-hitter. (William M. Anderson)

Scrappy George Moriarty played third base for Detroit during most of 1909–14 and made his mark as one of the club's best all-time base stealers. He specialized in stealing home, a feat he achieved a dozen times in one season. Moriarty managed the Tigers in 1927–28. (William M. Anderson)

ball club, finishing first or second in 10 of the previous 11 years, but that standard deteriorated in 1918 as Detroit batters ranked sixth. The pitchers were even worse, giving up the most earned runs (3.40) per game in the league. Right-hander Bernie Boland topped the staff with 14 wins. A Labor Day double-

Frank Navin purchased a kid named Harry Heilmann from Portland in 1913 for $1,500. A powerful batter, Heilmann hit the ball hard and often. He was a line-drive hitter who specialized in extra-base hits. Heilmann hammered 40 or more doubles in seven seasons. He valued bat speed, saying, "I don't care how strong and heavy a batter is, he can get a quick snap into a light bat much more effectively than he can one of those wagon tongue maulers the public is so fond of seeing." (William M. Anderson)

The main man of the 1908 pitching staff, Ed "Kickapoo" Summers notched 24 victories with a low 1.64 ERA for the league-leading Tigers. Summers had two fine back-to-back seasons but faltered in the 1908 and 1909 World Series, losing all four games he pitched. (Library of Congress)

header closed the war-shortened season and illustrated a lost campaign. In the final game, "Old Bill" Donovan, formerly "Wild Bill," started for Detroit. Ty Cobb hurled four innings, and Bobby Veach two in relief. Always an aspiring pitcher, Cobb made his mound debut in this game and earned the distinction of being the best-hitting pitcher in baseball since he was also the major league batting champ with a .382 average.

Nearly everything improved for the Tigers in 1919. They were slow out of the gate, but then showed signs of being a contender before losing their momentum in August and backsliding into fourth to finish only eight games behind the leader. Pitching improved as Dauss won 21 games, and the

Oscar Stanage had one of the longest tenures as a Tiger catcher, stretching from 1909 through 1920 and then catching three games in 1925. His 133 hits in 1911 represented Stanage's finest offensive season. (William M. Anderson)

Detroit purchased the contract of Ed Willett in 1906. Willett racked up a season-high victory total of 21 in 1909. He jumped to the Federal League in 1914. (Library of Congress)

Wahoo Sam, named for his hometown in Nebraska, patroled centerfield throughout most of his 15 years with Detroit. Crawford had few peers as a slugger, hitting an all-time career record 312 triples. (William M. Anderson)

Bobby Veach was one of the best hitters ever to wear a Tiger uniform. In 12 campaigns, he batted over .300 nine times and racked up a healthy .311 average while in the Motor City. When asked to discuss the techniques of successful hitting, Veach said, "I have found that the best thing to do is to develop a style which will insure your hitting the ball hard and then forget about it. Put your attention on the task at hand, namely on hitting the ball." (William M. Anderson)

▶ Oscar Vitt spent the first seven years of his career (1912–18) as an infielder with Detroit. A lifetime .238 hitter, he was traded to Boston following the 1919 season. (William M. Anderson)

hitters rebounded with Cobb first (.384), Veach second (.355), and new outfielder Ira Flagsted fifth (.331). It was Cobb's 12th and last batting title.

Cobb was his own master when it came to spring training, determining his own workout schedule and deciding when he would report to the team. The 1920 preseason was typical, as Cobb chose to skip the team's program and train with the Washington Senators in his home state of Georgia.

Bob "Ducky" Jones spent his entire nine-year major league career with the Tigers principally as a third baseman. Jones had his career season in 1921, Ty Cobb's first as Tiger manager. He played in 141 games and hit .303. (Ray Billbrough)

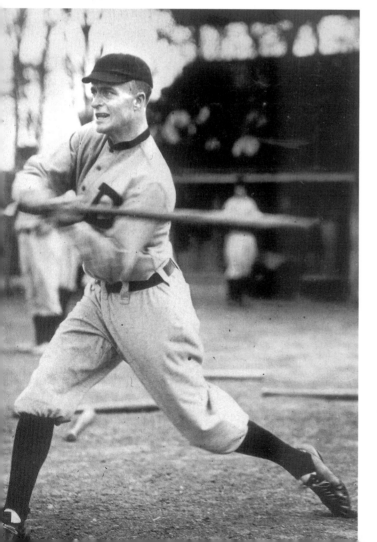

Tubby Spencer shared the catching duties with the regular receiver Oscar Stanage during most of his three years (1916–18) with Detroit. Nicknames were often suggestive of physical characteristics, yet ironically *The Baseball Encyclopedia* does not record the dimensions of Tubby Spencer. (William M. Anderson)

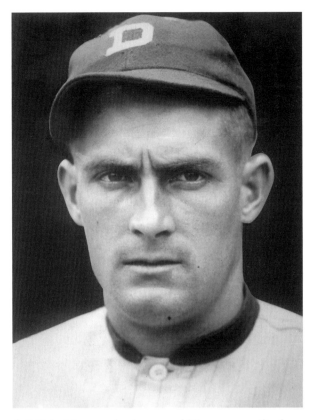

▼ Middle infielder Ralph Young played nearly 800 games at second base for Detroit during his seven seasons, 1915–21. He knocked out 173 safeties in 1920, which earned him a .291 batting average. (Ray Billbrough)

▲ Del Baker is best remembered as a successful Tiger manager, guiding the team to a pennant in 1940. He got his start in major league baseball as a part-time catcher for Detroit, 1914–16. He and several other Tigers, Bernie Boland, George Cunningham, Howard Ehmke, Bill James, and Red Oldham, served in the military during World War I. (Ray Billbrough)

During his eight-year major league career, outfielder Chick Shorten played alongside Ty Cobb during three seasons (1919–21). He batted a combined .293 but almost exclusively as a singles hitter. (Courtesy of the Burton Historical Collection of the Detroit Public Library)

Hughie Jennings is at the wheel of a new EMF 30 Studebaker touring car, accompanied by four of his players. Seated next to Jennings is Jim Delahanty. In the back seat behind the driver is Ed Lafitte with Oscar Stanage in the middle and Del Gainor alongside. (William M. Anderson)

Catcher Oscar Stanage (*left*) and star pitcher George Mullin were battery mates for five years, 1909–13. (Courtesy of the Burton Historical Collection of the Detroit Public Library)

Detroit suffered through 13 straight losses to open a terrible season of defeat. This outfit established a team record of 93 losses, compiled the lowest win-loss percentage ever, and finished farther behind the league champion Cleveland Indians (37 games) than any other Tiger squad in its 20-year history. Fortunately, an even more woeful Philadelphia team played in the same league and claimed the pit. In a revolutionary occurrence, Cobb failed to rank significantly in any batting or running category. Heilmann and Veach both hit over .300, but not a single pitcher had a winning season.

By the close of the 1920 season and even earlier, there had been several signs foretelling a changing of the guard, most noticeably the explosive emer-

gence of New York's Babe Ruth and the advent of the long ball, and, with it, the passing of Cobb's supremacy. The era of Hughie Jennings ended, too. Following a remarkable string of winning seasons during which Manager Jennings was credited with creating harmony, differences and dissension became increasingly apparent. Having Ty Cobb, the greatest player of his time, on his team was a huge advantage, but Cobb was also the center of tension. He had no friends on the field and few off the diamond. Among his chief adversaries were Crawford, Bush, and Marty McIntyre. Jennings had once called Cobb a genius, and the gifted one was about to replace the boss.

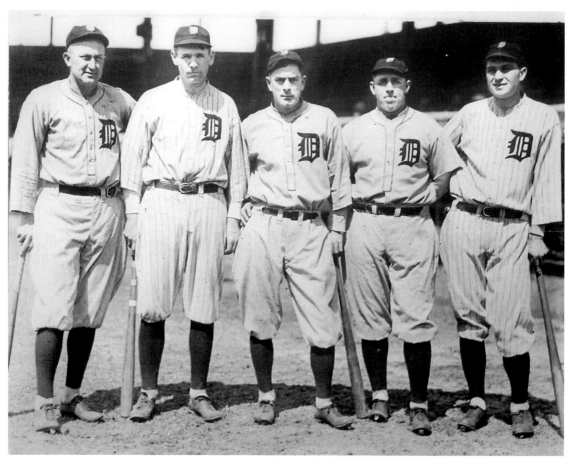

An awesome-hitting Tiger outfield in 1923. *Left to right:* Ty Cobb (.340), batting champ Harry Heilmann (.403), Bobby Veach (.321), Bob Fothergill (.315), and Heinie Manush (.334). (Courtesy of the Burton Historical Collection of the Detroit Public Library)

4
A Legacy of Great Hitters Continues
1921–1930

One of Hughie Jennings's greatest feats was his ability to coexist with Ty Cobb, allowing Cobb to function independently while holding the rest of the team together. He made obvious exceptions for the star and tolerated his extreme behavior. Both Jennings and the Tigers were ready for a change, but it would take a unique personality to succeed with this team. When it is apparent that a team has had its last winning season for a while or there are holes in the team, the manager is usually the first to know and the first to go. Jennings was experiencing battle fatigue, and he recognized the need to rebuild the team, knowing it would be a long process.

Knowing Cobb could handle Cobb and thinking Cobb's aggressive spirit would inspire the club, the Georgian was Navin's first choice. He declined the offer and, while others were being considered, pressure mounted for Cobb to reconsider. Tris Speaker's successful experience at Cleveland as player-manager and the potential selection of Clarence Rowland, whom Cobb considered incompetent, may have influenced his new decision. Cobb signed a contract to manage the Tigers in 1921, saying, "This thing has been forced upon me."

During his managerial honeymoon and while enjoying a great season as a player, Cobb's optimism ran high. He compared the Tigers to a broken-down machine shop. "There was a lot of strength in the club, but it didn't seem to fit. The parts had grown rusty and didn't coordinate properly. And the winning spirit was lacking," Cobb said.

Right-hander Haskell Billings played his entire and short major league career in Detroit, winning 10 games in three seasons, 1927–29. (William M. Anderson)

Surely no one doubted that Tyrus Raymond Cobb would light a fire under these Tigers, but his potential for oiling a disjointed machine seemed remote. Could anyone duplicate his concentration and intensity? Later, he wrote, "I tried to be as sensitive as a burglar alarm to every pulse of the game."

Many of the Tigers fell far short of his standards for hustle and determination. He tried to convert distance runners into sprinters and quiet players into boisterous firebrands. He pushed and pressed his charges and, failing his expectations, they suffered his wrath and many were discarded. "If a player wasn't doing his best, I got after him," said Cobb. "If he sulked or broke under the criticism I gave him, it merely showed he didn't have the stuff in him that was necessary for a fighting, winning ball club. I have small patience with a man who whimpers instead of fights."

Cobb's philosophy of how baseball should be played had been dramatically demonstrated for 16 years, and in subsequent interviews he expounded his combative principles. "I have been accused of taking all the law allowed and perhaps a little more. That accusation is just and I accept it without apology." Baseball is "a fight, a continuous nerve-wracking, exhausting fight . . . it is a game of merciless competition. Whether I was batting or running bases, I always played full-speed and the man who stood between me and victory was my enemy." No one should have been surprised when Cobb sought to transfer a playing style to a management style. Unfortunately, at times a fighting spirit became a feuding spirit.

Detroit played in the first division during the first half of the 1921 season but then gradually lost ground. Cobb led by example, exhorting his men and playing and managing with great energy. He

Stoner's given name was Ulysses Simpson Grant, though he was popularly known as "Lil." He won 10 games three times during his seven-year career with the Tigers. (Courtesy of the Burton Historical Collection of the Detroit Public Library)

Like many young pitchers, Whit Wyatt was slow developing and Detroit gave up on him after five stints. His level of performance did not improve with the White Sox and Indians either, but he became a fine wartime pitcher with Brooklyn, winning 41 games during the 1941–42 seasons. (William M. Anderson)

Roy Johnson takes a big cut and comes up empty in an exhibition game with the San Francisco Seals. The catcher is Pop Penebski. Johnson had a great rookie year with Detroit in 1929, collecting 201 hits en route to a fine .314 batting average. After tailing off the next two seasons, he was traded to the Boston Red Sox where he rediscovered his stroke with three consecutive .300 seasons. His brother Bob was also a fine hitter. (William M. Anderson)

a team batting average of .316. Heilmann was Cobb's prize pupil though, banging out a league-leading .394 average and beating out his tutor, who ranked second at .389. Cobb recognized the potential, having predicted earlier that "Heilmann is capable of batting .400."

Even the best-hitting team in baseball could not compensate for a second-division pitching staff; only Bert Cole compiled a winning record with seven wins and four losses, and the Bengals accepted sixth place in 1921.

Trying to bolster their pitching for the 1922 season, Frank Navin purchased Herman Pillette and Sylvester Johnson, two promising prospects from

A very solid player, Marty McManus played third base for Detroit for most of five years (1927–31). In 1929, he hit a career-high 18 home runs, drove in 90 runs, and scored 99. While playing in the big time for 15 seasons, McManus finished with a .289 lifetime batting average. (Courtesy of the Burton Historical Collection of the Detroit Public Library)

In one of the team's worst trades, Detroit swapped future Hall of Famer Heinie Manush and steady-hitting Lu Blue to the Browns for outfielder Harry Rice and two other players. Although not a long-ball threat, Rice (shown here) was a very consistent hitter, compiling a .303 average for Detroit, 1928–30. (William M. Anderson)

liked to tinker with the lineup and players' heads; staid Bobby Veach became a major project. Harry Heilmann was assigned to agitate Veach. The strategy apparently worked, as Bobby hit .388 yet acquired a lasting dislike for Mr. Heilmann. Other hitters responded as well, with only shortstop Emory Rigney among the regulars batting below .300. The 1921 Tigers set a new American League record with

West Virginia—born Del Gainor began his 10-year major league career with the Tigers in 1909. He was good enough to hang around for a decade but never rose above the role of backup first baseman. (William M. Anderson)

When the Tigers acquired Mark Koenig during the 1930 season, he had already played the best baseball of his career on several great Yankee teams. He managed a .247 average over two years with the Bengals as a middle infielder. (William M. Anderson)

Portland of the Pacific Coast League. Both contributed, but Pillette especially proved to be a good investment, as he racked up 19 wins to lead the staff.

Cobb injured his knee in spring training and the team got off to a sluggish start. By May they were above .500 in the standings and maintained that level for the duration, ending the season in third place, 15 games off the pennant pace of New York. Cobb had another great year, batting over .400 for the third time in his career. The Tiger tradition of great-hitting outfielders continued as Cobb hit .401, Heilmann .356, and Veach .327. The hitters combined for runner-up honors in batting and slugging averages and runs scored. Right-hander George Dauss, returning to past form, won 21 games.

Confrontations followed Cobb throughout his career, but at this stage, his adversaries were often umpires. During his first season as manager, an angry Cobb challenged umpire Billy Evans to "slug it out" after the game. Evans accepted, and a bloody

◀ Left to right: Johnny Bassler, Donie Bush, Bobby Veach, Bert Cole, Dutch Leonard, and Hooks Dauss, 1921. (William M. Anderson)

struggle occurred that eventually netted Cobb a suspension. Manager Cobb sat out a three-day suspension in 1922, again resulting from a fracas with an umpire. The tension started early in 1923, when a spring exhibition game argument caused a contest to be forfeited because Cobb would not leave the field after being thrown out by an umpire.

As the rebuilding continued, Detroit had a special knack for acquiring hitters, yet could not find similar talent in pitchers. In 1922, the Tigers called up rotund outfielder Bob Fothergill from Rochester, where he was hitting International League pitching at a .383 clip. He adjusted quickly to the big leagues but had difficulty breaking into an outfield crowded with outstanding hitters, such as Cobb, Heilmann,

Right-hander Ken Holloway started his major league career with Detroit in 1922. Over the next three seasons he consistently won in double figures as a member of the starting rotation. He won 57 games in seven years pitching for the Tigers. His top season performance came in 1924 when he went 14–6. (William M. Anderson)

A new automobile was an exceptional gift and Tiger manager Stanley "Bucky" Harris is the proud recipient of a shiny new black Ford—the standard color at that time. Harris has the distinction of being the only Detroit Tiger manager to be rehired for a second tenure. (William M. Anderson)

and Veach. Henry "Heinie" Manush, yet another outfield prospect, joined the Tigers in 1923, having impressed management with his outstanding Western League batting average of .375 the previous season. Major league pitching proved no mystery to Heinie either, as he connected for a .334 batting average in 1924, his freshman season. Struggling to develop a solid keystone combination, Manager Cobb welcomed the signing of impressive rookie Charles Gehringer in 1924. The "Silent Son of Fowlerville" (Gehringer, from Fowlerville, Michigan, was notoriously quiet) was farmed out for two years of seasoning.

Bucky Harris (*left*) gets acquainted with his new team and pitching ace Earl Whitehill during spring training, 1929. Whitehill was the mainstay of the Tiger pitching staff after his first season in 1923. He won 133 games for Detroit. (Michael Mumby)

Ty Cobb made Johnny Bassler his regular catcher in his first year at the helm. Bassler, a consistent hitter, compiled a .308 average over seven years with Detroit, 1921–27. In 2,240 times at bat for the Tigers, he managed only one home run. (Courtesy of the Burton Historical Collection of the Detroit Public Library)

improved pitching that ranked third lowest in earned runs allowed and the rapid development of Earl Whitehill, Cobb rung the best out of everyone. Catcher Johnny Bassler matched Heilmann's .346 batting average for team leadership, shortstop Topper Rigney drove in 93 runs, and second baseman Del Pratt added 77. Together they set the hitting standard for the league with a .298 average and in runs scored with 847. The scrapping Tigers were in and out of the lead through the summer in what proved to be the high watermark of Cobb's managerial tenure. Navin had anticipated correctly and

Although baseball didn't select a Rookie of the Year in the early 1920s, Lu Blue would have been a legitimate candidate in his first season in the majors (1921). The Tiger first baseman hit .308, scored 103 runs, and drove in an equal number. During his seven years with the Tigers, Blue hit .300 or better four times. He was even more highly regarded as a fielder. (William M. Anderson)

Cobb's third season at the helm in 1923 produced a second-place finish; however, the real race was with Cleveland to see who would capture second. That year the Yankees were unchallenged champions, winning by 16 games, while Detroit edged out Cleveland by a half game to claim the runner-up position. Detroit wins were produced by superior hitting, paced by Heilmann, who won his second batting title with a .403 average and ranked third in hits, RBIs, and home runs. The Tigers had the second-best team batting average at .300, far above the league average of .280. Pitching was second-rate, although Dauss won 21 games.

Under Cobb's tutelage, the Tigers continued to improve in the standings, finishing a close third in 1924, just six games back in a three-team race. With

erected temporary seating for a pennant race season that drew 1,015,136 fans, and the team's first one million spectator gate.

Fortunes reversed in 1925 as pitching and infield problems resurfaced and players were reshuffled. Detroit slipped to fourth position after surviving a horrendous beginning. They finished 16 1/2 games behind and eight games above, even in wins and losses. Hitting remained the constant and in-

cluded yet another high-average hitter in the outfield. Absalom "Red" Wingo, acquired a year earlier, enjoyed his best major league performance, hitting .370, fifth highest in the league. Cobb was fourth best with .378, and Heilmann "predictably" rebounded to his every-other-year hitting binge to win the crown at .393. Backup outfielders Fothergill and Manush hit .353 and .303, respectively.

Cobb's 22nd season at age 39 would be his last

Hack Wilson (*left*) and Bob Fothergill were both excellent hitters. Wilson had a lifetime batting average of .307, could hit the long ball, and is a member of Baseball's Hall of Fame. Fothergill, known as "Fat," could eat and hit for a high average. He played at 230 pounds and though he accumulated a .337 batting average during his nine seasons with Detroit (1922–29), all that bulk did not produce many home runs. (William M. Anderson)

Ty Tyson is about to interview the "Mechanical Man," Charlie Gehringer. Gehringer was a fixture at second base during most of his 19 years with the Tigers. Branch Rickey said, "He was a man of mechanical precision, obscure as far as showmanship but a very great player." (William M. Anderson)

in a Detroit uniform. The aging veteran reduced his playing time in 1926, particularly in the latter half of the season. When it was over, he had played in just 79 games, fewer than in any season since his rookie year. The season's record was almost identical to that of the previous year with a shift of two wins and two losses (79–75), yet Detroit ended the season in sixth place, only 12 games behind the winning New York Yankees. Whitehill was the star pitcher, winning 16 games. Detroit sluggers dominated the league's batting honors with Manush first (.378), Fothergill third (.367), and Slug Heilmann a close fourth (.367).

In November 1926, Cobb resigned. He was certainly glad to sever his relationship with owner Frank Navin, and the feeling was mutual. The two

had frequently clashed over salary negotiations and Cobb's independence. The ultimate measure of managerial success is winning pennants and in that regard Cobb failed. That ambition evaded Cobb's grasp and surely was a great disappointment. In a relative sense, the Tigers played improved baseball during his six-year tenure, and Cobb is often credited with being a good hitting instructor. The consistently high team averages seem to substantiate that recognition even though higher averages were the norm during the era. While Cobb managed Detroit, the Tigers ranked first or second in team batting average every year except one, and in that season were third best. That he lacked the requisite disposition to promote team harmony is even less refutable.

The Tigers owned minor leaguer Carl Hubbell for several years and were unimpressed with his fastball and discouraged his experimenting with a screwball, an odd-looking curveball. In 1928, they accepted the Giants' check for $30,000 in exchange for this rookie pitcher. (Ray Billbrough)

these star players were exonerated. Early in February 1927, Ty Cobb signed to play for Connie Mack and the Philadelphia Athletics. He retired after the 1928 season.

Former third baseman and umpire George Moriarty became the new mentor, leading the Tigers for the next two campaigns. When an organization changes leadership, it often selects a new leader whose strengths compensate for the deficiencies of the previous boss. That supposition seemed apparent in the selection of Moriarty as Cobb's successor. Moriarty was considered one of the finest men in baseball, and was very well liked, accommodating, and congenial. Although not a great player, Moriarty made his mark by frequently stealing home. That ability became the subject of a *Detroit News* editorial titled "Don't Die on Third," in which writer William Cameron used Moriarty's determination to score as a lesson for life.

The 1927 New York Yankees, considered one of the best teams in baseball history, ran away with the American League pennant, leading the field by 19 games while winning 110 games. Detroit rallied for a

"There were times," said former pitcher Harry "Rip" Collins, "when I couldn't even see Ty's face through the red haze that sprung up between us. I hated to work for him." According to Collins, Cobb was very demanding and hard to get along with. Yet time provides a more objective perspective and even this outspoken critic could recognize Cobb's management strengths and observe that, given the team's talent, no one could have done any better.

This was a time of transition for a baseball immortal who was terminating his long association with the Detroit Tigers and who was uncertain if this was the end of a brilliant career. Then, in December 1926, his integrity was seriously challenged when Commissioner Kenesaw "Mountain" Landis revealed that former pitcher Hubert "Dutch" Leonard had accused Cobb and Speaker of trying to fix a game in 1919. Following an investigation, both of

The Tigers signed a Jewish boy from the Bronx on February 5, 1930. Henry Greenberg, a recent graduate of Monroe High School, was signed by Detroit scout Jean Dubuc. (Detroit News)

► Harry Heilmann climbed up on a roof to toss a ball down to someone waiting to catch it. Under manager Ty Cobb's tutelage, he became one of the all-time great hitters in baseball. Winner of four batting titles, "Old Slug" hit a resounding .342 lifetime average. During Cobb's six-year administration, Heilmann averaged .377. (National Baseball Hall of Fame)

One of two "Dutch" Leonard pitchers in major league history, Hubert came to Detroit in 1919. In six previous years with Boston, his earned run average had never been above 2.72 for any season. Leonard was 49–49 during his five years in Detroit and left a negative memory by falsely accusing Ty Cobb and Tris Speaker of betting on baseball games. (Ray Billbrough)

Heinie Manush graduated from the Western League to Detroit in 1923 and immediately confirmed that he could hit as he compiled a .334 average. Two years after winning a batting title, the young outfielder was traded to St. Louis. He played 17 years in the big show, achieving a .330 lifetime batting average. His hitting philosophy was simple: "Any good batter can hit almost anything that's over the plate, provided he knows it's coming." (Ray Billbrough)

Johnny Neun hit with consistency (.288) during his four years with Detroit, but he is best remembered for making an unassisted triple play on May 31, 1927. (Brace Photo)

champion-to-be came out for the last round and nearly duplicated his heroics of the first game, going three-for-four, including a double and a home run. Seven hits in nine tries propelled Heilmann to a .398 average and the batting title. Fothergill hit a hefty .359 to rank fourth in the league, while Earl White-hill had 16 victories and the other five hurlers on the team each won 10 or more games.

Philadelphia challenged the Yankees in a two-team pennant race in 1928, while the Tigers fell to sixth place, 33 games from the top. Charlie Gehringer continued his emergence as a stellar player, but the dependable big hitters, Heilmann and Fothergill, slipped badly. The pitching was con-

first-division finish in fourth place, and the perennial hitters maintained the Tiger tradition. Harry Heilmann won his fourth batting title in seven years with a storybook finish. Al Simmons, his rival, had completed the season one day earlier and led Heilmann in the race by an eyelash, .392 to .391. Heilmann needed to hit .400 or better in the last two games of the season, a doubleheader at home against Cleveland, to surpass Simmons. In the opener, Heilmann had two doubles, a single, and a home run in five trips to the plate and grabbed the lead. Rather than sit out the last game with championship in hand, Heilmann tested ability, fate, and luck, saying, "I want to do it by playing the string out." Greeted by a standing ovation from an admiring crowd, the

Obviously hoping he could regain his previous form, Detroit obtained Yankee pitching standout Waite Hoyt in a five-player trade in 1930. In pieces of two seasons, Hoyt won 12 and suffered 16 setbacks before he was peddled to the National League. (Ray Billbrough)

Following the 1933 season, Detroit traded a fine young outfielder named Jonathan Stone for Goose Goslin. The Tigers bought three years of heavy run production in Goslin, but the acquisition wasn't cheap. Stone spent six years in Detroit hitting at a .304 clip and played five more with Washington, including a string of four .300-plus seasons. (Ray Billbrough)

sistently below average. Six pitchers posted losing records though college star Ownie Carroll showed his best stuff with 16 wins.

The future was still not in sight as Tiger ownership searched for a strategy that would produce a winner. Moriarty did not possess the magic and he was replaced by another friendly guy, boyish Stanley "Bucky" Harris. Harris had the distinction of being the only Tiger field boss to serve two terms in office, the first from 1929 to 1933, the second from 1955 to 1956. Prior to coming to Detroit, he had won pennants in 1924 and 1925 with Washington. He could not transfer his success with the Senators to Detroit, however. Harris had a lock on second-division fin-

ishes with seven Bengal teams.

During Harris's first tour with the Tigers, Detroit closed out 1929 in sixth place and made only slight improvement over the previous year. The diagnosis was fairly simple: the 1929 Tigers were the worst fielding team in the league and the most generous in giving up runs with a team ERA of 4.96 compared to a league average of 4.24. Gehringer and the outfielders continued to hit, but the old guard was aging fast. Heilmann was sent to Cincinnati following the season, and Fothergill played 55 games in 1930 before moving on to Chicago.

Eddie Wells pitched for Ludington in the old Central League in 1922 and the next season jumped all the way to Navin Field. He was 12–10 in 1926, his best season in Detroit before signing with the New York Yankees for the 1929 campaign. (Courtesy of the Burton Historical Collection of the Detroit Public Library)

Brought up through the minors, Absalom "Red" Wingo joined the Tigers in 1924 and played out the remaining five years of his career in the Motor City. In 1925, he batted .370 and scored 104 runs. (Courtesy of the Burton Historical Collection of the Detroit Public Library)

Larry Woodall spent his entire career (1920–29) playing for Detroit, primarily as a second-string catcher. He batted over .300 during three seasons. (William M. Anderson)

The home plate umpire goes over the ground rules with managers George Moriarty (*left*) and Don Howley of the St. Louis Browns. Moriarty was hired in 1927 and fired following the next season. Tiger catcher Johnny Basler stands off to the left. (William M. Anderson)

Heilmann closed out his career in Detroit by hitting .344 with 120 runs batted in, hardly the kind of season after which a team gives up on a star player, but arthritis was taking its toll. What a slugger he had been! Even including his first season when he played just 67 games, Heilmann averaged 98 runs batted in for each of his 15 years with Detroit.

In 1930, Gehringer hit .330, his fourth consecutive .300-plus season, promising to be the hub around which Tiger hopes would be built. That season introduced several of the supporting cast, including Hank Greenberg, Tommy Bridges, and Bill Rogell. The 1930 Tigers moved up a notch to fifth and won five more games.

The Tigers had struggled through a decade characterized by superb hitting, particularly among outfielders, yet counterbalanced by substandard pitching and an ever-changing infield. Cobb later

claimed, "No manager who ever lived can take a rag-tag and bob-tailed infield and an apology for a pitching staff and win a pennant." Detroit's crystal ball failed miserably when they traded Heinie Manush, principally to acquire disappointing pitcher Elam Vangilder, and then swapped pitcher Howard Ehmke for hurler Rip Collins. Ehmke promptly won 20 games for the last-place Red Sox. It was a time, too, when the pitching-starved Tigers were unable to see the potential of young Carl Hubbell or the talent of 19-year-old Floyd "Babe" Herman. This babe spent 13 years in the majors, whacking the ball for a .324 lifetime average. Yet another youngster with a great future slipped away in 1928. His name was Richard Ferrell. Both Hubbell and Ferrell would rate among baseball's greatest players and be enshrined in the Hall of Fame.

Catcher Rick Ferrell signed with Detroit in 1926. While Ferrell was playing for Columbus in the American Association in 1928, Commissioner Kenesaw "Mountain" Landis decided the Tigers were violating contractual rules and declared Ferrell a free agent. The future Hall of Famer signed with the St. Louis Browns and enjoyed a great 18-year major league career. Nineteen twenty-eight was a black year in Tiger player development history. (William M. Anderson)

After the team's near miss of a world championship in 1934, owner Frank Navin confers with team manager Mickey Cochrane during spring training at Lakeland the following year. (William M. Anderson)

5
Cochrane and an Era of Champions, 1931–1940

The Detroit Tigers continued to tread the waters of mediocrity for the next three seasons, providing little evidence that they were more than a losing proposition. Detroit's 1931 season proved to be a disaster: they lost 93 games and finished 32 wins below .500 and 47 games out of first, a gap unprecedented in the history of the franchise.

Hitting, which had been the hallmark of the Tigers, now reflected their overall level of play, and they ranked fifth, sixth, and sixth in the 1931, 1932, and 1933 seasons, respectively. Only in 1933 did the ball club have a hitter among the leaders, when Gehringer finished fifth at .325 and ranked in hits and total bases. The booming bats were gone.

Dale Alexander swung the biggest stick in the lineup, but not big enough to make up for his poor

The spoiler shakes hands with the near-perfect pitcher. On August 5, 1932, Detroit pitcher Tommy Bridges retired 26 straight Washington hitters before pinch hitter Dave Harris singled. (Courtesy of the Burton Historical Collection of the Detroit Public Library)

fielding. After compiling a .332 batting average for his first three seasons, Alexander was traded in 1932 to Boston, where he won the batting title with a .367 average.

Generally, pitching showed improvement after 1931 as the staff became more competitive. The following season, Earl Whitehill, in an oft-repeated role, led the staff with 16 victories. Then, in a two-for-one trade, the Tigers picked up pitchers Fred

Left to right: Pitchers Fred Marberry and Carl Fischer and outfielder Hank Greenberg run out to a scheduled practice at Henley Field in Lakeland, Florida, 1934. (Walter P. Reuther Library, Wayne State University)

Manager Del Baker (*center*) stops for conversation with two of the mainstays of his 1940 pennant-winning pitching staff. Schoolboy Rowe (*left*) had a comeback season, posting a 16–3 record, while Bobo Newsom led the starting rotation with 22 wins against only 5 defeats. (William M. Anderson)

Marberry and Carl Fischer from the Senators and parted with their ace left-hander. Whitehill immediately enjoyed his best-ever season in 1933, winning 22 games and helping Washington win the pennant. Marberry paced his new team with 16 wins, and Fischer chipped in with 11 more. Tommy Bridges was learning to control his splendid curve while steadily improving. In 1932, he flirted with greatness, retiring 26 batters in succession before pinch hitter Dave

Harris singled to ruin a perfect game.

Finishing fifth in 1932 turned out to be the high point of Bucky Harris's first tour of duty as Tiger pilot; these Bengals won one more game than they lost. This was the only winning season out of five under Harris. The next campaign was more of the same, fifth in the standings and a .487 winning percentage. Bucky resigned near the end of the schedule, claiming that five seasons was adequate

Birdie Tebbetts (*left*) enjoyed his best season with the Bengals in 1940 when he hit .296. Billy Sullivan shared the catching duties with Tebbetts during his two-year stay with Detroit and hit a highly respectable .295. (William M. Anderson)

opportunity to demonstrate success.

Hindsight would show that Harris led Detroit during a period when the Tigers were developing the players who would stock their powerful teams of the mid-1930s. Aside from Bridges, Gerald "Gee" Walker got his start in 1931; Jo-Jo White, another outfielder, broke in during the 1932 season. A banner crop of new talent surfaced the following year, with Hank Greenberg taking over first base, Ervin

"Pete" Fox earning a regular spot in the outfield, and Marv Owen playing full-time at third. Pitchers Elden Auker and Lynwood "Schoolboy" Rowe also made their debuts in 1933. Typically, young stars emerge sporadically or singularly; Detroit's assembly line farm system had an express lane, producing quality players in bunches.

The Tigers needed enthusiastic, aggressive leadership, so pronounced *Detroit Free Press* editor

Malcom W. Bingay, alias "Iffy the Dopester." Having enough of the congenial types, the Tigers should have returned to the style of Jennings and Cobb, but Frank Navin supposedly set his sights on a big-gate attraction, wanting to hire Babe Ruth. Although Ruth was available, his immediate commitments and ambitious compensation demands jinxed the deal. Then the potential of acquiring Mickey Cochrane emerged, offering the opportunity for both an outstanding catcher and a natural leader. After some ne-

gotiation, Connie Mack, owner of the financially strapped Philadelphia Athletics, agreed to sell Cochrane for $100,000. The Depression had drained Navin's reserves too and, after conferring with Walter Briggs, his partner readily provided the cash to purchase Cochrane.

No one wanted to win more than Mickey Cochrane, not even Ty Cobb, Frankie Frisch, or Jackie Robinson. "For the Tigers as a ball club," said Cochrane, "we have only one idea . . . fight and

Left to right: Schoolboy Rowe, Tommy Bridges, Vic Sorrell, Elden Auker. These four accounted for a lot of wins in 1934 with Rowe and Bridges the one and two starters for a fine pitching staff. (Ray Billbrough)

Cardinal pitching stalwart Dizzy Dean is carried from the field after being hit in the head by a ball, October 6, 1934. In game four of the World Series, Dean was sent in as a pinch runner. On a double-play grounder, he failed to slide into second and was struck in the head by the throw back to first. Catcher Mickey Cochrane, Marv Owen (#8), and the public address announcer can be seen in the foreground. (William M. Anderson)

hustle . . . and the ballplayer who doesn't whip himself mentally after losing a game isn't in the proper mental condition." Cobb, once his teammate on the Athletics, recalled how desperately "Black Mike" wanted to win. "One night in St. Louis after we had lost a game to the Browns we should have won, Mike came in the room, flung off his cap, and then walked over and jumped up and down on it."

Remarkably, the two Detroit player-managers were very much alike: both were great players, intelligent, extremely aggressive and enthusiastic, hard-nosed, angry combatants, and leaders by example. They were men of speed, and Cochrane liked to play Cobbian attack-style baseball: hit and run, steal, sacrifice and squeeze. Yet, in sharp contrast, what Tyrus the Untamed lacked, Black Mike brought to the game. Cobb managed a team consistently weak in pitchers and infielders; Cochrane, fortunately, inherited a young ball club where both of these crucial elements were potential strengths. Cochrane could skillfully handle pitchers and people, an ability Cobb lacked. Also different than his famous predecessor, Mickey Cochrane got along with umpires and

was generally admired by his competitors.

Prior to starting the 1934 season, the new Tiger skipper influenced a major trade, sending Jonathon Stone to Washington in exchange for outfielder Leon "Goose" Goslin. Goslin had starred on three

The mound crew of the 1940 Tigers. *Standing, left to right:* Lynn Nelson, John Gorsica, Al Benton, Tommy Bridges, Schoolboy Rowe, Buck Newsom. *Sitting, left to right:* Dizzy Trout, Hal Newhouser, Tom Seats, Archie McKain. (Courtesy of the Burton Historical Collection of the Detroit Public Library)

A horrible thud and Mickey Cochrane is felled by a pitch, May 15, 1937. Umpire Steve Basil and Yankee catcher Bill Dickey step forward to aid the Tiger manager. Cochrane recovered from a severe concussion, but his playing days were over. He was a lifetime .320 hitter, the identical average he had in 1934, his first season in Detroit. (National Baseball Library, Cooperstown, NY)

two challengers, the Tigers and the Yankees, with Cochrane carrying the flag to victory. The Tigers' 101 wins established a new team record. Aside from slugger Goslin, Detroit had great speed in the outfield with White, Fox, and Walker, who combined for 73 swipes, as Detroit ran to the stolen base championship. They were also leaders in team hitting and six other run-producing categories. The infield represented unsurpassed excellence, with Cochrane hitting .320, Greenberg .339, Gehringer .356 (second best in the league), Rogell .296, and Owen .317. Given this explosive firepower, the 1934 Tigers scored in multiples.

Two tigers with similar stripes tangled in the World Series, and the cats from Detroit were caged, Led by the cocky and talented Jerome "Dizzy" Dean, the St. Louis Cardinals came to town ready to do battle. Dean easily outdueled Alvin Crowder in the opener. In the next four engagements, the teams

Four future Hall of Famers have their pregame conversation interrupted by a photographer. *Left to right:* Mickey Cochrane, Jimmy Foxx, Charlie Gehringer, and Goose Goslin. (William M. Anderson)

championship Senator teams, and Cochrane wanted that winning attitude to rub off on his young players. In addition, Goose was a heavy hitter in the mold of Heilmann; he delivered for his new boss with three straight 100 RBI seasons.

Somewhat to Navin's chagrin, Cochrane "announced" that his team would win the American League pennant. Black Mike fueled a fighting spirit as the Tigers started fast. Led by the boss's inspiration, Greenberg, White, and Owen in particular exemplified Cochrane's aggressive style of play. Young hurlers Rowe and Bridges burst into greatness under Cochrane's skillful handling. Schoolboy, in just his second major league season, racked up a record-tying streak of 16 straight wins before being stopped in late August. Tommy Bridges had never harnessed his exceptional skills, winning no more than 14 games in any of his four previous seasons. These two gems, along with Auker and Marberry, turned in season performances to rank the staff with the best in baseball. Rowe won 24 to lead the mound corps, Bridges recorded 22 victories, and Auker and Marberry each racked up 15 wins.

As the season progressed, the field narrowed to

Hank Greenberg (*left*), Eddie Mayo, Rudy York, and Roy Cullenbine were the heart of the lineup for Steve O'Neill's 1945 world champion Detroit Tigers. (William M. Anderson)

First-inning play of the opening game of the 1935 World Series with Schoolboy Rowe on the mound. The Chicago Cubs won the first encounter, 3–0, but the Bengals prevailed to win the Series. (William M. Anderson)

Happy Tigers celebrate a big win by surprise starter Floyd Giebel. *Left to right:* Billy Sullivan, Giebel, John Gorsica, Del Baker, Rudy York. Hal Newhouser's smiling face is seen in the background. Rookie Giebel pitched the game of his life to best Bob Feller, 2–0, and clinched the pennant on September 27, 1940. (Ray Billbrough)

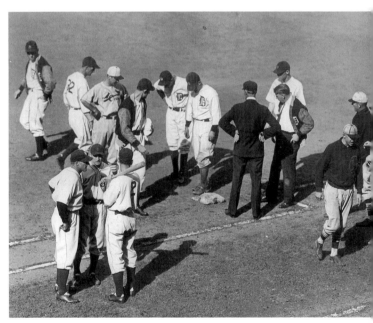

Tiger manager and catcher Mickey Cochrane looks down while standing at first base after being spiked in the knee during game six of the 1934 World Series against the St. Louis Cardinals. Goose Goslin is seen facing Charlie Gehringer (#2) along with Billy Rogell as the threesome converse in the foreground. Other Tiger personnel identified are (*left to right*) Coach Del Baker (#32), Elden Auker (*wearing warm-up jacket*), trainer Denny Carroll, and Coach Cy Perkins (#31) on the far right trying to catch a glimpse of the situation. (William M. Anderson)

Tigers' opening day lineup in 1940. *Left to right:* Barney McCosky, Bruce Campbell, Charlie Gehringer, Hank Greenberg, Rudy York, Pinky Higgins, Dick Bartell, Birdie Tebbetts, Bobo Newsom. (Courtesy of the Burton Historical Collection of the Detroit Public Library)

Elden Auker threw a fastball, a curve, and sinker from his submarine delivery. A product of the Tigers' farm system, Auker won 15 games in his first full season in helping Detroit win the American League pennant in 1934. He was an even bigger factor in 1935, chalking up 18 victories. The Kansas native pitched during six campaigns for Detroit. (William M. Anderson)

traded victories. Each time the Cardinals won, the Tigers countered to knot the Series. In game five, Bridges, helped by a circus catch from Jo-Jo White in the eighth inning, avenged an earlier defeat by besting the invincible Dizzy Dean. The Tigers were now poised to win their first world championship, and Cochrane handed the ball to his ace pitcher Rowe. As in game three, the other Dean (Paul) mastered the Tiger bats. Rowe was such a fine hitter that even with two out in the ninth and Detroit down 4–3, Cochrane sent him to the plate and the Schoolboy hit a long drive to centerfield for the final out. Dizzy the intimidator came back to tame the Tigers, blanking them on six hits while the Cardinals scored at will in a Series finale marred by frustration and anger.

Known as "Rowdy Richard," Dick Bartell was a first-team bench jockey. Although he played only one full season with Detroit, Bartell helped spur the Tigers to a pennant victory in 1940. (William M. Anderson)

Undaunted by defeat, Cochrane repeated his prophecy, claiming the Tigers would win again in 1935. The doubters cautioned, however, that Cochrane would not be so lucky in 1935 and experience an injury-free season. This time the Tigers stumbled out of the gate and played catch-up for several months. As the team got on track, they bore down on the Yankees, seizing the lead in July, and then set the pace to victory in October. These were very profitable years for Mr. Navin, for his winning teams drew 919,000 in 1934 and topped the million mark with a record-high attendance in 1935.

Detroit's attack was formidable, leading the league in hitting, slugging, and runs scored. Big Hank Greenberg hammered home 170 runs and batted .328, leading the parade of offensive weapons. Gehringer hit .330, Fox .321, and dependable Cochrane came through with a .319 average.

Bridges and Rowe traded places in pacing the pitching staff in victories, with 21 and 19, respectively. Auker won big with 18 victories, and the old veteran Crowder reached back for one last hurrah, winning 16.

In the 1935 Series opener against the Chicago Cubs, Cochrane played a different card, leading with one of his strongest hurlers, pitting strength against strength. Although Rowe pitched well, Cub hurler Lon Warneke was better, blanking the Tigers on four hits. Detroit took game two, but suffered a huge loss when Greenberg, the league's most valued player, was seriously injured and lost for the Series. Cochrane's boys rallied to win three in a row, putting

Tommy Bridges pitched for the Bengals during 16 seasons beginning in 1930. His best years were 1934, 1935, and 1936, when he won over 20 games in three consecutive seasons. Though he had a blazing fastball, hitters were even more impressed with his great curveball. Bridges tried to set up the hitter and then throw him something extra special. In his words, "If I put all I have on the first ball, the batter has looked over the worst he has to face." (William M. Anderson)

The two opposing moundsmen, Paul Dean (*left*) and Tommy Bridges, pose for a ceremonial photograph before game three of the 1934 World Series. Although the hits were nearly even, Detroit stranded 13 runners and St. Louis won the contest, 4–1. Bridges was gone after four innings and Dean went the full nine. (Walter P. Reuther Library, Wayne State University)

A lifetime .320 hitter, Mickey Cochrane hit .320 and .319 while leading his Tigers to successive American League pennants in 1934 and 1935. (William M. Anderson)

Roy Cullenbine hit 24 home runs, his best ever, during his last season in the majors. The one-time Tiger bat boy was given a brief trial in 1938 and 1939 and declared a free agent the following year. He signed with Brooklyn and then played for several other clubs before returning to Detroit in 1945. (William M. Anderson)

Ervin "Pete" Fox became a regular in his first season in 1932 after a banner year at Beaumont in the Texas League. A consistent hitter, Fox averaged .302 during eight seasons for Detroit. He hit most pitchers but found the fastball of future Hall of Famer Charles "Red" Ruffing the toughest. "The darn thing breaks three ways, up, out, and in," said Fox. (William M. Anderson)

The league's Most Valuable Player in 1937, Charlie Gehringer had an awesome season, getting 209 hits, scoring 133 runs, and batting .371. Gehringer had more than 200 hits in seven seasons. (William M. Anderson)

Babe Ruth (*left*) is sharing some batting advice as two sluggers converse during the 1934 World Series. Four years later Hank Greenberg would seriously challenge Ruth's season record of 60 home runs, falling just two short with his career best. (Detroit News Archives)

the Cubs in a must-win situation. In a repeat of the first game pitching matchups, Warneke again prevailed as Tiger batters could only muster a single run. The sixth and deciding game was a seesaw contest that went down to the final out. After Detroit scored a run in the sixth, the game remained tied until the tension-packed ninth inning. Stan Hack opened the Cub half of the inning with a long triple. Cochrane stayed with Bridges, and the Tennessean quickly retired the next three batters, stranding Hack at third. Detroit staged its own threat in the bottom of the ninth, with Cochrane triggering a rally by getting a safety and moving into scoring position on the second out of the inning. Then another old veteran of pressure, Goose Goslin, banged a single to right, and the Tigers were champions of the world.

The stage was perfect. Winning their first modern world championship at home set off a huge victory celebration. Cochrane, like Jennings, had begun his managerial career with two successive pennant victories, but only fiery Black Mike had seized the golden ring. And for owner Frank Navin, his patient faith and untiring determination had finally been rewarded.

There was joy in Detroit; yet within weeks, the city was jolted from its ecstasy by the news that Frank Navin had died. Navin was the rock upon which the foundation of the Tiger organization had been built. His stabilizing influence was all-important in the survival and development of the franchise. As a senior and respected executive, he played a similar cementing role in the American League. His death marked the end of a dynasty. Walter O. Briggs then claimed the reins of power, and he became sole owner of the team.

Through two glory-filled seasons the Tigers had escaped injury, but their luck ran out when Greenberg broke a wrist in the 1935 World Series. Early in the spring and after playing only 12 games, Hammerin' Hank reinjured his tender wrist, and the big slugger was knocked out for the season. Despite winning 19 games, Schoolboy Rowe pitched with a lingering sore arm. Then, in June, the always driv-

Alvin "General" Crowder had established a formidable record when the Tigers acquired him for the 1935 season. Crowder had led the league with 26 and 24 victories in 1932 and 1933 but had an off year in 1934. But he came up big for the American League champion Tigers winning 16 games and game four of the World Series with route going 5 hitter. (William M. Anderson)

ing, always intense Cochrane suffered a nervous breakdown. Directed to get away from the pressure of baseball, Black Mike rested and recuperated on a ranch in Wyoming. He returned in mid-July to complete the season, though he played in just 44 games. Cochrane and Greenberg, the league's most valuable players for the previous two seasons, played only a fraction of the games in 1936.

New York won the flag in a breeze, beating the second-place Tigers by 19 1/2 games, while only three games separated the second- and fifth-place teams in the standings.

Tom Bridges enjoyed a great season, topping all hurlers with 23 wins. The team's earned run average ballooned to 4.00, about average for the league, but average pitching does not win pennants. Charlie Gehringer had another sparkling year, getting 227 hits, good for a .354 average, 144 runs scored, and 116 runs batted in. New acquisition Al Simmons maintained his status as an outstanding hitter with a .327 average, and six-year veteran Gee Walker hit an impressive .353.

Once kissed by destructive fate, Cochrane could not reverse his personal fortune. Late in May 1937, while playing the Yankees, Cochrane was beaned by pitcher Bump Hadley and suffered multiple fractures of the skull. Miraculously, he survived and, following months of convalescence, resumed his managerial duties, but he would never play again. During both of Cochrane's absences in 1936 and 1937, coach Del Baker managed the team.

Elden "Chief" Hogsett was used primarily in relief during his tenure with Detroit, which began in 1929. He pitched extremely well during four appearances in the 1934 and 1935 World Series. (William M. Anderson)

Hard-throwing Fred Marberry was acquired from Washington prior to the start of the 1933 season. He was an important member of the mound staff in 1933 and 1934, winning 31 games while pitching both as a starter and reliever. (William M. Anderson)

Norman "Buck" or "Bobo" Newsom pitched for seven major league teams, including five stints with the Washington Senators, three with the St. Louis Browns, and two different sojourns with the Philadelphia Athletics. He was a most unusual fellow, fond of making predictions (which he often achieved) and calling people "Bobo," explaining: "You meet so many people in this racket you go nuts tryin' to remember them." Newsom won 50 and lost 35 in three years with Detroit (1939–41) and played a big role in Detroit's 1940 pennant win. (William M. Anderson)

◄ Switch hitter Billy Rogell made the big club with Detroit in 1930. He got into just 102 games the first two seasons but became the regular shortstop in 1932. Full-time duty was the chance Rogell needed, holding down the shortstop position for the next seven seasons. Over a 10-year period, he hit for a .274 average. Rogell had his career season in 1934, scoring 114 runs, driving in 100, and batting .296. (William M. Anderson)

After one season in a utility role, Marv Owen became the regular third baseman for Detroit in 1933. Owen had an outstanding season in 1934, compiling a .317 average and driving in 96 tallies. (William M. Anderson)

Lynwood "Schoolboy" Rowe appeared to be a pitching giant when he won 24 games in 1934, but his often ailing right arm curtailed expected greatness. He won 19 games in each of the next two years and then faltered. A great athlete and excellent hitter, he once made five hits in a game and batted .271 over 10 seasons for Detroit. (William M. Anderson)

The Tigers were runner-up to the Yankees again. They were first in hitting and seventh in pitching. Rowe pitched in only 10 games to begin a three-year stretch in which he won 12 and lost 18. Roxie Lawson won 18 and pitched as never before or again. Gehringer made lots of noise with his bat, hitting a league-leading .371 and promoting his selection as Most Valuable Player. During August, rookie slugger Rudy York went on a home run tear, hitting 18 circuit clouts to establish a new major league record. Greenberg came within one of the league season record for runs batted in, as he accounted for 183.

The erosion of pitching continued to plague Detroit in 1938. Cochrane and Baker used an array of arms; there was no stopper among this crew. Greenberg and York generated the greatest excitement with the Tigers, for they made up a two-man "Murderers' Row." Hank Greenberg blasted home runs with fury throughout the season, seriously challenging the Babe's record of 60. Hank clouted 58 round-trippers, and his partner hit 33, good for first and fourth in the league. And they were second and fourth in runs batted in.

In August, owner Walter Briggs decided it was

▲ After being injured for the fifth time in his career, Detroit gave up on Fred "Dixie" Walker and sold him on waivers to Brooklyn on July 24, 1939. From 1940 through 1948, Walker hit under .300 just once. (William M. Anderson)

▼ Mickey Cochrane had played with Al Simmons on those great Philadelphia Athletics teams in 1929–31 and wanted that big hitter to ensure a third straight flag for Detroit in 1936. The purchase was made in December 1935, and although Simmons did his job (112 RBIs and a .327 batting average), the team didn't win, and he was "transferred" to Washington following the season. (William M. Anderson)

Signed off the Wake Forest College campus, Vic Sorrell pitched his entire career (1928–37) in the Tiger organization. Interviewed in 1933, he talked about the settling influence of experience and losing close games. Sorrell stated, "Even hotheaded pitchers tend to grow philosophical with the passing of a few seasons." Sorrell won 92 and lost 101. (William M. Anderson)

time for change, relieving Cochrane and replacing him with Del Baker. Cochrane clearly was not the same leader on the bench as he had been on the field. The 1938 Tigers performed at a pennant-winning pace (37–20) under Baker's leadership. Their 84 wins and 70 losses bought the Tigers a fourth-place finish as the powerful Yankees made it three in a row.

Detroit lost further ground in 1939, slipping down a place in the final standings and finishing 26 1/2 games back in the pack. Owner Briggs continued to shake up the roster, completing his second blockbuster trade, this one involving 10 players. The key acquisition was pitcher Bobo Newsom. This most colorful character enjoyed making predictions and called almost everyone "Old Bobo," including Mr.

73

Briggs. Fortunately, he was quite a pitcher. Bobo quickly hit his stride in Detroit, winning 17 in less than a full season. Bridges returned to past form, matching Newsom's victory total, and Tiger fans had their first glimpse of future star hurlers Hal Newhouser and Paul "Dizzy" Trout. Other new faces included Mike "Pinky" Higgins, a third baseman acquired from Boston, George "Birdie"

Jo-Jo White was a Tiger outfielder from 1932 to 1938. Never a great threat with his bat, White "earned his keep" defensively and as a base runner. In game five of the 1934 World Series, White made a spectacular catch which, in the opinion of some observers, ranked among the best ever. That season he batted .313, easily his highest average. (William M. Anderson)

Speed merchant Gerald "Gee" Walker was a rookie sensation when he came up with the Tigers in 1931. Although erratic on the base paths, he stole a lot of bases. Walker was a very popular player and his trade to Chicago in 1937 caused a fan uproar. For seven seasons with Detroit, Walker batted .317. (William M. Anderson)

The Walker brothers, Gerald "Gee" (*left*) and Harvey "Hub," joined the Tigers together in 1931. (William M. Anderson)

Tebbetts, who became the regular catcher in 1939, and outfielder Barney McCosky, who played brilliantly in his first year while collecting 190 hits.

The farm system, which had steadily produced a bumper crop of fine players, received a terrible setback in January when Commissioner Kenesaw "Mountain" Landis decreed that Detroit had illegally manipulated minor league player contracts and transfers. The penalty declared free agency of 91 players.

There were plenty of other surprises in 1940, the most important of which was that New York did not run away with the pennant. The Tigers were given new opportunity in a more balanced competition among Detroit, Cleveland, and New York, and unexpected help because of internal dissension within the Tribe. All-Star first baseman Hank Greenberg was also surprised when he was asked to play left field so that a position could be opened for hard-hitting, weak-fielding Rudy York. Thanks to management's financial incentives and Hank's determi-

▲ Jack Zeller (*left*) and manager Del Baker chat before a game at Briggs Stadium. Zeller had a long baseball career, beginning in Texas in the minor leagues. He eventually became the Tigers' farm director and later earned a promotion to general manager. (William M. Anderson)

▼ Three Tigers stars celebrate a victory: Goose Goslin (*left*), Schoolboy Rowe, and playing manager Mickey Cochrane. (William M. Anderson)

◀ Rudy York was a two-dimensional player—he could hit and throw. His first full season with the Tigers was in 1937, and he belted 35 home runs. York explained that he changed his stance in the minors and said, "That's when I started sockin' 'em long." From August 2, 1937, through the end of the month, York went on a home run binge, "socking" 18 over the wall. In nine years with Detroit, he hit 239 homers and averaged 104 runs batted in a season. Rudy was swapped to the Red Sox after the 1945 campaign. (William M. Anderson)

Tiger broadcaster Harry Heilmann visits with Hall of Famer Grover Cleveland Alexander. The great pitcher never played for Detroit; he was performing some ceremonial function suited up in a Tiger uniform. (William M. Anderson)

Opposing hurlers had to bear down when pitching through the heart of the Tigers' 1935 lineup. These guys could hit. *Left to right:* Hank Greenberg (.328), Goose Goslin (.292), Charlie Gehringer (.330), Pete Fox (.321). (William M. Anderson)

After losing the World Series in seven games in 1934, Detroit readied for the new campaign with its fine mound corps intact. Shown here during spring training at Henley Field are the pitchers Manager Mickey Cochrane would rely on to bring another flag to Detroit. *Left to right:* Tommy Bridges, Fred Marberry, Elden Auker, Vic Sorrell, Alvin Crowder, Chief Hogsett, Schoolboy Rowe. (William M. Anderson)

Mickey Cochrane got his insurance policy when owner Walter Briggs agreed to purchase slugger Al Simmons (*left*) for the 1936 season as Detroit tried to win three pennants in a row. Despite Simmons's presence, Detroit finished a weak second. Shown here are three former members of the Philadelphia Athletics: Simmons, Mickey Cochrane, and Cy Perkins. (William M. Anderson)

The Tigers should have been highly favored in game two of the 1934 World Series with pitchers Bill Hallahan (*left;* 8–12) and Schoolboy Rowe (24–8). The game went 12 innings before a single by Goose Goslin scored the winning run for a 3–2 victory for Detroit. Rowe went the distance while Hallahan pitched into the ninth. (William M. Anderson)

It was common for former star players to make appearances during postseason games. Here Babe Ruth wishes both managers, Detroit's Mickey Cochrane and Charlie Grimm, good fortune in the 1935 World Series. (William M. Anderson)

nation, the experiment worked magnificently. Detroit stayed in close contention throughout most of the campaign, overtaking Cleveland on September 10. The season ended with a Detroit-Cleveland showdown. Bob Feller would start the all-or-nothing series for Cleveland and, with the luck of a riverboat gambler, Manager Baker selected rookie Floyd Giebel to oppose the Indian ace. Giebel pitched the game of his life, and York drove one of just three hits off Feller into the stands for a two-run homer and the victory. The win brought Detroit its sixth American League pennant, won by the slim margin of one game, yet a major vault upward from the previous season's finish.

Pitcher Izzy Goldstein (*left*), first baseman Harry Davis, outfielder Gee Walker, and shortstop Heinie Schuble were all considered legitimate prospects in 1932. Only Walker made a significant impact. (William M. Anderson)

This is a view of a packed Navin Field down in the left-field corner during the 1935 World Series. (William M. Anderson)

The Tigers parted with a younger hitter to obtain a veteran batsman. A recognized clutch hitter, Goose Goslin drove in 100 or more runs each of his first three seasons with Detroit. This great career hitter won election to the Hall of Fame in 1968. (William M. Anderson)

Greenberg and York were the crushers in the Tiger lineup, ranking first and second in runs batted in and first and third in home runs. In addition to leading the league in these two power measures, Hank Greenberg had the best record for total bases, slugging, and doubles. His great production earned him a second Most Valuable Player award. Detroit native McCosky was even more spectacular in his sophomore season, batting .340 and matching Greenberg's team-leading average.

Buck Newsom (he had several names) pitched masterfully, winning 13 straight en route to a 21–5 season and a strong 2.83 earned run average. Nearly as important to winning the pennant was the outstanding comeback performance of Rowe. He compiled a 16–3 record as the number two man in the rotation.

Detroit faced defending National League champion Cincinnati in the 1940 World Series. This Series opened in Ohio, and the visiting Tigers quickly

Pitcher Vern Kennedy (*left*) and outfielder Dixie Walker pose for the photographer. Journeyman Kennedy hurled for seven teams during his twelve-year big league career. Once a 21-game winner with the Chicago White Sox, he won 12 games for the 1938 Tigers. Though injured, Walker had a good season in 1938, batting .308. (William M. Anderson)

The Tiger field management team at spring training in 1933 in San Antonio. *Left to right:* Coach Wish Egan, Manager Bucky Harris, Coach Del Baker. (William M. Anderson)

got the upper hand with a decisive 7–2 victory behind Newsom. Unable to shake his World Series jinx, Schoolboy Rowe dropped his fourth postseason contest the next day. In game three, Tiger bats banged out 13 safeties, tallying seven runs, and the veteran Bridges went the route for a second Detroit win. There were no days off for travel, and the teams played every day. Detroit hosted game four, and Paul Derringer got even for his first game drubbing, stopping the Tigers on five hits. The advantage swung back to Detroit after Newsom hurled a brilliant three-hitter the next afternoon. Leading three games to two, Detroit was positioned for the kill but could not deliver the blow. Cincinnati shut out the Tigers in game six and, despite a valiant ef-

The game is about to begin as the Tigers square off against the Chicago Cubs at Navin Field during the 1935 World Series. (William M. Anderson)

fort on one day's rest, Old Bobo's superb pitching in the finale was not supported by enough offense and Detroit lost, 2–1.

The Motor City had survived the Great Depression. Now a new international crisis fueled its recovering economy as America became the arsenal of democracy. Amid economic, political, and military shockwaves, the Detroit Tigers and their city had flourished with three American League pennants, three one-million gate seasons, and a host of new heroes.

Having the opportunity to select any player on the San Francisco Seals club in 1928, Detroit ultimately picked Roy Johnson over Earl Averill. Averill became a star for Cleveland, and the Tigers eventually acquired him during the 1939 season. He spent the following season in Detroit before closing out his career with the Boston Braves in 1941. (William M. Anderson)

Two servicemen meet at Briggs Stadium before an Army-Navy game. Fred Hutchinson served in the Navy and outfielder Pat Mullin was an enlisted man in the Army in 1942. For some unexplained reason, he is out of uniform, according to military protocol. (William M. Anderson)

6
The War Years
1941–1950

World War II had a major influence on American life, and the entertainment business of professional baseball was not exempt. The war years stripped teams of numerous talented players and lowered the overall level of play. Many outstanding players lost several prime playing years while they served in the military, and less talented players were consequently given an opportunity to play major league baseball in order to fill up the ranks.

The first Tiger inducted into the armed forces was able-bodied and eligible bachelor Henry Greenberg, who became a soldier in 1941 and missed the entire season. Pearl Harbor and the American entry into the war in December extended Greenberg's

A contingent of the many Detroit Tiger players who served in the military during World War II. These returning veterans included (*left to right*) Al Benton, Red Borom, Les Mueller, Hank Greenberg, Tommy Bridges, and Walt Wilson, September 1945. (E. J. "Red" Borom)

Barney McCosky, a product of the Tiger farm system, was a highly regarded rookie who began his big league career hitting like a veteran. In his first season with Detroit, McCosky had 190 hits, scored 120 runs, and batted .311. In Detroit's pennant-winning 1940 season he led the league with 200 hits and hit a robust .340. Though a .312 lifetime hitter, his lack of power diminished his value and Detroit sent him to the Philadelphia A's in 1946 for third baseman George Kell. (Brace Photo)

military service, and Detroit lost a premier player until July 1, 1945.

Auto magnate Walter Briggs had been a silent partner for years, allowing conservative Frank Navin great latitude in directing the Detroit Baseball Company. Like future owner Tom Monaghan, he was a longstanding Tiger fan; he was also an exuberant one, having been once threatened with expulsion by an American League umpire if he didn't quiet down. He first met Navin when he was unable to purchase tickets for the 1907 World Series, and his persistence got him a seat.

The squad that pitched Detroit to the 1945 World Series. *Standing, left to right:* Art Houtteman, Walter Wilson, Les Mueller, Jim Tobin, George Caster. *Sitting, left to right:* Hal Newhouser, Al Benton, Dizzy Trout, Stubby Overmire, Zeb Eaton. (Courtesy of the Burton Historical Collection of the Detroit Public Library)

Catcher Birdie Tebbetts and pitcher Pat McLaughlin are caught in a lighter moment. (William M. Anderson)

Briggs liked aggressive baseball and players. As sole proprietor, he pitched into the game, ready to invest his wealth and make bold personnel moves to improve the club. Following Navin's death, Briggs enlarged the right-field grandstand and bleachers and two years later revamped the stadium to increase seating to 53,000. Although he loved Mickey Cochrane, Briggs fired his friend. He spent big dollars to acquire Al Simmons and to sign bonus players Dick Wakefield and Fred Hutchinson. The war would keep the best executive busy replacing the troops and marshaling a team that could mount an attack.

The Yankees outclassed the league in 1941, winning the crown by 17 games, while Detroit tumbled all the way down to a fourth-place tie, a huge reversal for the defending champions. Those Tigers

Baseball commissioner Kenesaw "Mountain" Landis raises his hat while attending a late-season game in Briggs Stadium as the Tigers scrap for a pennant in 1940. Seated with Landis are Tiger owner Walter O. Briggs and his son "Spike." (William M. Anderson)

One of the greatest single-season pitching tandems ever, Dizzy Trout (*left*) and Hal Newhouser had each won 26 games by September 23, 1944. Trout eventually won 27 and Newhouser led the league with 29 victories. (William M. Anderson)

George "Birdie" Tebbetts was a fine receiver and leader during nine campaigns with the Bengals. He was a talker who liked to distract hitters with his chatter. He accumulated an even 1,000 hits in his 14-year major league career. (William M. Anderson)

broke the string of seven consecutive winning seasons. Offensively, they were strictly a second-division club with a few bright spots: York, McCosky, Higgins, and rookie Pat Mullin. In a brief 54-game trial, Mullin hit .345 and then missed the next 615 games when a higher duty called and he went off to the war. Big winner Newsom became big loser Newsom as he languished through a league-leading 20 setbacks that ensured a change of uniform. Overall, the pitching staff was very average, with Al Benton's 15 victories the best among the lot.

Dick Wakefield received a big bonus when he signed off the University of Michigan campus in 1941. Although he hit .293 over nine seasons, even more was expected of this hot prospect. (William M. Anderson)

Virgil Trucks pitched brilliantly for the Navy during 1944–45, winning 28 and losing only once. He first joined Mickey Cochrane's powerful Great Lakes Naval Training Station team and in February 1945 was a star pitcher when two service teams played on several Pacific Islands. On April 10, 1945, Trucks wrote to Tiger General Manger Jack Zeller, "I guess you know that we have just completed a tour of the Pacific with two Navy teams. And had a wonderful tour. But boy being stationed here in the Marianas is really no fun. Hal White is here with me. McCosky is on another island." (William M. Anderson)

Boston mounted a challenge in the next campaign, but the Yankees were winning the wars on the home front. The toothless Tigers fell 30 games down the list, playing losing baseball and unable to muster a .300 hitter. Any cause for hope rested with a promising young mound corps that finished runner-up in earned run average. Virgil "Fire" Trucks, who had previously pitched only two innings in the majors, won a team-high 14 games and exemplified several young and strong arms in the Tiger arsenal.

▶ Dick Wakefield (*left*) and Hoot Evers shared similar backgrounds: both played at Beaumont in the Texas leaguer as minor leaguers and had served in the military during World War II. Wakefield never regained the level of performance he exhibited in 1943 but Evers's best years were yet to come. (Grand Rapids History and Special Collections, Grand Rapids Public Library)

Super scout Wish Egan is surrounded by the team of fine Tiger players he personally signed. *Left to right, back row:* Hal Newhouser, Roy Cullenbine. *Middle row:* Art Houtteman, Egan, Johnny Lipon. *Front row:* Gerald Burke, Billy Pierce, Barney McCosky. Egan also signed Hoot Evers, Stubby Overmire, Joe Ginsberg, Johnny Groth, Dizzy Trout, and Neil Berry. (William M. Anderson)

He had fanned an amazing total of 418 at Andalusia in 1938. Trucks, Newhouser, and Trout were the core of hard-throwing pitchers during a decade when Tiger hurlers were annually among the leaders in strikeouts. The other two flamethrowers, Newhouser and Trout, took longer to harness their heat. Both had spirited dispositions and blazing missiles. Trout lost 18 games in 1942, and Newhouser absorbed 17 defeats in 1943. They both got it together the following season and became big winners.

The Tigers on Uncle Sam's team kept mounting until, by 1943, President Roosevelt had a better outfit than President Briggs. Uncle Sam's roster included infielders Jimmy Bloodworth, Charlie Gehringer, Billy Hitchcock, and Johnny Lipon; outfielders Walter "Hoot" Evers, Hank Greenberg, Barney McCosky, Pat Mullin, and Dick Wakefield; and pitchers Al Benton, Tommy Bridges, Fred Hutchinson, Les Mueller, Virgil Trucks, and Hal White.

After two progressively poor finishes, Tiger ownership ousted Manager Baker and promoted another Detroit coach, Steve O'Neill. O'Neill, a fine former catcher, had previous managerial experience at Cleveland and in the Tiger minor league organization. A change in leadership brought improved per-

Shortstop Johnny Lipon, a seven-year Tiger veteran (1942, 1946–52), enjoyed his best year in 1950, hitting .293. (William M. Anderson)

A million-dollar outfield and a future Hall of Fame third baseman made for a formidable core on a fine 1950 Detroit Tigers team. *Left to right:* third baseman George Kell (.340), left fielder Hoot Evers (.323), right fielder Vic Wertz (.308), centerfielder Johnny Groth (.306). (William M. Anderson)

Detroit won 92 games in 1946 and finished 12 back of the pennant-winning Yankees. These four along with Freddie Hutchinson made up the starting rotation led by Hal Newhouser. *Left to right:* Dizzy Trout, Virgil Trucks, Al Benton, Hal Newhouser. (William M. Anderson)

Fleet outfielder Hoot Evers hit over .300 in three successive seasons for the Tigers and compiled a .290 average during his nine years with Detroit. Several years of military service during World War II and frequent injuries deprived Evers of an even more impressive career. (Grand Rapids History and Special Collections, Grand Rapids Public Library)

One of the many fine pitching prospects signed off the Detroit sandlots, young lefty Billy Pierce pitched in only 27 games for his hometown Tigers. Needing a catcher, Detroit traded Pierce for Aaron Robinson in a disastrous deal in 1948. Following his departure, Pierce won 208 games. (Detroit News Archives)

formances; the Tigers played two games above .500 and pulled up a little closer to the front. Even though repeating as fifth-place finishers, they were only six and a half games out of second place. Sensational and confident rookie Dick Wakefield made a serious run for the batting title. His .316 average made him second best, and fellow Detroiter Roger "Doc" Cramer was fourth in a year in which Luke Appling hit less than a usual champion mark of .328. During Greenberg's tour of duty, Rudy York took over as the main Tiger power broker. In this season, York led the junior circuit in home runs, slugging, runs batted in, and total bases. The team was first in hitting and fourth in earned runs allowed. Right-hander Trout mastered his skills and fashioned a 20-victory season.

As major league baseball players made an increasing presence in the armed forces, civilian teams were more and more armed with spear carriers. The

Detroit needed help at the catching position and assumed that left-handed hitting Aaron Robinson could readily reach the short fence in right field at Briggs Stadium. Having to decide which of their two prime young left-handers to trade, Ted Gray (*left*) or Billy Pierce, management decided to let Pierce go. Considered the worst trade in franchise history, Pierce went on to become an all-star. (Detroit News Archives)

A nine-year Tiger veteran, pitcher Al Benton joined the Tigers in 1938. He won 71 games for Detroit, dividing his pitching duties between starting and relief. (William M. Anderson)

One of the great power hitters of all time, Hank Greenberg led the American League in home runs and runs batted in four of the 12 years he played. Although twice named the Most Valuable Player, Hank lost the honor to Jimmy Foxx in 1938, despite hitting 58 home runs, scoring 144, and driving in 146. A great student of the game, a philosophical Greenberg once said, "The time to get mad at the man on the hill is when you are going up to the plate to face him, not after you've taken your turn." (William M. Anderson)

talent drain affected all teams and the Yankees in particular, perhaps accounting for a more interesting pennant race in 1944. In a rare circumstance in Detroit history, this team relied on the pitchers for their pennant-contending season. Even the big run producer York was off; his assistants were good for only a so-so performance. The return of serviceman Wakefield at midseason significantly bolstered the Bengal attack. Excitement was generated by awesome performances by Newhouser and Trout, the greatest one-season pitching duo in baseball history. From July 13 on, when Detroit made its move, those two went to the whip, winning 33 of 51 victories, often relieving each other. Detroit rode the Newhouser-Trout express as the tandem captured all season pitching records. Newhouser ranked first in wins (29) and strikeouts (187) and second in earned run

Charlie Gehringer had a fluid picture swing. He was a hard line-drive hitter and one of the best two-strike hitters. Satchel Paige said, "You couldn't fool him." In 19 seasons with Detroit, this great infielder batted .320. (William M. Anderson)

Manager Steve O'Neill gave Ted Gray his big league start in 1946. His best season was 1949 when he compiled a 10–10 record. Following the 1954 season he was traded to the Chicago White Sox. (Grand Rapids History and Special Collections, Grand Rapids Public Library)

Though a good player, Johnny Groth was haunted by an expectation of his being a Joe DiMaggio clone. He became the starting centerfielder in 1949 and played there through 1952. Traded to the St. Louis Browns following the season, he was reacquired by the Tigers in 1958. In all, he played 10 years for the Bengals and compiled a .293 batting average. (Grand Rapids History and Special Collections, Grand Rapids Public Library)

Some continue to believe that Roger "Doc" Cramer belongs in Baseball's Hall of Fame. The 20-year veteran collected 2,720 hits and had a career batting average of .296. He spent his last seven years with Detroit, including the 1945 season when he played a key role on the world champion team. (William M. Anderson)

▶ One of the better third basemen in Tiger history, Mike "Pinky" Higgins compiled a .280 batting average in six-plus seasons with Detroit. The Tigers acquired Higgins from Boston in 1939. (William M. Anderson)

Michigan native Walter O. Briggs owned and operated Briggs Manufacturing Company, a builder of automobile bodies. He became a minority owner of the Detroit Tigers in 1919 and when owner Frank Navin died in 1935, he purchased the majority shares owned by the estate and became the sole owner of the club. Mr. Briggs was a great Detroit Tigers fan, a passion developed from childhood. He greatly expanded the ballpark, which reopened in 1938 and was christened Briggs Stadium. (William M. Anderson)

average (2.22), complete games (25), shutouts (6), and innings pitched (312.1). Trout, the other half of this pitching machine, finished second in wins (27) and strikeouts (144) and first in earned run average (2.12), complete games (33), shutouts (7), and innings pitched (352.1).

The drama built to the very last series of the season, with Detroit holding a one-game lead and playing lowly Washington, while St. Louis engaged

Seated on a bench alongside the clubhouse at Henley Field in Lakeland are infielders George Kell (*left*), Eddie Lake, Eddie Mayo, and Roy Cullenbine. Mayo and Cullenbine were nearing the end of their playing careers in 1947. (Grand Rapids History and Special Collections, Grand Rapids Public Library)

After winning 25 games in 1939 for Seattle in the Pacific Coast League, Detroit purchased young Fred Hutchinson, considered a great prospect. Hutch joined the major league club in 1939 and pitched in the Motor City for 11 years, posting a 75–71 record. He was a control pitcher who finessed hitters by changing speeds. (William M. Anderson)

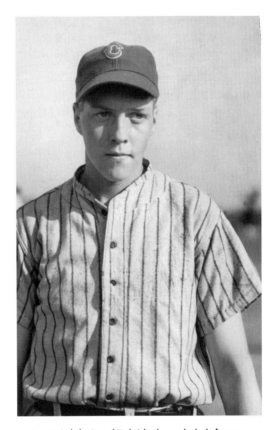

For years, Detroit Catholic Central High School was a hotbed of amateur baseball, and several young ballplayers graduated to the big time including John McHale, pictured here, and Art Houttleman, Ray Herbert, and Frank Tanana, all of whom eventually played for the Tigers. McHale played 64 games over parts of five seasons with Detroit from 1943 to 1948. He later became general manager of the team and an executive with other major league clubs. (Detroit News Archives)

contending New York. The Browns met the challenge, winning all four; the Tigers split their series, and St. Louis captured their only pennant as members of the American League.

Detroit took up where they left off the previous season and drove for the lead in 1945. Hitting again played a subordinate role as the pitchers blazed an outstanding 2.99 earned run average. Newhouser and Trout were joined by Al Benton, fresh from military duty, in giving the pennant-bound Tigers solid pitching. "Prince Hal" was the league's dominant force, besting all others in eight categories, including 25 wins and a 1.81 ERA.

Taking over first place in early June, the Bengals stayed at the front of the pack through the remaining months, holding off the challenge of the surprising Washington Senators. In a bad news–good news

exchange, Uncle Sam took Wakefield but gave Greenberg back. After a four-year absence from Briggs Stadium, Hank came hammerin' back with a home run announcement in his very first game on July 1. York continued his consistent slugging, and Detroit got some added punch when it reacquired outfielder Roy Cullenbine. Through some strange scheduling, Washington finished its season a week early and watched as the race between the Tigers and the Browns went to the last day. Weather forced a doubleheader, with the Tigers needing one victory to clinch. In a rain-soaked first game, Detroit rallied in the ninth, filling the bases with two outs and

93

Like many others of his generation, Pat Mullin's baseball career was interrupted by military service during World War II. In all, Mullin played the outfield for Detroit for nine-plus seasons. He was a .271 hitter for the Tigers. (William M. Anderson)

leaving it up to their best weapon, ex-army captain Henry Greenberg. Hank rocketed the ball into the left-field stands for a pennant-winning grand slam homer.

In the minds of most observers, the 1945 fall classic was not a showcase of vintage baseball. Two wartime teams, each with its quota of aged veterans, squared off in a loosely played Series. Detroit faced the Chicago Cubs for the third time in postseason play and lost the opener at home by a lopsided score of 9–0. In game two, recently released serviceman Virgil Trucks won his only game of the season with fellow patriot Greenberg supplying most of the fire-power with another clutch home run. Chicago left town after game three, leading the Series and follow-

ing a masterful one-hitter pitched by Claude Passeau. On a rainy opener in Chicago, Detroit countered with strong pitching from Trout and evened the contest at two games each. Detroit won again the next day and then, in a wild affair on October 8, the Cubs squandered a big lead, only to be handed victory with a bad-bounce single in the 12th inning. The Cubs' reprieve was momentary, for the Tigers took command earlier in the final game and cruised to a 9–3 victory.

The defending champs were preseason favorites to repeat, but, after an initial spurt, they drifted back behind the hard-charging Red Sox and Yankees. Newhouser pitched brilliantly, equaling his wartime

Originally signed by Detroit, the Tigers lost Eddie Mayo through a commissioner's decision. They later drafted him from Louisville in 1944 after an uneventful trial in the majors. The 34-year-old infielder played the best baseball of his career during a five-year stay with the Tigers. (William M. Anderson)

Hal White came up to Detroit from Buffalo in 1941. After being used as a starter for two seasons, White was switched to the bullpen. He pitched in relief during most of his career with the Tigers (1941–52), winning 40 and losing 49. (William M. Anderson)

dominance while posting a league-best 26 wins and the lowest earned run average. Trout, Trucks, Hutchinson, and Benton proved to be a strong supporting cast for one of the best pitching staffs in baseball. Though there were bright spots in the performances of Greenberg, Evers, Cullenbine, and newly acquired George Kell, Detroit could not

Paul "Dizzy" Trout believed that he would be a bigger draw if he acted crazy, behavior that came rather naturally. Signed by Wish Egan, his scouting report stated, "Great fastball, fair curve. Calls himself Dizzy and is known by that name throughout the league. Inclined to pop off around hotels." Aside from his propensity to clown around, Trout was an excellent pitcher, compiling 161 victories for the Tigers during 1939–52. (Grand Rapids History and Special Collections, Grand Rapids Public Library)

Left to right: first baseman Rudy York, second baseman Eddie Mayo, and shortstop Joe Hoover. (William M. Anderson)

mount a consistent offense. Greenberg finished his Detroit career with a flourish, smacking 44 homers and driving in 127 runs, the league's best marks. Unofficial Rookie of the Year Hoot Evers had an impressive debut as he played through serious injuries. Demonstrating that you have to give up something to get something, the Tigers had parted with highly regarded Barney McCosky to obtain future All-Star third baseman George Kell. The timing was perfect. Kell immediately blossomed into an outstanding hitter and fielder and the cornerstone of the Tiger infield. His .327 average was second to Cullenbine's

team-leading .335. Detroit finished with a rush to capture second, 12 games out of the winner's circle.

The end of the season meant the end of the line for two Tiger greats, Tommy Bridges and Hank Greenberg. Bridges would try unsuccessfully to gain reentry through the minors, and Hammerin' Hank played one more season with Pittsburgh. Speculating about "what if?" in baseball is pure fantasy, yet in Greenberg's case it is surely tempting. What would his numbers have been if he had not missed 814 games or the equivalent of five prime time seasons?

Jumping out in front, Detroit sustained a great

The Tigers' first night game began at 9:30 P.M. on June 15, 1948. Detroit bested Philadelphia, 4–1, on this historic evening before a sellout crowd of 54,480. The team played 13 more home games under the lights during the rest of the season. (Tony Spina/Detroit Free Press)

The Tigers experienced a drop off of 15 wins following their 1940 pennant-winning season. These three starting pitchers, Schoolboy Rowe (left), Bobo Newsom, and Tommy Bridges, had combined for 49 wins in 1940, but they produced only 29 total victories in 1941. (William M. Anderson)

Sometimes called the "meat of the order," these four Tigers were relied on to produce runs on a 1944 team that missed a pennant by a single game. Left to right: Doc Cramer, Pinky Higgins, Dick Wakefield, Rudy York. (William M. Anderson)

These three hurlers were at the heart of the Tiger rotation during the decade of the 1940s. *Left to right:* Dizzy Trout, Fred Hutchinson, and Hal Newhouser. Trout and Newhouser carried the pitching load during World War II and Hutchinson was a double-digit winner for six years following the war. (Grand Rapids History and Special Collections, Grand Rapids Public Library)

start for the first two months of the 1947 campaign. Then their weaknesses and the competition caught up to them. Pitching, the heart of recent team strength, slipped as Newhouser, Trout, Trucks, and Benton all faltered. Highly prized Freddie Hutchinson had his best-ever season, winning 18, but a basically good team lacked the essential extra needed for a legitimate run at the flag. Kell paced the offense as the only .300 hitter, and Detroit finished second best and 12 games back.

Still optimistic and expecting pitching prowess to return, Tiger management looked forward to a good season. For the first time in six years, the Tigers never entered the race. They made a brief appearance in the first division and then settled back to lead the other four teams. Detroit duplicated their 1943 record with 78 wins and 76 losses and fifth-place honors. Cleveland nosed out Boston and New

York, riding home to victory with superior pitching, as Indian hurlers combined for a 3.22 ERA, compared to a league average of 4.28.

This was an era of great Detroit fan support as the Tiger faithful swarmed through the turnstiles in record numbers. Throughout the 1945–50 seasons, Detroit drew an average season total in excess of 1.6 million. On July 20, 1947, 58,369 attended, setting the all-time record. The following season, Walter Briggs broke with tradition, leaving only the Cubs with an exclusive daytime home baseball schedule. Briggs Stadium was first illuminated for a night

▶ The bulk of the Tigers' wins in 1945 came from this group of pitchers posed with manager Steve O'Neill, far right. On the far left is Tommy Bridges, Al Benton, Dizzy Trout, Jim Tobin, Stubby Overmire, and the ace of the staff, Hal Newhouser. Bridges and Benton were recent World War II veterans. (Ray Billbrough)

George Kell (*left*), Johnny Lipon, Eddie Mayo, and George Vico made up the Tigers' infield for most games throughout the 1948 season. (William M. Anderson)

Among the many players lost to military service during World War II by the Detroit Tigers were Birdie Tebbetts (*left*) and Charlie Gehringer (*right*). Like all field bosses, Manager Del Baker had to shuffle his lineup constantly, hoping to fill in with raw rookies and over-the-hill veterans. Gehringer was in his last season when he entered the military in 1942, but the younger Tebbetts was the Bengals' first-string catcher. (William M. Anderson)

Detroit had what some writers called a million-dollar outfield in 1950 composed of Hoot Evers, Johnny Groth, and Vic Wertz. But when one or more of these guys weren't hitting, manager Red Rolfe didn't hesitate to pencil in Pat Mullin (*left*) and aging veteran Charlie Keller and they often produced big games. Pitcher Art Houtteman (*right*) was the beneficiary of their combined offense on this occasion. (William M. Anderson)

Hal Newhouser finally overcame the negative bias toward his wartime pitching prowess to gain election to baseball's Hall of Fame in 1992. Newhouser was a dominant pitcher during much of the 1940s, leading the American League in victories in 1944, 1945, 1946, and 1948. During that stretch, he won 101 games, twice earned the Most Valuable Player award, and finished a 17-year career with an impressive 3.07 ERA. (Grand Rapids History and Special Collections, Grand Rapids Public Library)

game on June 15, 1948. A couple of months later, the new evening entertainment attracted 56,586 consumers, the highest in history.

Newhouser regained his touch in 1948, winning the most games in the American League for the fourth time, but the other pitchers had undistinguished seasons. Evers continued to develop, leading Detroit in batting average and runs batted in. Dependable Kell struggled through an injury-plagued season and still managed to hit .304. General Manager Billy Evans called the 1948 Tigers a "lousy team," but their run of 18 wins in 20 games

Four of the mainstays of the Tiger rotation in 1950. *Left to right:* Hal Newhouser, Virgil Trucks, Art Houtteman, Fred Hutchinson. A sore-armed Trucks only contributed three victories and his off season probably cost the team a pennant in 1950. (William M. Anderson)

In game five of the 1945 World Series, Cubs first baseman Phil Caverretta has just laid down a bunt and Tigers catcher Paul Richards is rushing to field it. Detroit prevailed (8–4) to take a 3–2 advantage in the series. (William M. Anderson)

Back row, left to right: Johnny Groth, Lou Kretlow, John McHale. *Front row, left to right:* Gerald Burke, Billy Pierce, Art Houtteman. (Detroit News Archives)

in September rekindled optimism. The Tiger organization had expanded its farm system, and ivory hunters such as Wish Egan had signed a bevy of promising youngsters. Art Houtteman, Ted Gray, Johnny Lipon, Vic Wertz, and phenom Johnny Groth were all being counted on to bolster the talent already in place. Groth was touted as the next Joe DiMaggio and, in Egan's opinion, "The type a scout dreams about finding once in a generation." Baseball experts regarded Houtteman as a top pitching prospect.

Management fired Steve O'Neill following a

disappointing season and promoted farm director Robert "Red" Rolfe to lead this developing aggregation of talent. If one were going to identify a player with managerial potential, Red Rolfe would be a leading candidate. Known for his hustle and determination, Rolfe had been a clutch performer on Joe McCarthy's great Yankee teams. A Dartmouth graduate who coached at Yale and for the Yankees, Red approached the game in a studious manner and applied his personal style of play: "I inherited a complacent ballclub . . . at spring training camp in '49, I drove the easygoing Tigers until their tongues were sunburned."

The Tigers broke from the gate with renewed spirit and challenged the leaders for several weeks. At midseason they slumped back, not yet able to convince the baseball world of their contender rank. Detroit caught fire in late August, roaring back toward the top and losing third position by only two games in the final week. Detroit played 20 games above a win-loss split, a big improvement over 1948. The season confirmed management's enthusiasm over its young talent. Good hitting outfielders, long a Tiger tradition, flourished in 1949, with Wertz batting .303 and knocking home 133 runs, Evers hitting .303, and "can't miss" Johnny Groth adding a .293 mark. "Fire" Trucks hurled a 19–11 season and quieted the opposition with a fine 2.81 ERA. Newhouser contributed 18 wins, and Hutchinson and Houtteman each compiled 15 victories. After surviving a life-threatening auto accident in spring training, Houtteman made a miraculous comeback. In a photo finish, George Kell hit .3429 to shade Ted Williams for the batting crown.

Most of the ingredients were in place to win. Detroit completed several transactions to strengthen its team, the purchase of second baseman Jerry Priddy being the most important.

Detroit would go as far as their pitching would take them in 1950. They began on a fast pace and maintained the lead for most of the season. As usual, the Yankees were the team to beat. Dick Kryhoski and Don Kolloway combined to shore up first base and, as expected, Priddy teamed with Lipon to become a superb double-play combination. Detroit's outfield was the best in years: Evers .323, Groth .306, Wertz .308. Kell battered the ball at a .340 clip and led the competition in hits and doubles. The 1950 lineup hit .282 in a league that averaged .271.

The pennant chase went right down to the final week when Detroit was unable to overhaul New York, a slim margin of three games separating the two teams. The front four were tightly bunched, Boston four back and Cleveland in fourth, only six behind. In a closely matched struggle, injuries and slumps are sharply felt. The blow Detroit could not overcome was the loss of Virgil Trucks, who had a sore arm after pitching seven games. Coming off a 19-win season, Trucks won only three. Art Houtteman ranked among the best American League pitchers and stood third in victories with 19. Four other hurlers won 10 or more games.

Just a little more pitching and this bunch of Tigers could win it all, or so it seemed. The future, however, would demonstrate that these cats had peaked.

The "Yankee Killer," Frank Lary, won 28 games in 41 decisions against the mighty Yankees, seven straight in 1958. (Grand Rapids History and Special Collections, Grand Rapids Public Library)

7
Too Many Big Yankees in the American League 1951–1960

J. W. Porter (*left*), Al Kaline, Bill Tuttle, Red Wilson, and Ray Boone await their turns to take batting practice during the 1956 spring training. (Grand Rapids History and Special Collections, Grand Rapids Public Library)

Red Rolfe's 1950 Tigers had put a scare into the Yankees and were tied for the lead all the way into the final 10 days of the season. That near miss, a "million-dollar outfield," an All-Star third baseman, what were believed to be quality starting pitchers, and more led the Tiger faithful to expect a great future, maybe even the beginning of a dynasty.

To displace the New York Yankees would require a repeat performance by the Bengals; instead reality hit. Most of the big hitters took the season off, as team run production dropped to sixth and team batting averages became very average; only Kell's .319 and Wertz's slugging bore a resemblance to the powerful attack mounted by the 1950 Tigers. A seemingly talented yet fragile pitching staff lost ace Houtteman to the military and Newhouser to a sore wing. The twosome won six games—all by Newhouser, a big 25 fewer than the previous campaign. When the disappointment finally ended, Detroit was blown out of the first division, 25 games behind the mighty Yankees and eight games below .500. Their fifth-place finish represented a comparative winning percentage net loss of 34 games. But the worst was yet to come as the paper Tiger crumbled.

After 72 games of bad baseball in 1952, management began overhauling the team, and Red Rolfe

Former Yankee Cliff Mapes (*on the left*) competes for an outfield post with the old guard of Hoot Evers, Vic Wertz, and Johnny Groth. (Grand Rapids History and Special Collections, Grand Rapids Public Library)

Two Tiger broadcast pioneers, Ty Tyson (*left*) and Harry Heilmann, are seen in the booth at Briggs Stadium, June 2, 1951. Edwin "Ty" Tyson broadcast the first Detroit Tiger game on April 19, 1927, from Navin Field, and Heilmann became an announcer in 1934. (Detroit News Archives)

In just his third season in the majors, Tiger hurler Jim Bunning started the All-Star Game and posted 20 wins, tying him for league honors. Following the 1963 campaign, management misjudged his future and traded the right-hander to the Philadelphia Phillies. He won 106 games after departing Detroit, including his second no-hitter. (William M. Anderson)

Charlie Maxwell (*left*), Bill Tuttle, and Al Kaline made up a very solid outfield for Detroit in 1956. In his first full season with the Tigers, Maxwell hit for his career-high average of .326. Tuttle was not a big offensive threat but he hit enough and compensated by being a great centerfielder. After winning the batting title in 1955, Kaline drove in 128 runs in 1956, his best career mark. (Grand Rapids History and Special Collections, Grand Rapids Public Library)

became the first disposable part. Player representative and veteran pitcher Fred Hutchinson began his managerial apprenticeship in the midst of an awful season and a beleaguered team. The Tigers were no more inspired by Hutch than Red and kept on losing with consistency. The last day of the season mercifully terminated the agony as these Tigers made history, their first cellar finish and the first team to attract 1,000,000 fans while finishing on the bottom. And it was a dead-last finish, 14 games behind the lowly seventh-place Brownies. Their horrendous 50 wins and 104 losses equated to an all-time low winning percentage of .325. There were no heroes among the hitters, and the hurlers resembled a shell-shocked combat unit. The top three pitchers compiled nightmarish records: Gray 12–17, Houtteman 8–20, and Trucks 5–19. When scrutinizing this awful season, the only pieces of silver lining were two no-hitters thrown by Trucks and a record-tying 12 straight hits rapped out by now Tiger Walter

The right-handed pitching candidates at the 1953 spring training camp were (*left to right*) Paul Foytack, Dick Marlowe, Milt Jordan, Art Houtteman, Ned Garver, Ray Herbert, Hal Erickson, Kapursunski (first name unknown), and Dave Madison. (Grand Rapids History and Special Collections, Grand Rapids Public Library)

"Moose" Dropo.

Once the ax began to swing, a lot of vintage fixtures fell. In a blockbuster trade engineered in June, Detroit peddled Kell, Evers, Trout, and Lipon to Boston and accepted Dropo, Don Lenhart, Johnny Pesky, and Bill Wight in return. Two months later, they packaged a four-for-four deal with the St. Louis Browns, with Wertz and Ned Garver being the principal properties in the swap. The underpinning of hope and the future saw brief introduction in the personages of Harvey Kuenn and Billy Hoeft.

Changes in personnel continued to ship out the

Gus "Ozark Ike" Zernial was a prototype 1950s-era slugger, big and slow of foot. He knocked 237 over the fence in his 11-year big league career. During his six-year heyday, Zernial averaged 28 home runs a season. He came over to Detroit in a multiple-player trade with Kansas City in 1958. (William M. Anderson)

A baseball pioneer, Lary Doby was the first black player in the American League. Doby played 18 games for Detroit in 1959, his last season in the majors. (Brace Photo)

An excellent lead-off man known for his ability to induce a free pass to first base, Eddie Yost would occasionally cross up the opposition and "jump on" a first-pitch strike in the middle of the plate. After a long tenure in Washington, Yost was traded to Detroit and he had two fine seasons (1959–60) with the Tigers. He led the league in walks both years and hit a combined 35 home runs while batting .269. (Detroit News Archives)

core of the 1950 Tigers, with Johnny Groth and Virgil Trucks departing for St. Louis and Art Houtteman to Cleveland. As the trades turned out, the best acquisitions for Detroit were pitcher Steve Gromek and infielder Ray Boone. Boone in particular responded to his new opportunity and immediately started the Tigers moving. A great clutch hitter, Boone hit 105 home runs while batting .291 during his six-year career with Detroit. Well known for its conservative and stand pat posture, Detroit was struggling through a tough transformation. A fan truly needed a scorecard to know the names of players, and astute managers surely kept their bags packed. What had happened to this seemingly fine aggregation of talent? Certainly Detroit was an aging

team and some sources claimed they had been complacent. Walter "Spike" Briggs, Jr., who succeeded his father upon the senior Briggs's death, claimed that his dad had been too good to the players, fostering a very comfortable attitude. New general

▶ After winning 20 games for the last-place St. Louis Browns in 1951, Ned Garver was traded to Detroit during the following season and had to contend with an ailing arm. Always a considerate person, Garver responded to a fan's motherly concern by writing, "Dear Mom, Thank you for the very nice letter and also the liniment. I hope it will be as good as you say." He rebounded with his second-best season, posting a 14–11 record in 1954 for Detroit. (William M. Anderson)

Paul Foytack became a starter in 1956 after two earlier attempts to stick with the major league club. This hard thrower was plagued by control problems but won 81 games while a Tiger. (Grand Rapids History and Special Collections, Grand Rapids Public Library)

Detroit obtained 33-year-old pitcher Steve Gromek in an eight-player trade with Cleveland after the 1953 season had begun. He finished up his major league career with Detroit in 1957. His top mark with the Tigers was 18–16 in 1954. (William M. Anderson)

Detroiter Ray Herbert began his professional career in the Tiger farm system and was used primarily in relief during his four seasons with the Bengals, 1950–54. He had his best record (20–9) with Chicago in 1962. (Grand Rapids History and Special Collections, Grand Rapids Public Library)

Two Wisconsin boys—Harvey Kuenn (*left*) and Billy Hoeft—engaged in conversation. A highly sought high school pitcher, Hoeft signed a contract with the Tigers in 1950 and began two years of schooling in the minors. He would pitch seven full seasons before being sent to the Red Sox for Dave Sisler and Ted Lepcio. Hoeft hit his stride in 1955, winning 16, and bettered that personal record with 20 victories in 1956. (Grand Rapids History and Special Collections, Grand Rapids Public Library)

were shortsighted in giving away Kell, Trucks, and Wertz, all of whom registered several productive seasons after leaving the Motor City.

Success is relative, and Detroit made progress in 1953, completing the season in sixth place yet way behind the fifth-place Senators led by old friend Bucky Harris. University of Wisconsin star Harvey Kuenn became the Bengals' first Rookie-of-the-Year player, leading the circuit with 209 safeties and a fine .309 batting mark. New third baseman Boone was the other major piece of the offense. He topped all Tiger hitters with a .312 batting average and ranked among league leaders in home runs and slugging. No one among the pitchers left their mark dur-

manager Charles Gehringer attributed the team's collapse to players not being hungry enough.

Failure demands change, and Tiger fans got change in everything except winning. Trading players is a speculative business carried out by "experts" in an imperfect game of hunch. All of this maneuvering got Detroit a little more punch in Dropo, a bigger bang from Boone, and some short-term pitching help from Garver and Gromek. On balance, they

Like Tommy Bridges and Milt Wilcox, Art Houtteman got down to the last batter and the string of mastery and luck ran out. With two out in the ninth, Houtteman lost his no-hitter when Harry "Suitcase" Simpson singled. Houtteman won 19 games for the Tigers in 1950. (Grand Rapids History and Special Collections, Grand Rapids Public Library)

Frank Lary was tagged with several nicknames, but perhaps "Bull Dog" best captured his pitching disposition. "You never know what he is going to throw and he's got the guts to fight you all the way," said Ted Williams. Lary came up with the Tigers in 1954 and during his tenure won 123 games. He twice won more than 20. A sore arm shortened his career following a banner year in 1956. (Grand Rapids History and Special Collections, Grand Rapids Public Library)

in his life.

A spring training injury to veteran outfielder Steve Souchock in 1954 provided an opening for Kaline. He joined other first-year players Frank Bolling and Bill Tuttle as Detroit stocked its starting lineup with youngsters. Detroit left the starting blocks playing like a contender. After a month, they responded to earth's gravity and played like they were supposed to, while the Cleveland Indians ran off with the flag. Both New York and Chicago played well enough to win in any normal year. The records of the other five teams looked like first-year expansion clubs. Detroit did move up a notch among this bunch but lost ground on the winner, finishing 40-plus games behind for the third consecutive season.

ing this recovery season. A third piece of the future made a brief appearance at the corner of Michigan and Trumbull: Albert William Kaline.

If losing has a bright side, it is found in higher draft picks in professional sports or in the luring of a great baseball prospect because the opportunity for a youngster is more immediate. Al Kaline's fantastic prep career had scouts drooling. The day after graduation from Southern High School in Baltimore, Kaline signed a Tiger contract, influenced in part by the opportunities presented on a weak team. Five days later, he joined the team in Philadelphia and the next evening played right field in a major league game, the first time he had ever played that position

On April 17, 1955, Al Kaline smacked three home runs, two in one inning, in a game against Kansas City. A slender Kaline didn't look like a power hitter, yet he hit 399 home runs in his career, the most by any player in Tiger history. (Grand Rapids History and Special Collections, Grand Rapids Public Library)

Brought up to the parent club after only 63 professional games in the Three I League, this line-drive hitter impressed his new manager. Fred Hutchinson said, "This boy knows he's a good hitter." In his first full season in 1953, Harvey Kuenn was Rookie of the Year, and in 1959, his last year with Detroit, he hit .353 to capture the American League batting title. (Grand Rapids History and Special Collections, Grand Rapids Public Library)

Boone and Kuenn were again the major weapons in the Tiger attack, and Steve Gromek compiled 18 wins and a fine earned run average in his premier season with the Tigers.

Following Hutchinson's off-season resignation, Detroit elected to bring back Stanley Harris, the boy manager they first hired way back in 1929.

Detroit turned the corner in 1955, demonstrating the fruits of their rebuilding program. Once again, they made a dash for the lead but were not yet ready to run in front. The season became a close race among four teams, with Detroit pursuing the pack. The Tigers earned fifth place but, more important, their first winning season in five years.

Nineteen-year-old Kaline burst into All-Star class with the top batting average in the league at .340; he was also first in hits and among the best in home runs and RBIs. Kuenn and Boone also had big seasons as Detroit outscored the competition and hit second best in the circuit. And the young arms of Hoeft and Frank Lary caused some enthusiasm. Hoeft turned in a fine 16–7 record and Lary, practically in his freshman season, notched 14 victories. Fans got a peek at another young pitching prospect; former collegian Jim Bunning saw action in 15 games working mostly out of the bullpen.

Detroit played two entirely different seasons in 1956; they were a poor second-division outfit during

"Old Paw Paw," Charlie Maxwell, was a big favorite with Tiger fans. Maxwell got his chance to play regularly in Detroit and hit an impressive .326 in 1956. A consistent long ball threat, he hit 31 homers in 1959. (Grand Rapids History and Special Collections, Grand Rapids Public Library)

After several years of effective work coming out of the Cleveland bullpen, Don Mossi was swapped to Detroit. The Tigers acquired his services following the close of the 1958 season and converted the left-hander into a starting pitcher. He responded with his best season, notching 17 victories. (William M. Anderson)

the first four months, but then got charged in the second half and played the best baseball in the league. The organization had developed a core of excellent young players and just reviewing individual statistics would seem to justify a finish higher than fifth. Detroit boasted four .300 hitters in Kuenn, Charlie Maxwell, Kaline, and Boone and the best overall batting average. And they hit the ball hard enough to rank third in homers with star right fielder Kaline banging in 128 runs. Hoeft and Lary surged to the fore of the pitching elite, winning 20 and 21, respectively. Still another hard thrower emerged in Paul Foytack, who had an impressive total of 15 victories despite very limited big league experience.

Ownership's criticism of the team and the impending sale of the franchise certainly eroded team cohesion. In mid-July, the deal was made and John Fetzer and Fred Knorr bought out the Briggs family, paying a record price of $5.5 million.

For the third year in a row, the Tigers finished fifth in the league but 10 games above .500, making the 1957 team the winningest in a 10-year stretch. The expectation to keep on improving with this young nucleus of talent did not materialize.

Too lackadaisical, too complacent, and too comfortable with losing was the private and not-so-private assessment by Tiger brass. Finally, Bucky Harris was replaced with congenial but tough Jack Tighe in an attempt to arouse the Tigers. Owners Fetzer and Knorr wanted some of that old-time

Traded to the Tigers in 1952, J. W. Porter was a versatile athlete as a catcher, outfielder, and first baseman. He got into only 96 games during his three-year stay in Detroit. (Grand Rapids History and Special Collections, Grand Rapids Public Library)

Hard-throwing reliever Ray Narleski completed his big league career with Detroit in 1959, winning four and dropping 12 decisions. (Detroit News Archives)

The Tigers needed help at second base, and they purchased Jerry Priddy from the St. Louis Browns. From 1950 until injured in 1952, Priddy anchored the keystone base and provided consistent .267 hitting. (Grand Rapids History and Special Collections, Grand Rapids Public Library)

Former Bradley University outfielder Bill Tuttle broke in as a Tiger regular in 1954. He was an outstanding fielder and had his best offensive season in 1955, scoring 105 runs. (Grand Rapids History and Special Collections, Grand Rapids Public Library)

A 10-year major league veteran, Red Wilson was always a part-time player sharing the catching duties with another receiver. His best years (1954–60) were spent in a Tigers uniform. (Grand Rapids History and Special Collections, Grand Rapids Public Library)

Jennings, Cobb, and Cochrane fighting spirit and aggressiveness. Adopting a soon familiar pattern, the Bengals crawled through the opening half of the schedule. Many of their big guns fired blanks; Boone and Kuenn both had subpar performances. The great young pitching tandem of Lary and Hoeft won 20 together while being racked for 27 defeats. Once seeded in the starting rotation, Bunning stepped to the front with a 20-victory season along with other high pitching marks. Finally Kaline got hot and carried the Tigers on a late-season winning binge, himself salvaging a respectable season for a player from whom so much was expected. Detroit managed a seldom seen first-division fourth-place finish, though just above a split in wins and losses.

Still determined to antagonize the Tigers, those

in charge swung a major trade following the season and acquired an explosive competitor in Billy Martin. Martin professed, "The way I play the game, I always get mad."

A bunch of talented young players, a corps of quality hurlers, and the injection of an intense spark plug would surely produce a ball club capable of challenging the Yankees, but the bottom fell out of the 1958 season right from the start. Both pitching and hitting failed, sending the skidding Tigers deep into the second division. With Hoeft and Bunning out with injuries, the battered Bengals occupied the cellar and, in early June, Manager Tighe was cashiered. Detroit summoned minor league skipper Bill Norman with a common hope that a change would stimulate the team. Whatever the reason,

Fred Hutchinson became manager of the Tigers in July 1952 when Red Rolfe was fired. Hutch is addressing his team in a clubhouse meeting to which the photographer gained entrance. Walt Dropo is seen on the far left with Joe Ginsberg gripping a bat over his left shoulder. Outfielder Steve Souchock is holding two bats across the room. (Grand Rapids History and Special Collections, Grand Rapids Public Library)

After 11 years, Virgil Trucks (*left*) was traded to the St. Louis Browns following the 1952 season. Like several other players at this time, he was reacquired and became a teammate of Al Kaline (*right*) in 1956. (Grand Rapids History and Special Collections, Grand Rapids Public Library)

Kaline started banging the ball around and things picked up for the Detroiters. By July 1 they had climbed up to fourth, but, in an up-and-down season, the team slid all the way to seventh position in 30 days before reversing its field and ultimately closing out the year on the fifth rung. The all-powerful New York Yankees captured their seventh pennant in eight campaigns while the rest of the league was collecting white surrender flags. Statistically, Detroit appeared better than a fifth-place team, leading the league in fielding and placing second in hitting, fourth in runs scored, and third in team ERA, but there were too many holes made bigger by too many injuries. The bread-and-butter players, Kuenn and Kaline, had good seasons, finishing third and fourth with .319 and .314 batting averages. Frank Strong

▼ Tiger veterans gather for a locker room photo in 1952. *Left to right, back row:* Johnny Groth, Dizzy Trout, George Kell, Jerry Priddy, Hal Newhouser, Vic Wertz. *Front row:* Joe Ginsberg, Matt Batts, Virgil Trucks, Hal White. (Ray Billbrough)

In this Detroit infield, only Harvey Kuenn came up through the farm system. *Right to left:* Ray Boone, Kuenn, Fred Hatfield, and two-time batting champion Ferris Fain. (Grand Rapids History and Special Collections, Grand Rapids Public Library)

Lary individually mastered the Yankees, whipping them seven times, while Ozzie Virgil made Tiger history, becoming its first black player.

It couldn't get any worse—or could it? Bill Norman's "band-aid" fix came off in a hurry in 1959. By May 3, Detroit was buried in last place with two wins against 15 defeats and the field boss was found guilty. Enter manager number six (in the last eight years), veteran campaigner Jimmy Dykes. Under new leadership, the team rebounded, though their revival was impeded by injuries. Several preseason

▼ As a season approaches, managers are often asked, who will be in the starting lineup? Fred Hutchinson had penciled in this cast in 1953. *Left to right:* Harvey Kuenn, shortstop; Owen Friend, second base; Russ Sullivan, right field; Walt Dropo, first base; Bob Nieman, left field; Jim Delsing, centerfield; Johnny Bucha, catcher; Fred Hatfield, third base. (Grand Rapids History and Special Collections, Grand Rapids Public Library)

▲ These are a corps of the veterans on the 1953 squad including Hal New-houser (*left*), Jerry Priddy, Pat Mullin, Billy Hitchcock, and field boss Fred Hutchinson. (Grand Rapids History and Special Collections, Grand Rapids Public Library)

trades paid off, with new pitcher Don Mossi contributing 17 wins and third baseman Eddie Yost playing well for his new club, bringing his special talent for walking to first base. Kuenn and Kaline staged their private Detroit battle for the league batting title, ultimately finishing one-two—Kuenn on top with a .353 mark and Kaline runner-up at .327. Maxwell had a big year, smashing 31 round-trippers, his career best. The individual highlights could not, however, mask the "also-ran" status of this ball club.

After a disappointing finish in 1951, Detroit began trading players, hoping to revive the competitiveness they had enjoyed the previous season. In the first significant trade they acquired a catcher with a perfect baseball last name—Matt Batts. He played for five teams during his 10 years in the majors and had his best season in 1953 with the Tigers when he collected 104 hits and compiled a .278 batting average. (Grand Rapids History and Special Collections, Grand Public Library)

Knuckleballer Marlin Stuart began his career playing in the Tigers' minor league system. Promoted to the majors in 1949, he pitched for Detroit in parts of four seasons, leaving with a 10–11 record. (Grand Rapids History and Special Collections, Grand Rapids Public Library)

They finished fourth, 18 games back, two games below .500, with the worst winning record of any Detroit team in five years.

Something had to be done, and the owners took major action, employing Bill "Let's Make a Deal" DeWitt as president and general manager while alert players waited for the inevitable. The whole season resembled a baseball stock exchange in Detroit as DeWitt made wholesale trades in a commodity with apparently no untouchables. Whether credited to genius or luck, he did make one of the best swaps in

A steady performer during six seasons with Detroit (1954–60), second baseman Frank Bolling had his best season in 1958 when he collected 164 hits, stroked 14 homers, and scored 90 runs. (Grand Rapids History and Special Collections, Grand Rapids Public Library)

Pitching machines were an innovative device in the early 1950s when Detroit introduced their use. This one appears to have been custom built out of plywood and angle iron to enclose the gears and mechanism. Pitching coach Schoolboy Rowe (*left*), Billy Hitchcock, and manager Bucky Harris look it over. (Grand Rapids History and Special Collections, Grand Rapids Library)

After playing in the shadow of Lou Boudreau's legacy, Ray Boone escaped to Detroit following the start of the 1953 season. His release from the comparison to Boudreau lifted Boone to new stature as a consistent run producer for the Tigers. He hit 20 or more home runs in four of his six seasons with the Bengals and twice topped the 100 RBI mark. (Grand Rapids History and Special Collections, Grand Rapids Public Library)

Walt Dropo was the key player in the Tigers' big 1952 trade with Boston. While with Detroit, he tied a major league record by getting 12 straight hits. (Grand Rapids History and Special Collections, Grand Rapids Public Library)

A fine product of the farm system, Vic Wertz played in Detroit during nine seasons, compiling a .286 batting average. In 1949 and 1950, Wertz drove in 133 and 123 runs. During the early 1950s when management felt compelled to overhaul the team, Detroit prematurely traded Wertz to the St. Louis Browns. (Grand Rapids History and Special Collections, Grand Rapids Public Library)

When a team has lots of candidates for positions it signals a ball club in transition with starting roles up for grabs. Coming off its worst season in franchise history, the 1953 Detroit Tigers were seeking to rebuild a competitive team. All of these players hoped to patrol the Tigers out-field. *Left to right:* Jim Delsing, Steve Souchock, Don Lund, Pat Mullin, Bob Nieman, Rufus Crawford, Bill Tuttle, Russ Sullivan, Carl Linhart, Frank Carswell. (Grand Rapids History and Special Collections, Grand Rapids Public Library)

Ned Garver and Steve Gromek were counted on to carry much of the load in the 1955 starting rotation. Manager Harris was hoping to get needed wins from the other three hurlers, Ray Herbert, rookie Leo Constante, and Al Aber. *Left to right:* Garver, Herbert, Constante, Gromek, Aber. (Grand Rapids History and Special Collections, Grand Rapids Public Library)

Detroit history, acquiring Norman Cash for Steve Demeter. Some traders tinker with a ball club, but General Manager DeWitt was bold enough to replace one of the girders. On the eve of the season opener, DeWitt rocked Detroit with the announcement that batting champion Harvey Kuenn had been traded to Cleveland for home run king Rocky Colavito. It is almost safe to speculate that those

who approved of the deal could be counted on one hand.

It was back to their familiar bad start for the Tigers in 1960; new management and new players wearing the same uniforms could not change the outcome. This team would win a few and then lose a few more. As the season entered August, Detroit ranked sixth in the standings and the "handwriting

Right to left: Fred Hatfield, Al Federoff, Harvey Kuenn, Jerry Priddy and Walt Dropo. Three of these infielders became managers: Hatfield and Federoff in the Tiger minor league system, Kuenn piloting the American League Milwaukee Brewers. (Grand Rapids History and Special Collections, Grand Rapids Public Library)

Maury Wills was purchased by the Tigers from Spokane and placed on the 40-man roster in 1959. He was released at the end of spring training. A year later, he was the starting shortstop for the Los Angeles Dodgers, and Tiger fans don't want to be reminded of the rest of the story. Wills stole 586 bases and hit for a .281 lifetime batting average. (Detroit Tigers Archives)

Ozzie Virgil became the first person of color to play in a major league game for the Detroit Tigers when he started at third base against Washington on June 6, 1958. His home debut came on June 17, and he enjoyed a storybook first game, getting five hits in five tries. John McHale (*left*), general manager at the time, executed the decision to break the color line. Virgil played in 131 games for the Tigers before departing for Kansas City in 1961. (Detroit News Archives)

was on the wall." In Frank Lane, Bill DeWitt had his equal for compulsive traders; both hated to stand pat. These two had already completed three Cleveland-Detroit player exchanges in half a season. On August 2, they outdid all previous dealers by trading managers; Dykes went to Cleveland and Detroit received former coach Joe Gordon.

Detroit dug a deeper hole in the standings in 1960, winning 71 and losing 83. They placed sixth in a very unequal race in which the unlikable Yankees outdistanced Detroit by 26 games. The season was filled with disappointments: Kaline, Bunning, Mossi, Foytack, and Maxwell. Bunning's year was especially sad. He won just 11 to go along with 14 losses, despite leading the league in strikeouts and compiling a second-best 2.79 earned run average. When he

Former Yankees gather for a photograph: Aaron Robinson (*left*), Jerry Priddy, Manager Red Rolfe, Dick Kryhoski, Charlie Keller. (Ray Billbrough)

pitched, the runs were not there. Though Colavito hit a lot of home runs (35), he did not have the impact expected.

The wheels of change kept turning in Detroit. Joe Gordon promptly resigned when the season ended, stating, "I knew this wasn't a good club but I didn't realize it was this bad. Thank you, but I'm leaving." John Fetzer bought out his partners and decided to call the old ballpark Tiger Stadium. And like a lot of other folks, Bill DeWitt made his exit.

The season is 1959 and Harvey Kuenn (*left*), American League batting champion, is showing off his lumber to Eddie Yost, Rocky Bridges, and the league's the second-best hitter, Al Kaline. (Detroit News Archives)

The farm system produced many of the new cogs in the team that won it all in 1968 but the old veteran Al Kaline rose to the occasion, setting a standard of excellence for others to emulate. Kaline, finally getting to play in a World Series, hit a sizzling .379 in the fall classic. (Grand Rapids History and Special Collections, Grand Rapids Public Library)

8
Rebuilding a World Champion
1961–1970

The Detroit Tigers had suffered through a decade of not being a competitive team; they had six losing seasons out of 10 and only one inauspicious first-division finish. And they were not on an apparent course of improvement. They were rebuilding, yes, but with disappointing results.

Constant change headlined by seven managers in 10 years and multiple general managers and owners characterized the Tigers. Heavy player turnover defied the stock reputation of this tradition-based and conservative organization. At times, Detroit looked good on paper, but its weaknesses and the Yankees' strengths produced an era of mediocre seasons.

Still needing to be fixed, Detroit hired another new manager to start the 1961 season. Bob Scheffing had recently led the Chicago Cubs through three straight losing campaigns but, for some reason, was expected to inspire the Tigers.

Baseball was riding a wave of popularity, and the American League admitted teams from Los Angeles and Washington into its association. An expanded league, a new field leader in Detroit, and spring just might improve the outlook, though there was not any real reason to honestly expect a much better season in 1961.

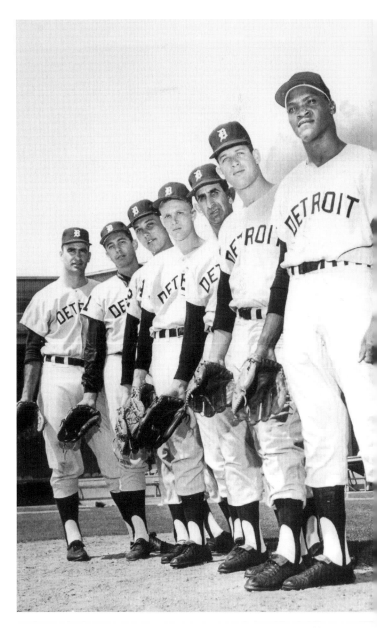

Every team needs several southpaw pitchers and here the Tigers display seven candidates for the team that will go north to Detroit to start the new season. *Left to right:* Dick Egan, Hank Aguirre, Doug Gallagher, Fritz Fisher, Don Mossi, Mickey Lolich, Willie Smith. (Ray Billbrough)

But the Tigers came out smoking, winning 10 of their first 14. They continued winning and acting like they belonged in Yankee company. The bats of Cash, Colavito, and Kaline were ringing. A winter trade that brought fleet outfielder Billy Bruton to Detroit and sent Frank Bolling to Milwaukee opened the way for rookie infielder Jake Wood, giving the Tigers a new speed dimension. Detroit ran in front with the big boys through July, fell back a stride in early August, and then closed in on the leader, heading for a showdown in New York. The moment of truth came on the first days of September when Detroit played a crucial three-game series in the Big Apple. Detroit, poised one and a half games back in the standings, lost a heartbreaking 1–0 decision in the series opener. New York countered with two more decisive blows, sending the challengers on an eight-game losing slide and the destruction of a legitimate pennant bid.

The Tigers were too good to lose, racking up 101 wins, matching the 1934 world champions and the best team victory total ever. This would have been enough in most other years, maybe, but the Bronx Bombers led by Roger Maris and Mickey Mantle were unstoppable. Detroit had its own battery of big guns: Colavito with 45 homers, 140 RBIs; Cash with 41 home runs, 132 runs batted in. Cash had a storybook season, coming from nowhere to lead the league in hitting at .361. Teammate Kaline was second with .324, and Detroit captured league honors in batting average and most runs scored. Frank Lary led a fine pitching staff with 23 victories, Bunning supported with 17, and Mossi pitched tough while winning 15. Amid all the big numbers and heroics, a new farmhand saw considerable action. Dick McAuliffe split time between shortstop and second and impressed management with his determination and hustle.

High hopes are often the kiss of death in baseball, but Detroit had reason for enthusiasm in 1962. However, they were playing like Detroit in the 1950s, winning and losing about the same number through early May. Then the team jelled and in the

Jim Northrup never got cheated when he took his cuts. He hit a mighty grand slam homer during game six of the 1968 World Series in an inning in which the Tigers scored 10 runs. (Mel Bailey)

next two weeks climbed into fourth place, three and a half back.

Tiger momentum had been generated by the sizzling bat of Al Kaline. Fighting to continue their drive, the Tigers won a battle but lost the war with New York on May 26. With two outs in the bottom of the ninth and a Yankee runner in scoring position,

Acquired from Milwaukee in 1960, Terry Fox (*left*) became the mainstay of the Tiger bullpen during most of his six years with the team. He notched 55 saves while pitching for Detroit. Hank Aguirre (*right*) pitched ten years (1958–67) for Detroit, winning 64 and losing 64. The talkative left-hander pitched his best baseball in 1962 when he was 16–8 with the league's best earned run average of 2.21. (William M. Anderson)

A fine number two hitter with speed and good bat control, Billy Bruton came over to Detroit from Milwaukee after the 1960 season. Bruton finished his major league career in the Motor City in 1964. He was a lifetime .273 hitter. (William M. Anderson)

Kaline made a dramatic diving catch to save a 2–1 victory, though breaking his collarbone in an all-or-nothing effort. At that time, Kaline led the league in hitting, home runs, and runs batted in. In his 61-game absence, Detroit fell out of contention. The other team-crippling injury was suffered by sore-armed pitching ace Frank Lary. He went from 23 wins to two.

On June 24, Detroit had another head-on collision with New York, losing in 22 innings, the longest major league game in history (as measured by time

lapsed). Late in July, Kaline returned to action and led a Tiger comeback for a fourth-place finish, 10 1/2 behind the Yankees, of course. Kaline hit .304 and was part of the trio that led the majors in homers: Kaline 29, Cash 39, and Colavito 37. The virtual loss of Lary from the rotation was reflected in a fifth-rate ERA. Aside from impressive power statistics, Detroit hitters slipped from best to eighth in one season. Bunning replaced Lary as the big winner with 19 victories, and left-hander Hank Aguirre unexpectedly came through with a sparkling 2.21 ERA and 16 wins.

The Tigers kept building and trading, and they hired a new trader. Jim Campbell became general manager after 12 years in the Tiger vineyard. One element was not new in 1963—another slow start. Losing more often than winning, the Tigers

A fine clutch hitter, Gates Brown played all of his 13 years with Detroit. Affectionately known as "The Gator," Brown had a phenomenal season pinch-hitting in 1968 when he batted .461. Brown said, "I'm as square as an ice cube and twice as cool." (William M. Anderson)

Norm Cash's acquisition from the Cleveland Indians in 1960 ranks among the all-time Tiger coups. Armed with a quick wit, Cash kept the emotional pot stirred. Cash had a dream season in 1961, slugging 41 homers, driving in 132 runs, and hitting .361. He never topped .300 again but hit with impressive power throughout his 15 years with Detroit. (William M. Anderson)

baseball for Dressen, good enough to salvage a tie for fifth position in the league. Outside of Kaline, Detroit didn't have any hitting stars, but overall they tied for second in team batting. The often injured Kaline produced another excellent season, finishing second in hitting and runs batted in. Tiger pitchers were roughed up and were among the league's worst in runs allowed. Fourth-year pitcher Phil Regan had his banner season with a team-leading 15 wins.

Detroit remained active in the market, trading in bigger commodities, as Campbell dispatched Bunning to Philadelphia for outfielder Don Demeter and Colavito to Kansas City for infielder Jerry Lumpe and two pitchers, Dave Wickersham and Ed Rakow. Campbell also claimed an untamed rookie named

An unmistakable stretching exercise characterized slugging outfielder Rocky Colavito's preparation to bat. Trading Colavito for Harvey Kuenn in 1960 rocked baseball fans everywhere. Detroit wanted a long ball hitter and Colavito pounded the ball for four years, averaging 35 homers and 94 runs batted in per season. (Detroit Tigers Archives)

slumped down into the standings and were 12 games below .500 when Scheffing, the fall guy, was discharged on June 19. Throughout Detroit history, when the team had faltered, the most commonly prescribed medicine was a new manager thought capable of lighting a fire under the sleeping Tigers. Fetzer and Campbell picked Charlie Dressen, a spirited senior helmsman who had managed four other big league teams. The team played .539 winning

Dennis McLain on waivers. Two other new names, Mickey Lolich and Bill Freehan, were introduced to Tiger fans.

For the next two seasons, Al Kaline, the franchise, was severely hobbled by a nagging birth defect that truly became his "Achilles' foot." Determined to play over the pain caused by a crippled left foot that had gradually worsened, Kaline managed to stay in more than 80 percent of the games.

Spring fantasies soon vanished in 1964 as Detroit went into a prolonged tailspin before leveling out in eighth place during May. Aside from an occasional short run, Detroit lingered near the bottom

Wanting a little insurance in the 1968 pennant stretch, Detroit purchased Elroy Face on August 31. Face had been an exceptional relief pitcher for Pittsburgh. He had no decisions in two relief appearances for the Tigers. (Mel Bailey)

Charlie Dressen "took some getting used to" when he took over the reins of the Tigers during the 1963 season. Dressen was a teacher and a demanding mentor, and his style did not meet with universal approval among the players. Over time, however, Dressen won their respect and the team improved. His managerial career ended abruptly when he died during the 1966 season. (William M. Anderson)

through most of July. Fortunately, a strong finish allowed them to climb up to fourth at the wire. In general, the pitching staff gave up too many runs. The bright spots were both pleasant surprises; Lolich won 18 and Wickersham piled up a career-high 19 victories. Young talent began to emerge among the position players, too. Freehan hit the top average at .300 and cracked 18 homers, while McAuliffe added needed punch with 24 home runs.

Detroit suffered an early setback in 1965. Manager Dressen had a heart attack, leaving the team in Bob Swift's hands until May 30. Under this unsettling adversity, the team rallied to make a quick start and contended in the early season. June was an up-and-down month until the team settled into fourth

Bill Freehan may have made his greatest contribution as a team leader. Freehan expected a lot of himself and his teammates. Following four straight losses to New York in late August 1968, the Tigers were discouraged. Freehan issued a challenge with a chalkboard message: "Anybody who thinks the world ended today doesn't belong here." (Mel Bailey)

In a major trade with Kansas City in 1963, the Tigers acquired a dependable second baseman in Jerry Lumpe. He finished his major league career in Detroit four years later. (Detroit Tigers Archives)

Minneapolis hoisted its first AL flag over Minneapolis–St. Paul. Detroit's repeat performance in fourth represented its best baseball in four years, 16 more games won than lost. Detroit's offense featured many players capable of delivering the long ball. Detroit native Willie Horton exploded on the scene with 29 home runs and 104 runs batted in. "Stormin' Norman" Cash blasted opposing pitchers for 30 long drives that reached the seats. Kaline battled multiple injuries to hit a team-leading .281. Wickersham was 10 wins off his previous season mark, but young Denny McLain took up the slack to register 16 victories, the best on the squad.

There were some very encouraging signs in 1966: a third-place finish just one game behind the runner-up Twins, the acquisition of big Earl Wilson, a power attack that led the circuit in homers (Cash

position. A rash of injuries to Kaline, McAuliffe, and Demeter squashed any serious hopes of competing for the pennant.

After winning five championships in succession, the mighty Yankees fell to a weak sixth, and

Shortstop Cesar Gutierrez played in 190 games for Detroit and made his greatest contribution as a defensive player. In 1970, his only full-time season, Gutierrez made history when, on June 21, he rapped out seven hits in seven official times at bat. (Mel Bailey)

Orioles. And then tragedy struck twice: death claimed courageous Charlie Dressen in August and former Tiger catcher Bob Swift two months later.

Now having assembled a bonafide contender, ownership again went outside the organization to hire a manager with major league experience. Fifty-two-year-old Mayo Smith had an undistinguished record mentoring the Phillies and Reds.

Kaline's hot bat carried the Tigers in a sustained drive to begin the 1967 season. They seemed to have it all going for them, even winning on April 30 while being held hitless by Oriole pitchers. But at the halfway mark of the season, Kaline was injured again, this one self-inflicted when the irritated star slammed his bat in the rack following a strikeout. The main man missed 26 games. And there were

32, Kaline 29, Horton 27, and McAuliffe 23), McLain's 20 wins, and the real potential shown by rookie flyhawk Jim Northrup.

There was hope, yes, but winning is the bottom line and much was expected of this 1966 club. Expectations are often cursed by disappointments, and Tiger bats did not immediately launch this team. In mid-May, after the team had it going, Tiger players were shaken by the news of Dressen's second heart attack. Bob Swift became interim manager again. The team bore down and made a serious run at the leaders. Detroit's talent, however, was thinly spread and unable to absorb frequent, though short duration injuries to key players, and the pitching generally failed. July was a horrible month. Swift became seriously ill, and coach Frank Skaff was pressed into service as manager. Detroit lost 20 games during July and virtually lost sight of the pace-setting Baltimore

Better known for his managerial talents, Whitey Herzog finished up an eight-year major league career with the Tigers in 1963. (Brace Photo)

other injuries, an obstacle only the lucky can dodge. Though Earl Wilson was superb and received lots of help from McLain and Joe Sparma, the bullpen couldn't rescue the starters.

Undenied by holes in the armor, the Bengals stayed in the hunt. As Boston, Chicago, Minnesota, and Detroit battled down the stretch, it looked like a dead heat in the closest four-way race in league history. Prepared for an almost certain playoff, the drama went down to the last game of a Detroit-California doubleheader in which the Angels were spoilers. The Detroit Tigers ran out of schedule, tied for second with Minnesota, one game behind the champion Red Sox. The alibis for this sliver of defeat were many of those already cited, but, during the final stretch run, the temporary loss of McLain following an alleged toe injury of questionable origin added special frustration.

Wilson and Boston's Jim Lonborg tied for most wins in the league with 22, and Kaline came back to bat third best with a .308 average.

Many past Tiger teams had started slowly and then, when it was too late, closed with a rush. The 1968 Bengals roared out of April and were seldom headed. It wasn't as easy as hindsight makes it appear, for these Tigers weathered the loss of Kaline

This big slugger was not easily intimidated. After being knocked down by an Earl Wilson fastball, Willie Horton shouted, "If you make me come out there, I can move you like a mountain!" Horton joined the Tigers in 1963 and hit 262 homers in 15 seasons with the team. (William M. Anderson)

Mickey Lolich became a regular starter in the Tiger rotation in 1964, only his second year with the big club. Lolich was the unexpected hero of the 1968 World Series, winning three games. In 1971 and 1972, he had back-to-back 20-game victory seasons. (William M. Anderson)

runs in fours, with four grand slam home runs during the regular season. On September 15, McLain won his 30th game, becoming the first to reach that pitching plateau in 34 years.

Detroit finished 12 games in front and won a team-record 103 games. McLain was the dominant player in baseball, winning 31 games and the Most Valuable Player and Cy Young awards. The team was first in home runs by a big margin and led in runs scored, slugging, fielding, and complete games. Horton paced the hitters; his .285 average ranked fourth in the league, and he hammered 36 home runs to place second.

with a broken arm, multiple "wounds" to expected star pitcher Wilson, and a generally battered starting rotation. There was one big exception to the pitching woes—confident and skillful Denny McLain. Pitching with incredible results, McLain had already posted 10 victories by June 13. During the season, he redefined the meaning of "stopper," winning 13 times following a Tiger loss.

The character of this great team surfaced most when behind in late innings. They rallied to win 40 games after being tied or trailing from the seventh inning on.

Gates Brown set the standard for pinch hitters with a blistering .461 mark. Jim Northrup packaged

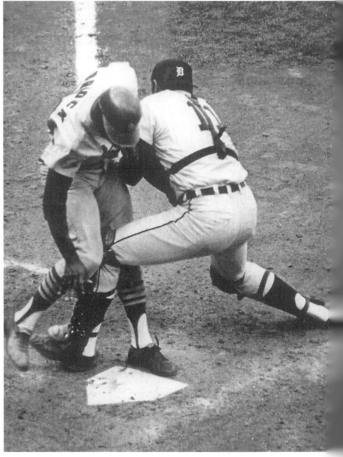

On Julian Javier's short single to left field, Willie Horton threw a strike to Bill Freehan and cut down the speedy Lou Brock at the plate. In a controversial play in game five of the 1968 World Series, Brock attempted to score standing up, but Freehan blocked him off the plate. Brock would later predict, "They will reprint the photos of that in baseball histories for years to come." (Tony Spina/Detroit Free Press)

Tiger rookie Mike Marshall pitched one season for Detroit in 1967 and posted an impressive 1.98 ERA. Following the 1968 season, he was lost to Seattle in the expansion draft and became one of the best relief pitchers ever. (Detroit Tigers Archives)

Eddie Mathews hit 512 home runs to gain membership in the Baseball Hall of Fame. He finished up his great career in a Tigers uniform, playing 67 games in two partial seasons. (Mel Bailey)

Dick McAuliffe came up as a shortstop in 1960 but after several seasons was moved to second base where he played equally well. An intense competitor, he fueled a fighting spirit on Tiger teams during his playing days. "The big difference in the Detroit club is McAuliffe," said Cleveland manager Al Dark. "He plays the game as it should be played—hard." McAuliffe also carried a big stick, smacking 192 home runs in his 14 seasons in the Motor City. (Mel Bailey)

A bear-down ballplayer and a left-handed batter who could hit left-handed pitchers, outfielder Jim Northrup became a regular in 1966. His 11-year career with Detroit spanned 1964–74. He was a lifetime .267 hitter who enjoyed hitting when the bases were loaded. Including the World Series, Northrup belted five grand slam home runs in 1968. (Mel Bailey)

A relief pitcher on the 1968 world champion team, right-hander Pat Dobson was traded away before he reached his prime. After departing the Tigers he won 111 games including being part of the amazing 1971 Baltimore Orioles rotation when all four starters won 20 or more games. (Mel Bailey)

Detroit's opponent in the 1968 Series was the defending world champion St. Louis Cardinals. Aside from dominant pitchers, the Series pitted the running Cardinals versus the slugging Tigers. In a major league gamble, Mayo Smith added Kaline to the already potent attack by shifting centerfielder Mickey Stanley to shortstop. Favored to win the Series, St. Louis hosted the opener, featuring a matchup of the two premier pitchers in baseball, Bob Gibson and Denny McLain. McLain was over-

◀ Denny McLain's flame burned bright and fast. He was the dominant pitcher in 1968 and 1969, recording 31 and 24 victories, respectively. McLain won 118 games in eight short years with Detroit. He pitched and played hard, and his stardom ended as abruptly as it had begun. (Detroit News Archives)

matched and chased in the sixth inning, while Gibson whitewashed the Tigers and struck out a record 17 batters. Detroit pitched their ringer in game two—unheralded Mickey Lolich. Tiger sluggers Horton, Cash, and Lolich belted homers in spacious Busch Memorial Stadium, and their left-handed hurler quieted Cardinal bats to even the Series. The Tigers dug an enormous hole by dropping the next two and forcing a must-win situation. The now familiar Lolich returned to face the Redbirds in game five and survived a shaky first. Manager Smith stayed

Mayo Smith inherited a homegrown team primed to win. He managed the Tigers to a near pennant in his first season in 1967, captured the flag and world championship in 1968, and continued as field boss through 1970. (Mel Bailey)

Born in southern Michigan, Phil Regan got his start with the Tigers in 1960. In a six-year stay, Regan compiled his best record in 1963, winning 15 and losing nine. Traded to the Dodgers in December 1965, he became "The Vulture" in the National League and a fine relief pitcher. (Grand Rapids History and Special Collections, Grand Rapids Public Library)

Centerfielder Mickey Stanley had exceptional fielding skills. "Getting a jump on the ball is a gift and Stanley has it," said Manager Mayo Smith. Stanley played his entire 15-year major league career with Detroit, and his "finest hour" came in the 1968 World Series when he was called on to play shortstop, and he performed like an experienced infielder. (Mel Bailey)

Only Brooks Robinson was considered a better defensive third baseman than Don Wert during his career. Following a brief apprenticeship in 1963, Wert became a fixture at third for the next seven years. He rapped out 927 hits during his tenure with the Tigers. (Mel Bailey)

Detroit-born Tom Tresh became a member of the Tiger organization in 1969, following a trade with the New York Yankees. Son of former Tiger property Mike Tresh, Tom spent his best years in New York when he slugged 140 home runs in eight seasons. (Tom Tresh)

with him, and the Bengals rallied to win. The Series shifted back to Missouri, and finally McLain would face someone other than Gibson. Tiger bats exploded for 10 runs in the third, including yet another grand slam by Northrup. Detroit drubbed the Cardinals, 13–1.

The Series came down to a close confrontation between the unbeatable Gibson and unexpected hero Lolich. Pitching on short rest, these two gladiators hurled scoreless baseball through six innings. In the decisive seventh, Detroit broke through for three big runs when centerfielder Curt Flood misjudged a long drive by Northrup. Both teams scored meaningless runs in the ninth as Detroit captured the world crown, only the third team in history to come back after being down three games to one.

Stanley fielded his position like a shortstop, Kaline made Manager Smith look like a genius, hitting .379, and Lolich was the toast of the team.

Baseball expanded again in 1969, adding two

new teams in each league and, for the first time, creating a division structure necessitating a league championship series. Washington joined the Eastern Division of Detroit, Cleveland, New York, Boston, and Baltimore, and major league baseball returned to Milwaukee in the Western Division of the AL.

Not surprisingly, Detroit was picked to repeat, but they were sidetracked by expectations, division, and a hungrier team in Baltimore. As the season got underway, Tiger hitters left their bats in the rack and slumped into fourth place by the end of April. A defending champion playing the same lineup puts extra pressure on itself, especially when most of its big hitters are slumping. Its propensity to rally in the late innings did not carry over to 1969. The fans, growing impatient, voiced their displeasure with the also-ran level of play. The target of their loudest criticism was Willie Horton, long a fan favorite but now someone to hold responsible for the team's failings. In mid-May, the abuse drove a frustrated Horton from the team; he was absent without leave and missed several games. Pitching star Denny McLain came and went as he pleased. The manager chose to ignore McLain's infractions, further eroding team morale and player respect. No one was able to awaken this uninspired Tiger team, and Baltimore didn't even get a fight when it took the crown away. Detroit completed the season a distant second, 19 games out of first and four games out of fifth. McLain and Lolich were very good, winning 24 and 19, respectively. Northrup was the team batting champ at .295, and the Tigers hit 182 home runs, 11 or more by nine different players.

Denny McLain self-destructed in 1970. It began in spring training with big news that he had been suspended indefinitely for gambling. Indefinitely became July 1, and the Tigers hoped to stay within striking distance until their ace returned. Instead of being the margin of victory, McLain pitched ineffectively upon his return to action. Far from reformed, the increasingly cavalier McLain poured ice water on two newspapermen and drew a quick suspension from Jim Campbell. About the time that penalty was lifted, he threw another illegal pitch by carrying a handgun; that cost him the remainder of the season.

Detroit had started fast in the new season, right on the heels of Baltimore; however, the renewed hope turned out to be a mirage. After the team stayed close to the top through the first half, Horton injured an ankle, forcing him out for the remaining season, and the Tigers fell apart around McLain. Denny got into only 14 games and managed just three victories. Their pitiful second half grounded them in fourth place, a long-distance phone call to Baltimore. Stars and outstanding performances were

Detroit obtained the services of big Earl Wilson after the 1966 season began by trading Don Demeter to Boston. Wilson responded to the change, going 13–6 after joining the Bengals. The next season he led the junior circuit with 22 victories. Often used as a pinch hitter, Wilson never got cheated on his cuts. In 1968, he deposited seven long drives into the seats. (Mel Bailey)

hard to find. Using earned run average as the bench-mark, Tiger pitchers represented the division's worst staff. The hitters played in even more inferior company with the lowest composite batting average in the league.

These former world champions had fallen a long way. Twenty-four fewer victories and 24 more losses represented the slippage from the team that played .636 baseball in 1968 and essentially the same team that won at a rate of .488 two years later.

In large part, the enthusiasm for baseball is sustained by that fountain of hope that is so easily primed during the off-season. In October 1970, Jim Campbell was guilty of larceny when he parted with McLain, Norm McRae, Don Wert, and Elliott Maddox and received Eddie Brinkman, Aurelio Rodriguez, Joe Coleman, and Jim Hannan from the Washington Senators.

Right-hander Dave Wickersham was part of a five-player swap with Kansas City, consummated after the close of the 1963 season. The change of scenery produced his top season pitching performance, 19 wins and 12 defeats. He remained with Detroit through 1967. (Brace Photo)

The "Major" is unhappy. Jim Campbell lured Ralph Houk out of retirement to manage the Tigers when they were a deteriorating team in 1974. After two years as tenants of the Eastern Division basement, Houk led the rebuilding process at Tiger Stadium. He resigned following the 1978 season, confident that the foundation was in place. (William M. Anderson)

9
Exiting Veterans and Custodians of the Cellar 1971–1980

I n the early 1970s, someone on high decided that to win, the Tigers needed a new field boss, not just a different manager but different leadership and a more aggressive personality. Periodically throughout Tiger history, similar assessments had been made, the underlying assumption being that the players were capable of better performances if properly motivated—the talent is there, just wake up the Tiger.

In October 1970, Tiger brass hired a Jennings-Cobb-Cochrane clone named Alfred Manuel Martin to fire up the old gang. While on a press tour in January, "Billy the Kid" laid out his philosophy: "I promise my players will give 100 percent all the time. When they don't give it to you, we'll give it to them." The change would be dramatic: from a "hands-off" Mayo Smith approach to a high-energy, all-orchestrated Billy Martin script.

A confident Martin was stung with a major misfortune before the campaign began, as his already marginal pitching corps fell apart with injuries and the loss of reliever John Hiller, disabled by a heart attack. General Manager Campbell rushed to acquire pitchers Dean Chance and Dave Boswell in a stopgap attempt to fill the breach. The 1971 Tigers began slowly but then started coming together, moving to within four and a half lengths of front-running Boston by the end of May. Through the first months of summer they leveled out, winning about the same number they lost. Then, in the last five to six weeks, Martin stoked the Tiger engine and it roared home like a winner, capturing runner-up honors in the Eastern Division. Detroit had won 91 games, played .561 baseball, and showed great improvement.

Billy Martin played for Detroit in 1957–58 and came back to manage the club in 1971. He led Detroit to a division title the following season. The ever-aggressive Martin said, "The way I play the game, I always get mad." (William M. Anderson)

Struck with early season injuries to the pitching staff in 1971, Tiger management purchased the contract of two-time 20-game winner Dean Chance. Chance, pitching in his final season, was 4–6 for the Tigers. (Mel Bailey)

The big trade with Washington paid major dividends: Joe Coleman had a superb season, winning 20 games, and the glovemen, Brinkman and Rodriguez, were important factors in Detroit's leading the league in fielding. Lolich, too, was outstanding, posting a league-high victory total of 25 and racking up other best pitching records. Left-hander Fred Scherman became the ace reliever, winning 11, saving 20, and holding opponents to fewer than three runs per every equivalent game. Detroit scored runs in clusters as hitters topped the circuit in homers. Stormin' Norman Cash rebounded to former greatness, belt-

ing 32 long blasts and driving in 91 runs.

The first-ever major league baseball strike delayed the start of the 1972 season until mid-April. Baseball is about as unpredictable as Michigan's weather, and instead of Tiger pitching being worrisome, the hitters let down. Martin worked all the angles, and the Tigers won enough to be in the second spot on May 15. Fortunately, this was a season without a dominant team, and Detroit stayed right in the fray into July. Following the All-Star Game, the team played poorly, but no one else took command of the

Detroit obtained slick fielding shortstop Eddie Brinkman in a larceny transaction with Washington in 1971. Brinkman held down the shortstop position for four years, won the Gold Glove Award, and set a major league record for playing 72 consecutive games without making an error in 1972. (Mel Bailey)

The complete player: Al Kaline didn't have to apologize for any dimension of his game. He could hit, field, throw, and run with equal skill. When signed by the Tigers, scout Ed Katalinas said, "To me, he was the kind of prospect a scout sees in his dream." In reflection, Kaline said, "I never was as good a player as I wanted to be." (Grand Rapids History and Special Collections, Grand Rapids Public Library)

ahead run in the 11th, then surrendered victory in the bottom half. They were shut down in the second game and pushed to the edge of elimination in this short best-of-five series. Coleman countered with a masterful shutout in the next contest. In game four in Detroit, the Tigers were handed a 4–3, 10th-inning victory. Like the previous four battles, pitchers dominated the finale and the A's scratched out a 2–1 victory. Detroit received superb pitching from Lolich, Coleman, and midyear acquisition Woody Fryman. It was a down year for Tiger hitters; they produced a subpar .237 average and slumped to .186 in the playoffs.

In a season shortened by injuries, Al Kaline surged for a fine .313 season. Credit for winning be-

Being traded to Detroit in 1970 was a bonanza for the younger Joe Coleman. "After pitching in Washington, I knew how to lose," said Coleman. In his first three seasons with the Bengals, he won 20, 19, and 23. (Brace Photo)

division. When the pennant season opened on September 1, the Tigers were a half game out; a month later they were tucked in a half game behind the leading Red Sox. When the Tigers went to the whip, it was Kaline who made the move. The old star had a brilliant stretch drive, consistently delivering the key hit and inspiring the team. Detroit prevailed in the final three-game do-or-die series with Boston, winning the east by a half game.

In its first league championship playoff, Detroit faced a powerful Oakland team in a series of closely shaved games. In the opener, Detroit scored the go-

Woody Fryman was claimed on waivers during the 1972 season. His 10 victories were a major factor in the Tigers' divisional championship. (Mel Bailey)

victories, and the mainstays of relief faded; yet, John Hiller came back from a career-threatening heart attack to set a major league record 38 saves. Certainly the play of Baltimore accounted for Detroit's drop to third and inability to repeat. The Birds won 97 games in capturing the flag, 11 more than Detroit's total in 1972 when no club took charge of the race. Hitting continued to suffer. Although Horton batted .316 in two-thirds of a season, the Tigers lacked the punch to drive in runs, most notably illustrated by the fact that Rodriguez led the team with 58 RBIs and Stanley accounted for the second highest total with 57.

A disgruntled Billy Martin made one bad decision after another in his relationship with Tiger brass, ensuring his departure ticket. With 19 games to play, Martin walked the plank, and coach Joe Schultz finished the season at the helm.

Mark "The Bird" Fidrych, pitching during his dream season in 1976 when he won 19 games and mesmerized the baseball world. A knee injury the following year began a painful descent. (Lloyd Wallace)

longed primarily to a good defensive team and the pitchers: Lolich, 22 wins; Coleman, 19 wins; Fryman, 10 wins in 16 games; and a solid bullpen.

Billy Martin had squeezed all of the juice out of the aging Tigers in 1972 and, without major repairs, the inevitable would soon become obvious. He saw the reality but was unable to manage his circumstance, and an impetuous Martin acted with little restraint. The bedrock of the divisional winners, fielding and pitching, remained fairly constant; Detroit recorded the fewest errors and the best fielding percentage for the third consecutive year in 1973. Newcomer Jim Perry replaced Fryman's 10 wins with 14, Coleman won 23, Lolich slipped to 16

The patching was over; Detroit needed a major overhaul. In the minds of many, they had waited too long and had tried to stretch the old guard too far. Northrup was traded for a player to be named later, Cash was given his outright release, and the most complete player in Tiger history, Al Kaline, would bat in his final season as the designated hitter only. Restructuring a ball club requires patience, and Detroit hired an experienced and patient skipper in

Canadian-born John Hiller was a premier relief pitcher in franchise history. Among all Tiger hurlers, he ranks first in career games and third in saves. Hiller made a remarkable recovery from a January 1971 heart attack. In 1973, he established a new major league record with 38 saves. Tiger skipper Ralph Houk had some great relievers when he managed the Yankees, yet he claimed that Hiller could "pitch as well as anybody I've ever had." (Mel Bailey)

On September 24, 1974, as his career was coming to a close, Al Kaline stroked hit number 3,000 in his former hometown of Baltimore. After watching him in the batting cage years before, the great Ted Williams said of him, "There's a hitter. In my book the greatest right-handed hitter there is." (Mel Bailey)

Ralph Houk. A close friend of Jim Campbell, the 54-year-old Houk was counted on to guide the team through the frustration of rebuilding.

From first to third to the pits in three short years, the Tigers were relative strangers to the cellar, having finished last only once before in 1952. They played 18 games under .500, and only California in the other division played worse in the junior circuit. These Tigers gave up lots of earned runs (most in the league) and didn't hit much, ranking above only two teams. Lolich, who had been a tower of

Al Kaline finished his brilliant career on October 2, 1974, and was unanimously elected to the Hall of Fame on the first ballot in 1980. (Mel Bailey)

league baseball. The season mercifully ended on October 2 with Detroit sitting on the bottom, 55 below (.500), sounding more like a temperature in Alaska. The pitching was just as frigid; only the Cubs had a worse ERA in all of baseball. No Tiger hurler won as many games as he lost, and both Lolich and Coleman were defeated 18 times. Mickey had weathered through two miserable seasons, losing 39 games in all, no doubt arranging his

An aggressive hitter and negotiator, outfielder Steve Kemp played five years in Detroit before being sent to Chicago in exchange for Chet Lemon following the 1981 season. His best season was 1979 when he batted .318 with 26 homers and 105 runs batted in. (Mel Bailey)

strength, toiled through 21 defeats. Hiller continued his remarkable comeback, winning 17 in relief, and Detroit needed a lot of relief. Paroled prisoner Ron LeFlore made his entry in the big show, flashing his unpolished talents. In sharp contrast, the curtain came down on a brilliant playing career when Al Kaline played his last game. Among numerous team records, Kaline got his 3,000th hit, joining an elite of only 13 players in baseball history. In his last season, he batted .262 with 13 homers and went out with a team-leading RBI total of 64.

As for new manager Houk, one would have to feel secure and confident to take a job like this, and there was more losing to come. Detroit went bust again in 1975 in an agonizing year that saw them lose 19 in a row during one stretch of counterfeit major

A vintage Mickey Lolich snaps off a hard slider. Lolich ranks with Hal Newhouser as the two best left-handers in franchise history. Winner of 207 games while pitching for Detroit, Lolich had many admirers. Billy Martin, his manager in 1972–74, said, "Lolich is amazing in finishing off a hitter. You don't find anybody better when it comes to making a pitch in a two-strike situation." (Mel Bailey)

Ron LeFlore was discovered in the Southern Michigan State Prison at Jackson and signed by Detroit in 1973. After brief seasoning in the minors, this rookie, with loads of raw talent, got his chance in the majors in 1974. In six seasons with the Bengals, he hit a combined .297 and averaged 49 stolen bases a year. (Mel Bailey)

The Tigers gained the services of pitcher Joe Niekro via trade with San Diego after the 1969 season. He experienced modest success with Detroit (21–22) during the next three seasons. After his departure, Niekro learned how to throw the knuckleball and had several big years with Houston. (Mel Bailey)

transportation to New York in exchange for out-fielder Rusty Staub. Hiller saved only 14 games in a season when there were not many games to save.

Among the position players left from the 1968 world champions, only Freehan played regularly in the field. Stanley had become a role player, and Horton took Kaline's place as DH. Horton enjoyed his last big year with the Tigers, belting 25 home runs and driving in 92 runs.

For those who love baseball, there is little that can top the unexpected, the occasional bright stars that suddenly appear like Cinderella. Many were aware of Ron LeFlore's raw talent, yet he made a

Regrettably, Detroit never fully appreciated the talents of Ben Oglivie. He was traded to Milwaukee in 1978 and given a full-time job in "Brew Town." Oglivie prospered in Milwaukee, socking 171 home runs in the next 10 seasons. (Mel Bailey)

quantum leap from prison obscurity to a brief minor league apprenticeship to the majors. Teams that are hurting provide amazing opportunities. LeFlore came out of the blocks like the sprinter he was, blazing a 30-game hitting streak in the first 30 games of the season. Unlike the "flash in the pan," LeFlore kept on flying; he hit .316, stole 58 bases, and made the All-Star team. Only a late season injury could derail this flying boxcar.

Though phenomenal, LeFlore's feats were over-shadowed by a nonroster pitcher who flew in his own special orbit. Mark "The Bird" Fidrych pitched well enough in spring camp to earn the last spot on the big team's roster. Typical for a pitcher of his sta-

Detroit acquired Aurelio Lopez in the off-season in 1978 in what has to be one of the great trading bargains. "Señor Smoke" became one of the finest relievers ever for the Tigers, winning 53 games and saving 85 during his stay in Detroit. In 1979, Sparky Anderson claimed, "Every team has to have a guy it considers to be the automatic man. For us, it's Lopez." (Mel Bailey)

A great glove and a rocket-throwing arm made Aurelio Rodriguez a fixture at third base for nine years (1971–79) in Detroit. (Mel Bailey)

A product of the Tiger farm system, Fred Scherman made the team in 1969 and became the bullpen stopper in 1971, winning 10 and saving 20. After the 1973 season ended, he was traded to Houston. (Mel Bailey)

tus, Fidrych hung out in the bullpen and on the bench during the first weeks of his major league career. Then on May 15, with Cleveland in town, Manager Houk decided to start Fidrych. That day the fans were introduced to a strange bird who ran on and off the field, congratulated teammates after they made a good play, talked to the ball, and contoured the mound with his hands. A modest crowd of 14,583 saw him pitch no-hit baseball into the eighth inning before he was touched for two hits en route to his first major league win. From then on, the house would be full when Fidrych pitched. His numbers were spectacular: 19 wins, the lowest earned run average in the majors, and the most complete games in the league. Equally astounding, he pitched before a combined audience of 900,000 in the 29 performances in which he was cast in the lead

role. The support players, in addition to LeFlore, were principally Rusty Staub, who batted .299 and drove in 96 runs, and new pitcher Dave Roberts, acquired from Houston; he helped out with 16 victories. In all, the Tigers showed vast improvement in climbing up the ladder one rung and winning 17 more games than in the previous season.

Detroit moved up another notch in the standings in 1977, but its fourth-place finish was inflated by the addition of an expansion team in Toronto, which took its expected place at the bottom of the ladder. The two season records were almost identical though; Detroit was buried in fourth, 23 1/2 games behind third-place Boston in 1977.

The previous season's pitching phenomenon Mark Fidrych could not dodge the sophomore jinx. A spring training knee injury required surgery, and

Drafted number four by the Tigers in 1975, Jason Thompson was a highly prized prospect. In just his second season in the majors in 1977, Thompson hit 31 home runs and made the All-Star team. Three years later he was traded to California for Al Cowens. (Mel Bailey)

Gourmet cook Rusty Staub collected 2,704 career hits. The Tigers parted with longtime favorite Mickey Lolich to obtain Staub for the 1976 season. During the next three years, he became the big RBI man for the Bengals, averaging over 100 each year. Continuing contractual problems ended his relationship with Detroit in 1979. (Mel Bailey)

when he pitched in his 11th game after returning to the Tigers he developed a sore shoulder, ending his season. So Fidrych won six, and Roberts, the number two starter of the previous year, notched four, and Houk had another pitching-starved ball club. Fortunately, another rookie, Dave Rozema, came out of the woodwork to nail down a club-high 15 victories, but that was far too little compensation.

LeFlore, Staub, and rookie Jason Thompson sparked the offensive with impressive statistics. The speedy LeFlore collected 212 hits and banged out a fine .325 average. Staub and Thompson both drove in over 100 runs, the first such Tiger combination since Cash and Colavito in 1961. The Bengals also introduced the new future with Steve Kemp, Jack

Versatility and pinch-hitting ability made John Wockenfuss a valuable role player for the Detroit Tigers for 10 years, 1974–83. Hitting out of a highly unorthodox stance, Wockenfuss could "sting" the ball. (Mel Bailey)

Morris, Lance Parrish, Alan Trammell, and Lou
Whitaker seeing their first action.

Although the future was in the wings, the Tigers
needed some carryover help in bolstering a very
marginal pitching staff. Campbell engineered two
deals that provided immediate benefit, acquiring
Jack Billingham from Cincinnati for the price of two
minor leaguers and Jim Slaton for Ben Oglivie in a
swap with the Brewers. Billingham gave Detroit 15
wins, and Slaton earned the most victories on the
staff with 17. The short-run pitching transfusion was
expensive, though, for Slaton skipped town for more
money the following season, and Oglivie went on a
tear in Milwaukee.

Detroit played well in opening the 1978 season,
and the evidence of a developing ball club was becoming more and more apparent. The Tigers had
passed through a phase when their overwhelming
weaknesses were commonly accepted; their developing respectability now kindled a growing expectation
to win. Ron LeFlore put together a third straight
season of high production, leading all others in the
American League in stolen bases and runs scored
and banging out 198 hits, good for a .297 batting av-

Everything about Frank Howard was big: his size (6'7", 255 lbs.), his expectations, and his prodigious home runs. Howard hit 369 home runs before coming
to Detroit near the end of the 1972 season. He played 99 games for the Bengals
in 1972–73, driving 13 more into the seats, before retiring as a player. (Mel
Bailey)

Acquired in a trade with Cincinnati, Jack Billingham had been a mainstay in the Reds' starting rotation. He was a big contributor with Detroit in 1978, his first season, when he rung up 15 victories. (Mel Bailey)

allowed Moss just 53 games to show his stuff and then demoted him in favor of the more experienced and effervescent George "Sparky" Anderson. The new spirit did not catch this year, and the Motown Tigers flattened out in fifth and stayed there.

Staub had a disastrous season, holding out for weeks trying to renegotiate his contract and unsettling the team. He finally signed in May but was then peddled to Montreal and had a lost season. Among the established nucleus, only LeFlore performed up to previous standards, swiping 78 bases, scoring 110 runs, and batting an even .300. In general, Tiger hitting and pitching reflected their level of play. The enthusiasm was generated by the new corps of Morris, 17 wins; Whitaker, .286; Trammell, .276; and Parrish, 19 home runs. The bullpen received a big boost from ex-Cardinal Aurelio Lopez, who responded to Anderson's confidence and heavy workload.

Sparky finished his first season philosophizing about the future: "This is the last I want to hear of us being a young club. From now on we can't live on the excuse that we're young."

Although Anderson predicted Detroit would win 90 games in 1980, his ever-flowing enthusiasm could not cover up his shortage of pitchers. Needing a left-hander, Detroit went into the market and made a major deal, trading All-Star LeFlore for highly regarded Dan Schatzeder. Hindsight would demonstrate that LeFlore had seen his best days; unfortunately, Schatzeder developed a sore arm after a few starts and struggled through a disappointing season. Often a team parts with an established regular when it is eager to make room for a bright prospect. The "can't miss" rookie was outfielder Kirk Gibson, but he injured his wrist on June 7 and sat out the rest of the season. The best-laid plans went down the drain.

The team never really jelled, although it did climb out of an early season hole to finish in a familiar fifth place. Compared to the previous season, the Tigers traded one win for two losses and gave no assurance they were ready to make a move.

erage. Staub and Thompson continued to drive in runners in big numbers; the duo accounted for 222. Alan Trammell and Lou Whitaker played regularly and began a unique keystone dynasty, while youngster Steve Kemp showed fans that he was for real by hitting .277.

In 1978, the Tigers enjoyed their best season since 1972 in finishing 10 games over .500. Although finishing in fifth, they were only 13 1/2 games back. Houk, who had signed an open-ended contract with the Tigers in 1974, decided his purpose had been fulfilled, and he retired from baseball again.

For 1979, Detroit went inside for its next manager, hiring coach Les Moss, who had managed many of these young players at Evansville. With sights raised on being a contender, the organization

◀ Someone in the batting cage has just hit one out as (*left to right*) Bill Freehan, Tony Taylor, and Al Kaline follow the flight of the ball. (Mel Bailey)

Left-hander Dave Roberts pitched in the majors for 13 seasons, winning 103 games. In his only full season with Detroit, he won 16 but was tagged with the loss 17 times. (Mel Bailey)

The team ERA was a whopping 4.25. Morris and Lopez were again the mainstays; the big right-hander led the starters with 16 wins and "Señor Smoke" won 13 and saved 21. Milt Wilcox showed some consistency, winning 12 or 13 each of the previous three years, and hard-throwing rookie Dan Petry looked promising in earning 10 victories. Sparky's lineup gave Detroit a balanced attack with six regulars hitting between .286 and .300, and they led all AL teams in scoring runs.

Since 1973, the Tigers had gotten younger, and a major transition had occurred. They had been playing for the future and their hopes had been raised on the farm. Having failed as a prophet the past season, Manager Anderson hedged his bet: "We will win at least 37 games in 1981."

▶ In 1977–78, Milt May was the Tigers' first-string catcher. Milt played for five teams in his 15-year big league career. (Mel Bailey)

Tiger ace Jack Morris has just hurled his second complete game victory in the fourth game of the 1984 World Series. Congratulating Morris are Alan Trammell, Marty Castillo, Dave Bergman, Tom Brookens, Darrell Evans, and Lance Parrish. (Ron Rossi)

10
The Farm System Produces Another Winner
1981–1990

The face of baseball was changing dramatically, becoming less of a game and more of a business. Huge television contracts, rapidly escalating salaries, free agency, and unionization were all dominant influences in the transformation of major league baseball.

Known for its conservatism and solid financial standing, Detroit struggled with the new contractual dynamics, preferring to stay out of the free agent market. As its young players developed into quality performers, management's conservative stance would be tested. Detroit lost all of its first arbitration cases and rightfully decided that Ron LeFlore was too high priced, so they shipped him to Canada.

Continuing disputes over free agent compensation festered into the longest general strike in base-

A great pitcher longs to take a turn in the batting cage. Jack Morris watches Lance Parrish wait for a "fat pitch," and former backstop Bill Freehan gets his annual spring training workout, March 1985. (Dan Anderson)

Second baseman Lou Whitaker (*left*) and Alan Trammell rewrote the definition of "fixture" in baseball language. These two stellar performers anchored the Tiger keystone combination for 19 years and their hitting statistics are amazingly comparable. (Mike Litaker)

ball history. Beginning on June 12, 1981, the 50-day work stoppage split the season in two, causing the Tigers to lose 53 games of their schedule. The first half was too short and the second too long. After a slow start they came on with a rush, closing fast on the leaders before the strike grounded their momentum, three and a half games behind the pace team. When play resumed in August, Detroit regenerated its winning drive, getting into the pennant race for the first time in nine years. With only 10 games left, Detroit held a game and a half lead, but the slide had already begun. Ten games later, they were one and a half games behind and both of their seasons were over.

Naturally, a short season suppressed everyone's numbers and Gibson, who was accustomed to playing shortened seasons because of frequent injuries, led the Tiger offense with a .328 batting average. No major league pitcher won more than 14 games in 1981; Jack Morris equaled that while Milt Wilcox

▼ Tiger leadership: Jim Campbell, president; Sparky Anderson, manager; and Tom Monaghan, owner, February 26, 1984, at Joker Marchant Stadium, Lakeland, Florida. (Detroit News Archives)

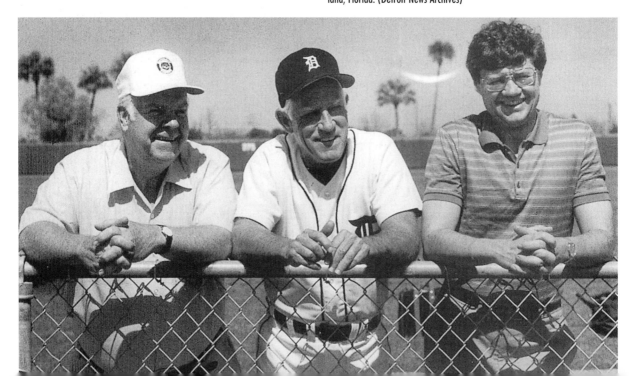

Frank Tanana, Alan Trammell, and Lance Parrish relax during spring training, 1986. (Richard Dancz)

won 12 and Dan Petry 10. New relief hurler Kevin Saucier ranked among the leaders in games saved.

The annual off-season team maintenance repairs were fairly significant in 1981–82, starting with the conclusion that Mark Fidrych could no longer pitch major league baseball. Then, convinced they could not sign their principal run producer, management swapped Steve Kemp for outfielder Chet Lemon. Dan Schatzeder, unable to fill Detroit's need for a dependable left-handed starter, was peddled to San Francisco following two disappointing seasons. In return, Detroit picked up another right-handed hitting outfielder in Larry Herndon.

Though they played out the entire 162-game schedule in 1982, Detroit played the season in three modes—great on the front end, horrible in the middle, and like an average ball club at the finish. By mid-June they were 36–19. For the next two months, Detroit lost 32 and won 16 and then played "one for you and one for me" the rest of the way. Pitchers posted the lowest ERA in the league, but that impressive record masked the failure of the bullpen. Sore-armed Aurelio Lopez saved only three games, and space cadet Dave Rozema was lost for the season following a May injury in an impromptu karate exhibition when he joined an on-the-field altercation. Jack Morris continued his ascendency as the main man in the Tiger rotation, topping all Bengal hurlers with 17 victories. New outfielder Herndon looked like a steal, displaying uncharacteristic power and accumulating a .292 batting mark. His heavy hitting along with the booming bat of Lance

George "Sparky" Anderson was inducted into the Hall of Fame on the merits of his managerial abilities and accomplishments. He is recognized for his exceptional human relations skills. He loved to tinker with his lineup, the minds of others, and the English language. Someday someone will surely catalog his colorful and original expressions. Following their spectacular start in 1984, the Tigers sputtered and Sparky said, "No one out of perfume could help the ugly games we played recently." Though a reformed prognosticator, Anderson could not resist making predictions. (Lloyd Wallace)

Parrish fully compensated for the absence of de-
parted slugger Steve Kemp. Parrish surpassed the
season home run record for catchers with his whopping total of 32. Although the Tigers expected to
contend, Milwaukee outdistanced the fourth-place
team by 12 games.

Confidence intact, management concentrated
on locking in its main weapons for the future, signing Morris, Whitaker, Lemon, and Herndon to multiple-year contracts. And Sparky Anderson, their
philosophic skipper, assured, "We're not a kid's team
anymore." Detroit's enthusiasm fizzled when the
team floundered in April. The ever-expected bright
star of Gibson remained dimly lit in 1983, and
though he played his longest career season, the hits
weren't there and he experienced his worst, a

Known for his outstanding fielding ability, first baseman Dave Bergman was
more than a defensive player. He hit a career-high .294 in 1988. (Mike Litaker)

Doyle Alexander came to Detroit in a late-season trade with Atlanta in which the
Bengals parted with highly regarded prospect John Smoltz. Alexander pitched
brilliantly down the stretch. His nine straight victories were a major contribution
to the Tigers' divisional title. (Dianne Chapman)

frustrating .227 batting average. Responding to un-
sympathetic fans, Gibson retorted, "I don't have to
be reminded how terrible I am."

The early 1983 season misfire was soon cor-
rected, and this team got rolling. Detroit charged
into the race and contested for the crown throughout
the remaining season. They battled Baltimore late
into September before conceding by six games, their
best drive in 12 years. These Tigers won 92 victories
and ended an encouraging season, 22 games above
.500. Statistically, Detroit had the horses to win.
Morris and Petty teamed to become a formidable
double-ace hand, winning 20 and 19, respectively,
and Lopez was "smoking" hitters again. The Tigers'

Though his successor was always on deck, Tom Brookens played third base for 10 years, 1979–88. (Dianne Chapman)

Potential is a two-edged blessing. Kirk Gibson signed a big bonus in 1978 and inherited the burden of an equally big expectation. He battled his unpolished skills and frequent injuries through several seasons with the Tigers. He played his longest season in 1985 (145 games), batting .287 with 29 homers, 96 runs scored, and 97 runs batted in. He became a free agent following the 1988 campaign and signed with Los Angeles. (Mike Litaker)

lineup boasted four .300 hitters, led by Whitaker's .320 and Trammell's .319, third and fourth in the league. Parrish continued to hammer opposing pitchers for 114 runs batted in and 27 drives over the fence. Lemon, Herndon, and Enos Cabell were important factors, too. And the Tigers were excellent in the field, featuring three Gold Glove winners in

Trammell, Whitaker, and Parrish, the first time in the history of the award that one team captured more than two trophies.

In giving the benediction for the 1983 season, junior philosopher Cabell said, "It's not far off." In October, this grand old franchise changed hands when pizza magnate Thomas S. Monaghan purchased the club for a record price estimated at $43 million. A caring John Fetzer carefully selected the right person with whom to entrust his Tigers.

The few holes that needed fixing if Detroit were going to claim the top prize included obtaining another starting pitcher, as well as strengthening the bullpen, first base, and third base. Chief trader Bill Lajoie skillfully solved these personnel problems. Wilcox had been campaigning for a better deal, and Lajoie wished him Godspeed in some other place. When other options for both parties didn't materialize, they reconsidered, and Wilcox got a new two-year license to pitch in Detroit. Detroit gave up Glen Wilson and John Wockenfuss to acquire reliever Willie Hernandez and first baseman Dave Bergman. In an unprecedented move, the organization took the plunge and signed highly sought free agent Darrell Evans, a man who played both first and third bases. Insider Howard Johnson was counted on to stabilize the hot corner.

In a history-making season, Detroit exploded on opening day to set a blistering pace while flying in their own orbit for the first 40 games. They opened with nine straight wins, lost a game, and reeled off seven more victories to stand 16–1 on April 26. During that euphoria, Jack Morris threw a no-hitter, blanking the White Sox, 4–0, in a nationally televised no contest. The Tigers were 26–4 in their first 30 games and 35–5 in the first 40 contests, both high watermarks in baseball history.

This runaway team reentered earth's orbit, and the roaring Tigers looked like ordinary cats in the next 40 games, winning 20 and losing 20.

Like any great team, the 1984 Tigers demonstrated a unique flair, its most notable trait being an ability to score early and force the opposition to play catch-up. The ignitors were Whitaker and Trammell;

batting first and second in the lineup, these two scored 175 runs to pace the best run-producing team in the American League.

Pushing aside the charge that they were riding the lead produced by their phenomenal start, Detroit cranked it up again, winning 49 games in the second half of the season to close out a fine Toronto team by 15 lengths. Only twice before had a team gone wire-to-wire in capturing the flag. Its 104 victories and winning percentage of .642 registered new highs in club history.

Detroit outbid the competition in its first-ever quest of a name free agent and signed Darrell Evans in December 1983. Evans was a major contributor of home runs, runs batted in, and leadership during his five years with the Tigers. He hit 40 home runs to lead the league in 1985. (Dianne Chapman)

During the last days of spring training in 1984, General Manager Bill Lajoie engineered a significant trade with Philadelphia, securing the services of left-handed reliever Guillermo Hernandez. In 1984, Hernandez was almost perfect, gaining 32 saves in 33 opportunities, and compiling a 9–1 record and an uncharitable 1.92 earned run average. He again pitched brilliantly during the following season. In six seasons with the Bengals, Hernandez saved 120 games, leaving only John Hiller, Mike Henneman, and Todd Jones with a better record with Detroit. (Dianne Chapman)

This team combined great pitching and run production to win it all. Wilcox became the other needed starter; with his best season, he notched 17 victories. The other freight haulers were predictable, Morris with 19 wins and Petry with 18. The staff combined for a 3.49 earned run average, best in the

In 1987, his first season with the big team, Mike Henneman emerged as the stopper in the Tiger bullpen. Armed with a great split-finger pitch, Henneman compiled a low 2.90 earned run average in his first four major league seasons. (Dianne Chapman)

The Tigers acquired outfielder Larry Herndon in 1982 in a trade with San Francisco. His first two seasons with Detroit were his best career performances, hitting .292 and .302. (Mike Litaker)

competition. And, oh, how Willie Hernandez restructured the relief corps. Nearly perfect, he won nine, saved 32, and consistently slammed the door, limiting opponents to fewer than two runs a game.

The big hitters were Parrish with 33 homers and 98 runs batted in, Gibson with 27 home runs and 91 RBIs, and Trammell with a .314 batting average. The bench was the best in years.

In its second-ever playoff experience, Detroit swept three straight from Kansas City as Gibson's bat thundered and the pitchers allowed just four runs. The San Diego Padres, an expansion club in the Western Division, represented the National League in the World Series. Opening on the West

Coast, Detroit drew first blood, defeating the Padres behind a complete game performance by Jack Morris. San Diego took game two, dealing the Tigers what would be their only postseason loss in this remarkable year. Good pitching from Wilcox and Hernandez produced a victory for the Bengals in game three. Morris and Trammell overmatched the National League's best team on the following day; the Tiger ace pitched a five-hitter and Tram drove two into the left-field seats. The stage was set for a dramatic finale, with Detroit needing only one to win. Each manager used four pitchers in this pivotal game. The knockout blow was swung in the eighth inning, when Padre relief ace Goose Gossage elected

Chet Lemon came to Detroit in a straight one-for-one trade with the Chicago White Sox in 1981. A superb fielder, he agreed to give up his regular centerfield post to adapt to the capabilities of other flyhawks. Lemon was a .273 lifetime hitter. (Mike Litaker)

hitting reflected the struggle after July; he hit a very subpar .258. The entire team ranked 11th in batting, worst in the Eastern Division. Pitching slipped, too, with Morris still among the leaders in several categories but down in wins with 16. New addition Walt Terrell helped fill the void with 15 victories. Hernandez continued to be the top fireman, rescuing 31 games. Overall, the staff's 3.78 earned run average placed them fourth in the junior circuit. Though batting averages were modest, this team could score quickly with the home run. They produced the second-highest total, led by Evans with 40, Gibson 29, Parrish 28, and Whitaker 21.

Expected by some observers to be in the driver's seat when the 1986 season closed, Detroit played through a second straight season of frustration.

While struggling to score runs and stay in the pennant race, Detroit traded several minor leaguers in August 1988 to obtain veteran star Fred Lynn. In his only full season with Detroit (1989), Lynn batted .241 with 11 home runs. (Mike Litaker)

to challenge Kirk Gibson, and the Tiger right fielder drilled a fastball into the upper deck for a three-run homer. The "Bless You Boys" had been blessed.

Amid the celebration, Detroit's No. 1 prophet, George Anderson, promised another pennant in 1985. Generally winners need only minor adjustment between seasons, and this Tiger outfit seemed pretty well set. Wilcox's ailing arm caused concern, and Lajoie parted with still-promising Howard Johnson to entice the Mets to surrender pitcher Walt Terrell. Sparky Anderson tinkered with the infield after being impressed by rookie Chris Pittaro, but that long shot missed the mark.

Toronto took charge in 1985, and Detroit put up a fight until the All-Star Game. During the second half of the schedule, Detroit didn't play anything like a defending champion, losing more than they won and skidding to a third-place finish. Trammell's

was riding, were largely ineffective and, on April 22, Gibson severely sprained an ankle, forcing him off the field for nearly six weeks. Manager Anderson recognized the depth of the problem, stating, "We've got to get better pitching because even with 24 Kirk Gibsons we couldn't win."

Through 40 games they were 20–20 and trailing most of the competition. By the All-Star break, the

Jack Morris was a dominant pitcher throughout the 1980s, and his pitching was as predictable as his usually outstanding performance. There was very little guesswork about how he would confront opposing hitters. Morris, a power pitcher, challenged hitters with an assortment of effective deliveries, supreme confidence, and an intense desire to win. (Mike Litaker)

Detroit secured four-time National League batting champion Bill Madlock during the 1987 season and he immediately sparked the light-hitting Tigers. His timely hitting was instrumental in Detroit's divisional championship. (Mike Litaker)

Admittedly concerned about his fielding, Sparky Anderson rested his pennant aspirations on a strong starting rotation and a lineup that could hit with power.

The campaign began on a sour note with a sputtering start and star shortstop Trammell nursing a sore throwing arm. The pitchers, on whom so much

During his 14 seasons with the Detroit Tigers, Jack Morris won 196 games, twice topping the 20-victory mark. Manager Sparky Anderson claimed that "Morris is the horse of baseball." The winningest pitcher of the 1980s averaged 256 innings of work during the first nine years of the decade. Morris threw a high velocity fastball, hard slider, and a nasty split-finger pitch. (Dianne Chapman)

Tigers posted a 43–44 record. They turned it around, getting hot in July with Jack Morris reeling off three consecutive shutouts and earning American League player- and pitcher-of-the-month honors.

Though Gibson returned in June, his presence was offset by the loss of Petry. The casualty list grew worse when Parrish, after hitting 22 home runs, had his season ended on July 27 by an ailing back.

Detroit worked its way into contention in August, trailing the Red Sox by just four and a half games, but two disastrous confrontations with Boston shattered Tiger dreams. The final six weeks were academic. Detroit repeated its 1985 finish in third position though closer to the leader.

Morris finished in whirlwind fashion with 21 vic-

tories. Darnell Coles, Alan Trammell, Lou Whitaker, Darrell Evans, and Lance Parrish made history as the first infield where each member hit 20 or more home runs in the same season.

Other than signing Evans, Detroit had for the most part opted to avoid the bidding wars of free agency since its inception. In 1987, the Tigers lost their first premium player to the new system. Lance Parrish, one of the very best catchers in Tiger history, suffered with increasing back problems in 1986, forcing him out of action during a good portion of the season. The Tigers were unwilling to sign him to a multiple-year contract, and Parrish entered the free

The loss of Lance Parrish through free agency pressed new catcher Matt Nokes into service in 1989, and he lit up the scoreboard with 32 home runs and a productive .289 batting average. (Dianne Chapman)

agent market and eventually signed with Philadelphia. Instead of creating a major weakness, the combination of two fairly recent acquisitions, catcher Mike Heath and Matt Nokes, surprisingly more than filled the offensive void. Heath performed credibly and Nokes hit like he owned most American League pitchers. The young catcher slammed 32 home runs while batting .289. In addition to this stroke of good fortune, Manager Anderson boldly moved Trammell to the clean-up position in the lineup, raising many an eyebrow.

The Tigers were beaten 19 times in their first 30 games, and it looked like the makings of a long season. The team was too dependent on Morris, it lacked a stopper in the bullpen, and left-handed

Given his youth, Dan Petry was off to a great career start when elbow problems curbed his rising status. He had big seasons in 1983 and 1984, winning 19 and 18, respectively. The well-liked pitcher was admired by his manager. Sparky Anderson said, "He won't change . . . some guys are like that. They are good people to start with and they don't change, no matter what." (Mike Litaker)

In 1982, Sparky Anderson said, "Lance [Parrish] can become anything he wants in this game." The Tigers made Parrish their first selection in the June 1974 draft, and he became the first-string Tiger catcher in 1979. He set a major league home run record for catchers with 32 in 1982 and bettered the mark by one in 1984. He left the Bengals after the 1986 season, signing a free agent contract with Philadelphia. In 10 years, Parrish hit 212 home runs, more than any other Detroit catcher in team history. (Mike Litaker)

pitchers stymied their weaker right-handed hitting lineup. But then the right combinations began to generate run production, and Detroit started winning. They won 70 of the next 103 games. General Manager Lajoie went searching for more bargains to bolster a revived contender, and he found two veterans who absolutely provided the margin of victory. First he picked up Bill Madlock in June, and this old campaigner delivered many timely hits. Two months later, he traded prize rookie pitcher John Smoltz to

Paul Gibson emerged as a major cog in the Tiger bullpen. He pitched in 60 games in 1990, posting a 3.05 ERA. (Mike Litaker)

games of the season, Detroit eked out 4–3, 3–2, and 1–0 wins to claim the Eastern Division title.

Offensively Detroit led the league in runs scored, home runs, and slugging. They were third best in team batting average and third best in pitching as measured by earned run average. Sparky's decision to hit Trammell fourth made him look like the ultimate genius, for Trammell had an MVP-type season, hitting .343, with 28 home runs and knocking in 105 runs. For the ninth consecutive year, Jack Morris led his team in victories.

The playoffs had been expanded to a best-of-seven series, and Detroit faced the Minnesota Twins

Grand Rapids native Dave Rozema had an outstanding rookie season, winning 15 games in 1977, a career high. During his eight-year tenure with the Tigers, Rozema was the resident free spirit. (Mel Bailey)

Atlanta for a seasoned hurler. All newcomer Doyle Alexander did was win nine victories in 11 starts while shutting down hitters with a 1.53 earned run average.

Beginning in mid-July and for the next 10 grueling weeks, Detroit and Toronto dogged each other, jockeying for the lead never more than a game and a half apart. And the schedule makers provided the ultimate confrontation, seven meetings in the last 11 days of the season. After dropping the first three in Toronto, Detroit appeared doomed, but a ninth-inning rally forced the game into extra innings, and the Tigers squeezed out a victory. Still one behind when Toronto came to town for the final three

Hard-pressed for a left-handed starter, Detroit obtained Frank Tanana from Texas in a midseason 1985 trade. Tanana prospered in his hometown, averaging 12 wins a season, 1986–90. (Dianne Chapman)

Picked in the June 1983 draft, Jeff Robinson made it to Detroit after fours years of minor league development. He enjoyed his best season in 1988, matching 13 victories against only six defeats. (Mike Litaker)

for the 1987 league championship. Perhaps spiritually drained by their desperate struggle with the Blue Jays, the Detroit Tigers were no match for Minnesota in this anticlimactic series of games. They immediately dug a hole by dropping the first two contests, as Minnesota hitters decoded Alexander's secret mastery and roughed up Morris, and their fans alienated all Tiger faithful with their homer hankies, whistles, and uproarious enthusiasm. In game three, the Tigers pushed across five quick runs then frittered away the lead, and only an eighth-inning homer by Pat Sheridan averted a three-game sweep. Gasping for air, Detroit escaped the homerdome hoping for a reversal in friendly

Although considered a hot prospect, Tiger management decided Howard Johnson was expendable in their quest for more pitching. Traded to the New York Mets following the 1984 season, Johnson became a star as his booming bat connected for 119 home runs in his first four seasons with New York. (Mike Litaker)

Tiger Stadium, but the Twins brought their hand-kerchiefs and whistles and Frank Viola with them. Minnesota wasted no time in pinning defeat on the Tigers, whipping them 5–3 and 9–5 to clinch the pennant. Detroit didn't hit (.240 BA) or pitch (6.70 ERA) well, and it was all over.

Free agency beat Detroit again in early 1988 when an arbitrator emancipated Kirk Gibson and the snarling Tiger sold his talents to Los Angeles. Reflecting on his contractual woes with his former employer, Gibson said, "They're as hard-line as they come."

Surgery had not restored Petry to his previous level of performance, so he was traded for fleet cen-

terfielder Gary Pettis. Lajoie shopped around for other affordable players to strengthen the soft spots and landed Ray Knight and Luis Salazar.

The 1988 season may have been Sparky Anderson's greatest managerial performance because he kept an aging and above-average team in the pennant race for a majority of the season. Morris and Evans, two of the main weapons, malfunctioned during the early season, and Nokes's bat cooled off considerably from 1987.

Detroit sent third baseman Howard Johnson to the New York Mets for Walt Terrell in order to strengthen its pitching for the 1985 campaign. Terrell had three strong seasons for Detroit, including a 17-win performance in 1987. An off-the-field injury wrecked his 1988 season, and he was dealt to San Francisco in 1989 for a hitter. The Tigers reacquired Terrell for the 1985 season. (Dan Anderson)

What did the Tigers think of Alan Trammell before he ever played a game in the majors? Hoot Evers, director of player procurement, reported early in 1977, "He does everything well. He's so good now at 18 that the instructors are teaching him how to finesse at shortstop instead of the fundamentals. You have to run him off the field [because he wants to practice all day]. A great kid." (Mel Bailey)

holes were not enough liabilities, Detroit was clobbered by injuries. Before the season started, Walt Terrell slipped on ice and wrenched his knee, effectively aborting most of his season. Later in the campaign, Whitaker injured his knee while dancing, and he sat out the remainder of the season. All-Star Alan Trammell was twice struck in the arm by pitched balls, severely slowing his ability to perform. And, in late August, Jeff Robinson developed an ailment in his pitching hand that ended his fine season. With the ranks thinned by casualties, Lajoie rushed new troops into the battle, acquiring outfielder Fred Lynn and pitcher Ted Power among others, but the reinforcements couldn't quite produce a miracle, and Detroit finished a close second, surrendering to Boston by just one game.

A battered Trammell ranked seventh in hitting with a .311 average, and Pettis stole 44 bases, second best in the AL. And that was about it for batting and run-producing feats in 1988. Once again Morris won the most games on the staff with 15. Robinson recorded 13 victories and a team-leading ERA of 2.98. Alexander, Frank Tanana, Henneman, and Gibson rounded out the foundation of this very successful season.

Tiger success in the 1980s had been stretched to the limit, and the collapse came in 1989. The often dominant Tigers became consistent losers in the last season of the decade. Weaknesses were soon exposed when players expected to anchor the corners of the infield were gone from the scene by the end of May. The 17-game absence of an exhausted Sparky Anderson five weeks into the season was yet another telling sign of distress.

An already thin cast of front-line players was riddled by a continuous string of injuries afflicting 16 different players in the course of the season. The combination of injuries, losses, and changes in the

Yet the Tigers won without scoring runs, or at least not very many. During a season-long drought, Tiger pitchers, particularly the starters, were superb, carrying the team into contention. Jeff Robinson emerged as the stopper, and surprising rookie Paul Gibson teamed with Mike Henneman to form a solid bullpen.

Tom Brookens likened his cohorts to a blue-collar team, while Dave Winfield thought the Tigers resembled a turtle in the pennant race. The media scribes called them "misfits," "bargain basement irregulars," and a "warehouse outlet team."

As if protracted slumps, age, and conspicuous

Alan Trammell connects for one of two home runs he hit in game four of the 1984 World Series, October 13. (Ron Rossi)

roster caused Manager Anderson to make frequent references to fielding "warm bodies" and his role as "a professional greeter."

By the All-Star Game break, the Bengals were mired in last place, and it only got worse. On July 17, they broke out of a 10-game losing streak and a month later went on a 12-game road trip and lost every game.

Detroit finished the season dead last with a 59–103 record, the third worst winning percentage (.364) in franchise history. Their worst record in major league baseball in the 1989 season left the Tigers completely out of any contention, 30 games behind the division winners, and 14 games back of the fifth-place New York Yankees. After losing their 100th game in late September, Sparky Anderson remained philosophical. "Any time you lose one more than you win you stink," said the Tiger skipper. "Why worry about how bad you stink? One hundred, that's just a different degree of smell. It's been a

stinko year."

Among the few bright spots in an otherwise dismal season was the ringing bat of Lou Whitaker. Assigned to bat third, Whitaker became the punch in the lineup, leading the Tigers in most offensive categories, including a career-high 28 home runs.

The Detroit Tigers had ridden the wave of the winningest decade in their history. Fans support winners, and attendance also ranked the best in the team's 89-year history, averaging over two million in each of seven seasons during the decade. Just as hitting comes and goes, so does winning. Although dynasties are becoming a phenomenon, a consistent winner is most often the result of a productive farm system. An outstanding team like the Tigers of the 1980s was built from within the system and relied on a core of key players around which the team was molded. Every era of Tiger greatness has had this characteristic, and it is difficult to identify a more critical nucleus than Morris, Trammell, Whitaker,

Louis Rodman Whitaker, known everywhere as "Sweet Lou," steps into the batter's box amid admiring cries of "Lou-Lou-Lou." Once a skinny "cripple shooter," Whitaker acquired some punch, hitting 21 and 20 home runs in back-to-back seasons in 1985 and 1986. Along with his considerable offensive contributions, "Sweet Lou" was a slick fielder and had a strong, accurate arm. (Dianne Chapman)

Following several mediocre seasons, Detroit purchased the contract of pitcher Milt Wilcox and sent him to Evansville. Wilcox caught on with the major league club in 1977 and became a member of the starting rotation the next season. He strung together seven straight double-digit winning seasons, capping it with a career-high 17 wins in 1984. (Dianne Chapman)

and Parrish, each ranking among the very best in Detroit Tiger history.

After a disastrous 1989 season, the Tigers were once again a team in transition; its core had been significantly weakened and they had a fairly empty minor league cupboard. Rebuilding from within usually is a slow, patient process, but Tom Monaghan and company radically broke with a tradition of conservatism and went into the free agent market determined to buy some reinforcements. Although their generous offers to star players were rejected, the Tigers did land Tony Phillips, Lloyd Mosby, Cecil

Fielder, and Ed Romero.

When Jim Campbell would retire had been a source of speculation for several years. However, his elevation to chairman of the board and the appointment of former University of Michigan football coach Bo Schembechler as president of the Tigers came as a surprise. Schembechler had just completed his first year on the Tiger board of directors and had recently resigned his dual posts as football coach and athletic director at Michigan.

The new decade began with old problems. Major league baseball's master agreement was due to expire, and the two parties, players and owners, were engaged in a tough, prolonged negotiation. On February 15, 1990, owners closed their training camps to major league players; the lockout continued well into March. Finally, after the second longest work stoppage in baseball history, a settlement was reached, and exhibition games began on March 26, a scant two weeks before the show began in Detroit on April 9.

A now not-quite-so-sparky George Anderson predicted that his team would "be a lot more improved over 1989." Free agents and other acquisitions had strengthened the offense, but pitching remained questionable. The starting rotation featured Jack Morris, Frank Tanana, Jeff Robinson,

Although a valued young player, outfielder Glenn Wilson was dealt to Philadelphia just before the opening of the 1984 season. He batted .278 while playing for the Bengals in 1982–83. (Neva Weidig)

San Diego relief pitcher Richard "Goose" Gossage elected to pitch to Kirk Gibson with first base open and runners on second and third in game five of the 1984 World Series. Gibson hit a dramatic eighth inning home run to cook the Padres' goose. (Detroit News Archives)

Kevin Ritz, and Urbano Lugo as needed for a fifth starter. Six weeks into the season, Ritz and Lugo were sent down in Toledo, and reclaimed pitcher Dan Petry was filling in admirably.

April and most of May saw the Tigers struggle. They opened with three consecutive losses and by mid-May were in the cellar with an 11–22 record, worst in baseball. Yet just four days later, amid a seven-game winning streak, the Bengals permanently left the basement for the remainder of the season.

A weak division makes weak teams seem respectable, and Detroit continued to move up in the standings. By midseason, they were winning at a .482 clip, six and a half games back of the leaders, and in fourth place.

Boston and Toronto dueled for the crown, while the rest of the division played in another competition. The contenders were dead even on August 20, but the Red Sox ultimately prevailed, winning the

▶ Jack Morris "gassed" the San Diego Padres with a five-hitter in winning his second complete-game World Series victory on October 13, 1984. (Dianne Chapman)

To start the 1990 season, the Tigers needed a right-handed batter who could hit with authority, and they found one in Cecil Fielder. (Mike Litaker)

flag by two games in a division in which only two teams played above .500 ball. The Tigers closed out 1990 in third place with a 79–83 record, nine games back in the standings.

Cecil Fielder just wanted to be an everyday player, and he struck with lightning once given the chance. He led a potent Tiger attack and quickly served notice that he was no fluke.

On May 6, he hit three homers in Toronto and duplicated the feat a month later against Cleveland. The big guy finished with a major-league high of 51 round-trippers and drove in 132 runs, also baseball's

Another of the Tigers' free agent acquisitions for the 1990 season was Tony Phillips. He played in 152 games, batting .251 and scoring 97 runs. (Mike Litaker)

including a superb relief corps. The right and left combination of Mike Henneman, Jerry Don Gleaton, Edwin Nunez, and Paul Gibson compiled a 17–14 win-loss record, saved 44 games, and allowed a stingy 2.54 runs per game.

Sparky Anderson was right: the Tigers did improve over their horrible previous season by winning 20 more games, but the next step up would be even tougher unless the farm system produced more than an occasional starting lineup player.

Returning from Japan, Cecil Fielder found a home in Detroit and his career blossomed. On October 3, 1990, he parked his 50th home run of the season at Yankee Stadium. (Lloyd Wallace)

best. He finished second in MVP balloting yet won numerous other awards for his spectacular season.

Shortstop Alan Trammell enjoyed another fine year, finishing fourth in hitting (.304) in the American League and leading the Tigers in several offensive categories. Tony Phillips contributed significantly with his solid all-around play and versatility, while rookie infielder Travis Fryman played above expectation, hitting .297 in 66 games.

Among the starters, Jack Morris returned to his familiar role as the ace, compiling a 15–18 record. This season unveiled several pleasant surprises

◀ Lloyd Mosby anchored a restructured outfield with strong defensive play in centerfield. Offensively he contributed 14 home runs in 1990. (Mike Litaker)

The Tiger organization hosted a very memorable experience for the capacity crowd at the final game. Sixty-five former players were present, paying respect to this hallowed place. During the closing ceremonies they came trotting out from behind the centerfield fence as they were announced and took their natural position on the field. The last and emotional event is portrayed here as these old players formed a line through the diamond as the U.S. flag was retired and passed from player to player and ultimately handed to team captain Brad Ausmus. (Lloyd Wallace)

11
A Franchise in Transition
1991–1999

The first half of the 1990s brought more of the same at the corner of Michigan and Trumbull. The decision to rebuild a ball club takes courage and patience, but the presence of a strong nucleus of excellent players argues for a different strategy: acquire the missing pieces via free agents and trades and win sooner rather than later. Many observers of the game seemed to agree that the farm system needed improvement as it continued to be unproductive. Baseball publications consistently rated the Tiger minor leagues among baseball's worst.

Junior Felix being congratulated after hitting a two-run homer in Milwaukee. Kirk Gibson (*left*) and Skeeter Barnes (#9) are seen in the foreground while Tim Belcher and Travis Fryman (#24) wait to congratulate Felix. (Lloyd Wallace)

A pensive pair of future Hall of Famers wait their turn to hit. Lou Whitaker and Alan Trammell rank in the top 10 of almost every Tiger career offensive category. (Lloyd Wallace)

New ownership in 1992 brought new confidence and expectation, yet it would become clear that many changes were in store and a longer solution to winning would be required. Hoping to soon field a contender, Detroit stayed with its solid core of players—primarily infielders—and tried to purchase the rest of the team. It did not work.

During the first half of the decade, the Tigers

The ever-popular Alan Trammell is always willing to accommodate fans. (Lloyd Wallace)

relied on the long ball and had an imposing cadre of free swingers who frequently led the league in home runs, runs, and strikeouts. Trying to outscore the opposing team became an increasing problem, though, as Detroit continued to be a pitching-poor franchise. During this five-year period, Tiger hurlers ranked no higher than 11th among American League clubs in earned runs allowed. Management tried to buy a pitching staff; six free agent hurlers were signed in 1993 alone.

On Monday, April 8, a crowd of 47,382 saw the Tigers win the 1991 season opener at home against the Yankees, and Detroit began the new campaign tied for first place in the American League East. A good start is every team's hope, and Detroit stayed competitive in the early going. The high watermark

of the season came on August 26 when Detroit reeled off its seventh straight victory, besting California and raising its record to 69 wins against 57 losses. That winning streak produced another tie on top of the standings, a place held for three days. Eventually Toronto captured the division title before losing the AL pennant to Minnesota. Detroit finished its season tied with Boston and Milwaukee in second place, seven games back. The Bengals had played respectable .519 baseball.

Free agent pitcher Bill Gullickson gave the Tigers their first 20-game winner in years as he tied for league leadership in victories. Mickey Tettleton, picked up in a trade with Baltimore, added his big bat to an already potent Tiger attack. Detroit batters hammered opposing pitchers for a league best: 209

homers, 32 more than their closest competitors. Cecil Fielder again claimed individual home run honors with 44. Detroit's home run hitters represented the latest version of a "Murderers' Row": Fielder 44; Tettleton 31; Rob Deer 25; Lou Whitaker 23; Travis Fryman 21; and Tony Phillips 17. Detroit used 19 pitchers throughout the season.

Bullpen mainstay Mike Henneman continued his late-inning mastery with a 10–2 record along with 21 saves.

Competitiveness in 1991 did not carry over in the new campaign as Detroit plunged immediately into a six-game losing streak and by April 20 had won only three of the first 14 games. By the All-Star

A very familiar scene at Tiger Stadium: another long home run hit by Cecil Fielder. Tony Phillips and Mickey Tettleton greet Fielder as he crosses home plate. Taking an unscientific approach to hitting, Fielder stated, "I just try to see the ball and hit it." His 245 home runs while playing for Detroit place him seventh among all Tiger hitters in team history. (Lloyd Wallace)

break, the Tigers were mired in sixth place, 13 games off the pace. In one stretch during the summer, they won just two games while dropping 11. Short winning streaks were frequently followed by hard times. The Eastern Division really had two levels of performance in 1992, an upper division of Toronto, Milwaukee, and Baltimore and a lower division of the also-rans. Toronto prevailed before going on to win its first world championship.

In August, business entrepreneur Michael Ilitch bought the organization he once played for and ushered in renewed optimism for the future. The wheels of change had been set in motion. As part of the purchase package, seller Tom Monaghan released team president Bo Schembechler. Even broadcasting legend Ernie Harwell and his longtime partner, Paul Carey, were replaced by a new play-by-play team.

One thing did not change: lots of runs scored whenever the Tigers played. Tiger hitters repeated as team home run champs, while the other AL teams

Seattle's Ken Griffey, Jr., banters with a very social Tony Phillips. During his five seasons with Detroit, Phillips became the consummate lead-off batter, averaging 100 walks and 100 runs scored each year. (Lloyd Wallace)

feasted on Bengal pitchers for a combined batting average of .277. Gullickson and ageless Frank Tanana led a weak starting rotation, and Henneman performed at a level expected of the pen's top fireman. Travis Fryman's outstanding season earned him a place on the All-Star team, and Tony Phillips emerged as one of baseball's premier lead-off hitters.

Following a disappointing sixth-place finish in 1992, Detroit rebounded in 1993, winning at a .525 clip and garnering a tie for third place in the final standings. Detroit opened the season poorly with a six-game West Coast road trip. Back in the familiar surroundings of Tiger Stadium, booming bats pro-

Three good friends who frequently expressed their mutual admiration with barbs. *Left to right:* Mike Henneman, Cecil Fielder, and Mickey Tettleton. (Lloyd Wallace)

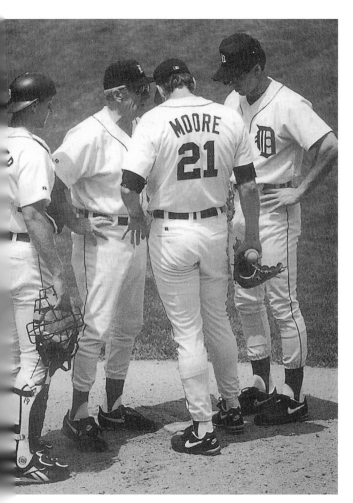

The Tigers hoped Mike Moore would become the mainstay of the starting rotation, but he toiled through three years of disappointment, piling up earned run averages in excess of 5.00. An all-too-frequent situation for Moore shows Chad Kreuter, pitching coach Billy Muffet, and Travis Fryman at the mound. (Lloyd Wallace)

Philadelphia en route to their second consecutive world championship.

A great offensive team could not overcome its lack of consistent pitching. Fielder, Fryman, Trammell, Whitaker, Phillips, Tettleton, Scott Livingstone, and newcomer Chad Krueter all had fine seasons. Management brought back old warhorse Kirk Gibson, and he produced a remarkable season given his age and absence from the game most of the previous year. Among the bevy of free agent pitchers, most was expected from Mike Moore. Though he topped the staff with 13 victories, he allowed more than five runs per game. Ace reliever Mike Henne-

A modest and unassuming Lou Whitaker has made a lot of noise with his bat. Seemingly out of character, Whitaker is confident that both he and Alan Trammell will join the Hall of Fame. His offensive numbers—2,369 hits, 244 homers, 1,084 runs batted in—rank among baseball's best middle infielders of all time. (Mike Litaker)

pelled the Tigers through a 12-game stretch in which they lost only once. Winning margins of 20–4 and 20–3, followed by a three-game series at the Metrodome in which Detroit swept Minnesota by scores of 12–4, 17–1, and 16–5, demonstrated the firepower of this explosive lineup. That series vaulted the Tigers into first place, a position they maintained for the next 65 days. A 10-game losing streak near the end of June cost the Bengals what could have been a bright season. The Blue Jays dominated postseason play, disposing of Chicago and

man racked up 24 more saves to become the all-time save leader in Detroit baseball history.

Baseball realigned in 1994, creating three divisions: East, West, and Central in each league and a three-tiered postseason championship series, all intended to generate greater fan interest. The new design and strategy failed when the players struck, shortening the season to just 115 games for the Tigers. Tragically polarized adversaries canceled the fall classic; baseball's showcase had been played uninterrupted since 1905.

Detroit remained in the Eastern Division, now with just five clubs. Detroit started and finished the 1994 season in the cellar, winning 53 and losing 62. At the traditional halfway point in the season, Detroit stood fourth in the divisional race, 11 1/2 games behind, but the rest of the year got progressively worse.

If the opposing pitcher glances into the Tiger dugout, there is no doubt as to who is anxiously waiting his turn to bat. Cecil Fielder and Manager Sparky Anderson are ready to do battle. (Lloyd Wallace)

▼ Mickey Tettleton (*left*), Travis Fryman (*center*), and middle reliever Joe Boever enjoy a relaxed time in pregame preparation. (Lloyd Wallace)

Detroit's Hall of Fame broadcaster Ernie Harwell (*left*) on the air in the radio booth at Tiger Stadium. His broadcast partner, Rick Rizzs, is on the right. (Lloyd Wallace)

Earned run averages continued to escalate in baseball, and Detroit's mound corps was one of four in the American League in excess of 5.37. Henneman finally experienced a substandard performance, saving only eight games. Joe Boever won nine games as a long reliever, only two shy of the team leader in victories.

Gibson, at 37, demonstrated the impact of a player with fire in his belly, turning in a remarkable .276 season with 72 runs batted in and 71 runs

A very disciplined Travis Fryman quickly honed his skills to become a three-time American League All-Star. His slugging consistently produced 20-home run, 90-runs-batted-in seasons. On May 5, 1993, Fryman hit for the cycle, the first Tiger to do so since Hoot Evers achieved the feat back in 1950. (Lloyd Wallace)

Tony Clark was considered among the best position players in the organization. Former general manager Joe Klein had predicted a bright future for Clark when he said, "Tony Clark's potential is unlimited. I think he is a 35 to 40 home run guy." He led the young Tigers with 32 home runs and 117 runs batted in during his first full season in 1997. (Mike Litaker)

scored in a short season. The Bengals continued to field a power-laden lineup.

Media reported ownership's desire for a new stadium with increasing frequency, while the team experienced the lowest attendance in the American League. With obvious concern for the state of baseball's affairs, Mike Ilitch said, "I think if I had known the shape baseball was in specifically . . . I don't think I would have bought the club."

And it did not get any better for quite a while in 1995. As the deadlock continued, the time to begin spring training loomed just weeks away, and owners began scrambling for replacement players and determining who could be used from within their farm systems. With no settlement in sight, all of the clubs except Baltimore began spring training with only minor leaguers and replacement players in camp. Baseball held its breath wondering how this mess would end.

Chad Curtis led the Tigers in runs scored and hit a career-high 21 home runs in his first year with the team (1995). In assessing his new team's winning potential, Curtis stated, "Sometimes talent doesn't cut it. You've got to have attitude." (Lloyd Wallace)

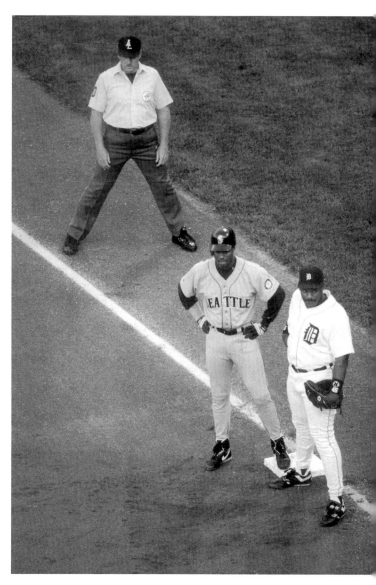

Ken Griffey, Jr., about to take his lead off first as Cecil Fielder attempts to hold him close. (Lloyd Wallace)

During his long 17-year tenure as Tiger manager, Sparky Anderson enjoyed the uncommon luxury of playing the same all-star-caliber shortstop. Alan Trammell was a recognized leader on the team. The testimony of pitcher David Wells is typical: "If Alan Trammell sees a conflict, he will step in and resolve it." (Lloyd Wallace)

Detroit's Hall-of-Fame-bound manager, Sparky Anderson, walked out of camp, unable to tolerate what he called counterfeit major league baseball. "I did not do this for the players or to hurt ownership. I cannot bargain my integrity. . . . I am not going to tarnish this game," said Anderson. Toledo manager Tom Runnells became interim manager while Anderson returned to his California home on unpaid leave.

Just before the season would have begun, owners and players agreed to a "no settlement." After 232 days, baseball ended the longest strike in professional sports history. The late start dictated a second consecutive shortened season; this time teams would play a 144-game schedule. The Tigers had little reason to expect much more than another year of struggle in 1995.

They came out of the gate slowly but then surprisingly put together a sustained stretch of winning, closing the first half of the season three games over .500 and just three games behind the leader. Then realism struck without compassion as these would-be contenders suffered through an eight-game losing streak. Bad became worse as Detroit won only 10 of the next 46 games.

John McHale, Jr., president of the Detroit Tigers, and his father, John McHale, Sr., former player and executive with the team, are being interviewed about their common and unique Tiger heritage. (Mike Litaker)

Detroit native Michael Ilitch began his professional sports career as a Tiger minor leaguer in the early 1950s, then built the Little Caesar's Pizza restaurant enterprise in Michigan while acquiring several professional sports teams along the way. His purchase of the Detroit Tigers in 1992 fulfilled a lifelong dream. (Little Caesar Enterprises, Inc.)

After three disappointing seasons, starter Mike Moore was released and Kirk Gibson elected to leave, finding it difficult to roar on a team with so little spark. Detroit had an awful second half and finished with a losing percentage of .417 among the dregs in the AL. As a team, they were mediocre in nearly every pitching and hitting category. There were small glimmers of light: new centerfielder Chad Curtis enjoyed a fine first season in the Motor City, and some rookies were on the team who might develop into real ballplayers. The day after the season ended, George "Sparky" Anderson left the Tigers for good.

Predicting a long season of futility for the 1996 Detroit Tigers required little special foresight or

Bill Gullickson won 20 games in his first season in the Motor City. Other than Jack Morris, who did it twice, Gullickson was the first to win 20 since 1974. (Mike Litaker)

The commitment of management to a new rebuilding plan evolved throughout the season. John McHale, Jr., became the new president and chief executive officer in January 1995. Mission: put together the package to finance the development of a new stadium. Popular and productive Tony Phillips, age 36, was traded to California for outfielder Chad Curtis, age 26. After the Tigers crashed to earth in the second half of the season, management actively wrote off the remainder and shopped its best two pitchers, David Wells and Mike Henneman, to contending teams. Youth replaced veterans as Detroit picked up prospects Phil Nevin, C. J. Nitkowski, and Mark Lewis.

Anderson closed out his illustrious career as the winningest Tiger manager (1,331) while compiling a career major league total of 2,134, placing him third overall in baseball history behind the leader, Connie Mack, and his closest record rival, John McGraw. (Mike Litaker)

The often injured David Wells put together his best career season in 1995. Selected for the All-Star team, Wells won 10 games for the Bengals before being swapped to Cincinnati as Detroit sought to acquire several young prospects. (Mike Litaker)

analytical ability. Detroit still had Fielder and Fryman, but its pitching staff was woefully weak and inexperienced, resembling a modern-day expansion team in its inaugural season.

The youth, inexperience, and personality of the new skipper, Buddy Bell, seemingly suited him well to withstand the beating his team was about to take. Bell's young Tigers got off to a horrendous start; by the end of May they were buried in last place, 18 games behind the division leader. In about a six-week period spanning April 17 through the month of May, Detroit salvaged only five wins while absorbing a staggering 34 defeats.

Playing almost .500 ball for the 30 days preceding the All-Star break provided a spark of encouragement, but fortune turned sour again. Detroit suffered through an eight-game losing streak in August followed by 12 consecutive losses in September. The inept Tigers gave writers and cartoonists plenty of substance to creatively describe what simply was bad baseball.

Placed in historical context, 1996 ranks as a horrible season. The Tigers set several franchise records: most earned runs allowed, most runs scored by opponents, most walks issued, and most losses. On an even higher level of futility, Detroit set major

Acquired in 1991 from Baltimore, Mickey Tettleton became one of the best trade acquisitions in recent years. In his three full seasons with Detroit, Tettleton hit 96 home runs with remarkable consistency, 31, 32, and 33. (Mike Litaker)

league baseball records for most home runs by opponents and the most strikeouts by a team. Detroit finished dead last in its division and in all of major league baseball, piling up 109 losses.

New general manager Randy Smith spent the season urging patience and reinforcing the reality that there was no quick fix for the Bengals: "This is a much bigger job than we had in San Diego, a much more major rebuilding than what we had with the Padres."

Smith shuffled players in and out of Detroit, searching for some combination that could reverse the flow of losing baseball. His actions tied the all-time club record for players used in a season, match-

ing Hughie Jennings's total of 53 in 1912. Late in July, the Tigers granted Cecil Fielder's wish and traded him to a pennant contender, the New York Yankees.

As in the previous 19 years, Alan Trammell started the 1996 season at shortstop. Although slated for part-time duty, old number 3 filled in for a few games and then gave way to a series of five other shortstops.

Despite the gloom, there were some bright spots in 1996. Travis Fryman continued his excel-

"They looked at how my ball moves, my awkward way of throwing, and decided if I was going to make it in the major leagues, I was going to be a reliever." The best pitcher to come out of the Tiger farm system in nearly 20 years, Mike Henneman spent his entire Tiger career being the chief firefighter out of the bullpen. Before being traded to Houston late in 1995, Henneman compiled 154 saves, second best in franchise history. (Dianne Chapman)

During an era when the Tigers struggled to win games, Bobby Higginson was often their best offensive weapon. Here he shows Red Wings coach Scotty Bowman his favorite weapon. (Mark Cunningham)

lent play, driving in a career-high 99 runs. A team that is not supposed to win can afford to give its young players extended opportunities to demonstrate their capabilities, and a couple emerged as legitimate big league players. Tony Clark hit 23 home runs in just 95 games. Bobby Higginson put together a whole season batting a sparkling .322 with 26 home runs. Help came from Melvin Nieves, one of Smith's trade acquisitions, who hammered out 23 home runs. Clearly pleased with Buddy Bell's performance, Tiger management extended his contract through the 1998 season. The Tigers signed an affiliation agreement with the West Michigan Whitecaps. This Grand Rapids–based team had

Given a starting role in 1993, pitcher John Doherty posted a team-best 14 victories. A sinker ball pitcher, Doherty's approach was fairly simple: "I'm after ground-ball outs." (Mike Litaker)

Few practitioners of baseball would challenge Connie Mack's well-known conclusion that pitching is 85 percent of the game. Assembling a quality pitching staff is both difficult and exceptional in present-day major league baseball. "One's approach is based on a philosophy. I believe in acquiring and developing power arms; pitchers with greater arm strength have a greater margin for error. In the past, the Tigers went after sinkerball pitchers who generated a lot of groundball outs. This type of pitcher has little room for error in locating the ball. I'm seeking power pitchers who will produce more strikeouts," said Randy Smith, vice president of baseball operations and general manager, on September 17, 1996. (Photos courtesy of Mike Litaker)

Pictured are Justin Thompson (*left*) and Brian Moehler.

developed into a premier minor league fan attraction and gave the Tigers their first in-state minor league team in more than forty years. The year also recorded a favorable decision by the Michigan Court of Appeals, clearing the way for the expenditure of state funds and a new Tiger stadium.

When a team has the worst record in major league baseball, there is one relatively safe bet for the new season: things will surely improve. Better than that, the Detroit Tigers made more progress in 1997 than anyone had a right to expect.

There were many new faces when the season began; only seven were left from the team that opened the 1996 campaign. Its lineup included a new centerfielder, new catcher, new double-play combination, and an overhauled pitching staff.

Buddy Bell's decision to start a newly acquired relief pitcher and a shortstop who had not played above A ball did not instill optimism.

Opening at Minnesota's Metrodome, the young Tigers played like the old Tigers of 1996 as the Twins swept Detroit in a three-game series. In games two, three, and four of the season, Bell used six pitchers in each contest. It looked like more of the same.

April's unseasonably cold weather reflected the team's start as it finished the month in the division's basement, already seven games behind the leader while performing at a .407 winning percentage.

A month later, the team showed signs of a new level of improved play and by the All-Star break were just three games below the coveted .500 mark.

During the 1996 season, the Tigers called up replacement pitcher Mike Christopher from their Toledo farm team, and he turned in an impressive performance with a 4–0 record and a 3.82 earned run average in 36 games. (Mike Litaker)

Here on September 13, 1995, Alan Trammell and Lou Whitaker are about to play in their 1,915th game together, breaking George Brett's and Frank White's record. "I have had a lot of best friends. Tram and myself were the first to join together as companions, working associates and professionals," said Whitaker. (Mike Litaker)

On the 75th anniversary of the birth of the Negro Leagues, the Tigers and Kansas City Royals wore Negro League–styled uniforms in a game at Tiger Stadium, July 8, 1995. Lou Whitaker, Juan Samuel, and Franklin Stubbs (*left to right*) wear replica uniforms of the Detroit Stars, the city's major league black team. (Mike Litaker)

The Bengals had won nine of their previous 12 and were 41–44 for the season. Remarkably, the Tigers' representative on the All-Star squad was a pitcher, Justin Thompson. Midseason prosperity followed by a dive back to reality had become a recent Tiger phenomenon, but this club broke the pattern.

Despite the improvement, Tiger GM Randy Smith remained committed to the long haul, swapping two-fifths of the starting rotation to Seattle in return for young prospects. Detroit overcame this loss of pitchers and continued to play respectable baseball. Quickly recovering from a broken jaw after being struck in the face by a line drive on May 4, Willie Blair won six games in July. Justin Thompson continued to pitch well despite his team's lack of

offensive support when he was on the mound.

Mike Hargrove's recognition of the improved performance of the Detroit club reflected the team's growing respect. The Cleveland manager said,

Al Kaline (*left*) and manager Buddy Bell commiserate during the miserable 1998 season when Detroit lost 97 games. Bell succeeded the winningest manager in franchise history and faced the challenge of rebuilding a winner. A four-time American League All-Star brought the experience of an 18-year playing career and two years of coaching with the Cleveland Indians to his new leadership role. He was fired on September 1, 1998, when a season of expected improvement turned sour. (Mark Cunningham)

To maximize the skills of a base stealer, the hitter must first get on base. Brian Hunter's highly successful first season with Detroit was directly attributable to his playing every game, collecting 177 hits, and walking 66 times. Hunter led all base stealers in 1997 with 74 thefts. (Mike Litaker)

Right-hander Willie Blair had never won more than seven games in a season before joining the Tigers in 1997. In his career season, Blair led the pitching staff with 16 victories. (Mike Litaker)

"They're a much better team—absolutely much better." Tiger players were also verbalizing a new confidence as expressed by cheerleader Bobby Higginson: "We're in every ball game."

During spring training, Manager Bell had stated his desired goal of playing some meaningful games in September. That month proved to be the high point of the season when the young Tigers mustered an impressive stretch drive. In its 157th game, Detroit achieved its 15th victory in its last 20 games and moved one game over .500 at 79–78. For the month, they won 16 and lost 11, a marvelous improvement over their record of 4–22 the previous September.

The Tigers finished third, 19 games behind a strong Baltimore team in a division in which only the

General Manager Randy Smith liked power pitchers and stocked the Tiger bullpen with several. Doug Brocail was a prototype of the Smith model. He became the set-up man and pitched brilliantly during his first two seasons with Detroit. (Mike Litaker)

Detroit acquired Todd Jones to be its closer and to strengthen an often maligned bullpen during the 1997 campaign. Jones became an impact player, racking up an impressive total of 31 saves. "All I know is he has been almost perfect for the last three months," said Manager Bell in 1997. (Mark Cunningham)

Yankees challenged the winners. Detroit seemed to run out of gas at the wire though, finishing the season with five consecutive losses. That aside, it had been a wonderful season of improvement. Detroit won 26 more games than it had in 1996, a record-setting turnaround. Bell, the highly regarded teacher, and the much improved pitching and defense accounted heavily for the gains. The Tigers also had better players, thanks in large part to the shrewd dealing of Randy Smith.

Detroit had three fairly consistent starting pitchers in Willie Blair, Justin Thompson, and Brian Moehler, all finishing with more than 10 wins. Smith

Shortstop Deivi Cruz was the cornerstone of a greatly improved team defense in 1997. He was so impressive that Manager Buddy Bell determined to play him even if he did not hit. "He makes so many good plays," said Bell. "It's amazing what this kid does." (Mike Litaker)

Although highly regarded, Damion Easley had never produced; injuries always seemed to be his adversary. He conquered that nemesis in 1997, playing in 151 games and hitting 22 home runs. His strong performance earned him a spot on the All-Star team in 1996, a season in which he drove in 100 runs as the Tigers' regular second baseman. (Mike Litaker)

set out to shore up the bullpen, and his December trade with Houston worked miracles. Stopper Todd Jones finished among the league leaders with 31 saves while Doug Brocail pitched brilliantly in the second half of the season as the set-up man, compiling an ERA of 3.23. Speed is often associated with good defense, and in Brian Hunter the Tigers had their first major league stolen base champion since Ty Cobb. Another special defensive weapon came

Considered an exceptional prospect and an important part of the Tigers' future, Juan Encarnacion never played up to that level of expectation. His best and only impressive hitting season came in 2000 when he compiled a .289 batting average with 14 home runs and 72 runs batted in. Encarnacion's disappointing fielding contributed to the decision to trade him to Cincinnati for Dmitri Young. (Mike Litaker)

Every franchise has a list, ideally a short one, of blown trades. Detroit gave up on Phil Niven (1995–97) too soon and he had several fine seasons with San Diego. He enjoyed a monster year in 2001, hitting 41 home runs and driving in 126 runs. (Mike Litaker)

Omar Olivares pitched for Detroit during the lean years (1996–97) when quality hurlers were in short supply. Used exclusively as a starter, he managed 12 victories in his brief career in Detroit. (Mike Litaker)

Gabe Kapler had a great season for Jacksonville in 1998, hitting .322, 28 home runs, and driving in a Southern League record-setting 146 runs. His outstanding season won him the league's Most Valuable Player award. *USA Today* named him minor league player of the year. (Mike Litaker)

from Bobby Higginson's strong and accurate throwing arm. He led all American League outfielders in assists. Tony Clark, Travis Fryman, and Higginson each drove in more than 100 runs and along with Damion Easley and Melvin Nieves combined to hit 123 home runs.

The Tigers had a cadre of young and talented players expected to be factors in a more competitive future. Management's decision to sign Todd Jones, Damion Easley, Bobby Higginson, and Tony Clark

◀ The Tigers selected fire-balling Matt Anderson as the first overall pick in the June 1997 draft. He was rated the best pitching prospect in college baseball prior to the draft by *Baseball America*. Anderson initially lived up to his billing but he never recovered his velocity after several occasions on the disabled list with a sore arm. (Mike Litaker)

to multiple-year contracts was indicative of a new confidence. Along with optimism was a keen awareness that much remained to be accomplished before the Tigers could compete in postseason play. Yet perhaps even more heartening for a winning future was the accelerated progress of the team's farm system. According to Howe Sportsdata International

Robert Fick was another outstanding young prospect in the Tigers organization. He starred at West Michigan and Jacksonville in back-to-back seasons and was then promoted to the big team. Although a natural hitter, the Tigers could never find a position in the field where he could perform at a satisfactory level. Fick's greatest moment in a Tiger uniform came in the ninth inning of the final game at Tiger Stadium when he hit a mammoth grand slam home run. (Mike Litaker)

The Tigers saw Frank Catalanotto as a utility and role player and included him in the trade that brought Juan Gonzalez to Detroit. Once given the chance to play regularly, Catalanotto showed how much he belonged in the everyday lineup. (Mike Litaker)

and *Baseball America*, the Tigers' minor league system was the best organization in 1997. Basing the acclaim on the organization's winning percentage of .531, fifth best among 30 major league baseball organizations, Howe reported that the team "completely rebuilt what had been the division's weakest farm system." Both Howe and *Baseball America*

Trading Luis Gonzalez after just one season in a Tiger uniform (1998) proved to be one of the team's worst player transactions in franchise history. In his first five seasons with the Arizona Diamondbacks he averaged 34 home runs, drove in over 100 runs, and had a batting average of over .300 in every year except one. (Mike Litaker)

in the weaker Central Division. Reality struck with unmercifully suddenness as the team staggered through the first month of the season. An Associated Press wire story released on May 1 reported, "The Detroit Tigers undoubtedly are happy to have April behind them. . . . The Tigers were 5–18 in April and were often their own worst enemy." During that awful April, the Tigers suffered through two five-

Although always considered a fine receiver and player, Detroit hung on to Brad Ausmus for only two full seasons. The first time they traded for him (1996) he finished the season having played only 75 games before being swapped to Houston. In 1999 the Bengals acquired him again via a trade and he played the next two seasons, making the All-Star Game in his first year back. Following the 2000 season he was dispatched back to Houston, where he finished his career. (Mike Litaker)

In return for Gonzalez Detroit received once highly regarded prospect Karim Garcia. It took only 104 games, most in his first season, for the Tigers to decide that he wasn't the ticket they had hoped he would be. Although he played in parts of 10 seasons he never reached his expected potential, ending his career with a .241 lifetime batting average. (Mike Litaker)

recognized that the organization has quality arms at all levels as well as quality depth at most positions. *Baseball Weekly* chose its first minor league all-star team and selected West Michigan Whitecaps starter Clayton Bruner and reliever Francisco Cordero. In a separate assessment, it named Jacksonville outfielder Juan Encarnacion among the top 10 minor league prospects in baseball.

The Tigers began the 1998 season with renewed confidence, hoping and even expecting to compete

Like many other teams, Detroit occasionally sought a fading star, hoping to squeeze out a season or two of his past glory. Eric Davis played in 60 games spread over two seasons, 1993–94. (Mike Litaker)

In his first full season (1997), Justin Thompson won 15 games and compiled a sparkling 3.02 ERA. He ranked among the top 10 American League pitchers in ERA, innings pitched, complete games, and batting average against. Considered untouchable, he saw his career dashed by persistent sore arms. (Mike Litaker)

game losing streaks and a seven-game drought. The miserable start matched the worst in franchise history.

At the midpoint in the season, they were 34–50, and 15 1/2 games behind the powerful Cleveland Indians.

Detroit absorbed three more sustained losing streaks, the worst in early August when the team couldn't buy a win in nine consecutive games. August resembled April—Detroit won only eight of 30 games.

Frustrations mounted throughout the season. After being battered in April, Manager Buddy Bell

said he was "tired of babysitting" his players as the mental errors piled up. The off-season player acquisition strategy of replacing the previous year's tendency to strike out too often with more consistent hitters failed. By the end of July a frustrated Bell stated, "I wish I knew what to do with our offense. We're going backwards offensively for some reason. I don't know if our guys are looking at numbers at this time of year, but we're not taking the walks when

▶ Following the 1997 season, Detroit let their best player leave through free agency. Leaving a major hole at third base, they signed Joe Randa but after one season decided he was no Travis Fryman and traded him to Kansas City where he promptly showed them how good he was by hitting .314 with 197 hits. (Mark Cunningham)

Ruben Sierra got into 46 games in 1996. (Mike Litaker)

Vince Coleman finished his career with Detroit playing six games in 1997. (Mike Litaker)

▶ The Tigers signed their first Japanese player, pitcher Masao Kida (*left*), in 1998. Tomo Ohka, also a hurler, broke in with the Red Sox the following year. (Mike Litaker)

A career .289 hitter, free agent Greg Jefferies signed with Detroit after the 1998 season and played his final two years in the Motor City. (Mike Litaker)

General Manager Randy Smith wanted a high-profile star player to pump up attendance at the new Comerica Park and he packaged a deal with Texas to acquire slugger Juan Gonzalez. Smith remained confident he could re-sign the free agent eligible Gonzalez, though he had already expressed displeasure with the depth of the left-field power alley fence. The injury-prone long ball hitter soon was on the DL, playing in only 114 games while having a very subpar season. Following the season he turned down Detroit's big contract, preferring the offer of and surroundings in Cleveland. (Mike Litaker)

they're there." On August 1, the Tigers terminated seven-year hitting coach Larry Herndon.

Amid a season of constant losing and disappointment, the Tigers' game face of "we're going to get better" eroded and fell off. The veterans started to talk. Damion Easley claimed the team lacked aggressiveness. Bobby Higginson said, "You keep trying to compete—and win—but let's be honest, we're really going to battle a little short." A normally restrained owner expressed doubt and the field boss

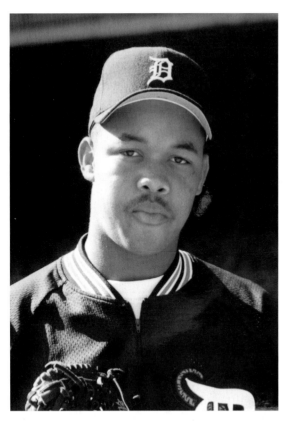

There are usually promising young players in a big trade and Detroit lost hard-throwing reliever Francisco Cordero, who became the quality closer anticipated. Over two seasons with the Rangers he saved 86 games and earned a berth on the National League All-Star team in 2007 with the Milwaukee Brewers. (Mike Litaker)

Tiger ownership had been a reluctant buyer of star-quality free agents for years. When the team signed Dean Palmer after the 1997 season they began to turn a corner in franchise attitude toward competing in the new contractual environment. Third baseman Palmer finished his career with the Bengals and put together his best string of run-producing seasons, featuring three straight years in which he knocked in over 100 runs. (Mike Litaker)

apparently felt a need for reassurance. The pressures of a miserable season squeezed all the decision makers and Buddy Bell lost his job.

During the previous season, the Tigers were so pleased with Bell's work that he had been given a new two-year contract. His successful leadership and the progress of the team were widely recognized by baseball officials. His firing shocked many and although explanations varied, the young team's reversal and the strain of losing were surely at the heart of the decision.

Vice president and general manager Randy

During an era when the ace of the Tigers' pitching staff meant winning more than a dozen games, Detroit acquired right-hander Dave Mlicki from the Los Angeles Dodgers in 1998 and he produced a career-high 14 victories. (Mike Litaker)

In the expensive trade for Juan Gonzalez, Detroit lost two quality young players, Francisco Cordero and Frank Catalanotto. Before an arm injury shortened his career, Danny Patterson was an effective set-up man in the Tiger bullpen and the only real value the team received in its player swap with Texas. (Mike Litaker)

Smith promoted bench coach Larry Parrish to replace Bell. Teams often respond with improved play for a while under a new manager, yet given Bell's popularity with the players, something more than the normal psychology must have occurred as the team gained new respectability during its last 25 games, playing over .500 with a 13–12 record.

This late surge averted what had looked like another 100-loss season. The bad news, however, was a very disappointing 65–97 season, a last-place finish

24 games behind the pennant-winning Indians, and a losing record equaled by one expansion team and only slightly better than the other brand-new franchise.

When a team "crashes and burns," there are many contributing factors that account for its agonizing season. Despite several acquisitions, these new players did not replace the loss of Willie Blair's 16 wins and consistency, or Travis Fryman's steady play and leadership. GM Smith tried to rebuild the starting rotation, but Scott Sanders, Frank Castillo, and Tim Worrell did not produce. Brian Hunter, Todd Jones, and Joe Randa all had mediocre seasons. Shortstop Deivi Cruz broke an ankle during winter ball and did not play until late April, yet despite his return, Tiger defensive play was way off the excel-

Opening day, April 5, 1999, and the last such occasion at Tiger Stadium. Introducing all of the players is an opening day tradition, and here are the members of the Detroit Tigers and Texas Rangers lining up during the ceremonies. The Tigers won big, 11–5, on this day and would occupy first place in the Central Division for about 24 hours of the 1999 season. (Lloyd Wallace)

Honorary team captains Al Kaline and George Brett, representing the visiting Kansas City Royals, meet the umpires and present the starting lineups for the final game in Tiger Stadium's major league history on September 27, 1999. (Mike Litaker)

lence shown in 1997. Fielding and base-running lapses were common, as the 1998 Tigers did not execute the basics very well. Youth and lack of experience certainly contributed to these shortcomings, as the Tigers had as many as 10 rookies on the team during the season and were one of the youngest squads in all of major league baseball. Perhaps the bottom-line explanation for the Tigers' futile performance in 1998 is fairly simple: they just didn't have enough good players. Some would argue that a franchise cannot win unless it spends the money to acquire quality players. That conclusion seems to be supported by the fact that 11 of the teams that played in postseason competition in 1998 had payrolls nearly double that of Detroit.

Yet not all was dark in 1998. The nucleus of this young team continued to play well. Tony Clark enjoyed his best season, leading the team with 34 homers, 103 runs batted in, 175 hits, and a .291 batting average. Free agent Luis Gonzalez hit 23 home runs and contributed regularly to the Tigers' offense. The rest of the power hitting came from Clark (34 homers), Damion Easley (27 home runs), and Bobby Higginson (25 home runs). Brian Moehler led starting pitchers with 14 wins and a 3.90 earned run average. Highly regarded Justin Thompson fell short of expectation with a 11–15 record, continuing his jinx of not getting much run support. The brightest aspect of Tiger pitching came from the bullpen, where the staff combined for a 4.25 ERA, sixth best in the American League. Doug Brocail produced a second consecutive strong season with a 5–2 record and a 2.73 earned run average. Youngsters Matt Anderson and Sean Runyon also pitched very effectively.

Former star shortstop Billy Rogell at age 94 throws out the ceremonial first pitch for the final game. Standing behind Rogell is former pitcher Eldon Auker at the grand age of 89—two living links to the storied memories of Tiger Stadium. Current Tigers gathered around the two old veterans are, from the left, Dean Palmer, coach Perry Hill with hands on hips, hitting coach Alan Trammell, Damion Easley, manager Lance Parrish, Karim Garcia, Willie Blair, and Matt Anderson (*on the far right*). Tall Tony Clark is back behind Trammell. (Mike Litaker)

The last decade of the twentieth century witnessed a major changing of the guard in Detroit: new ownership, new front office leadership, new managers, new coaches, new players, a new short-stop and second baseman combination, and a new team ready to begin the new century in a new place. During the last years of the century the Tigers parted with some big elements of their history: the keystone combination of Alan Trammell and Lou Whitaker, two star players who anchored the middle of the infield for a record-setting nineteen seasons; Mike Henneman, the best relief pitcher in the

The Tigers' best starting pitcher, Brian Moehler, delivers the first pitch in the final game at the old ballpark. (Mike Litaker)

Tigertown, the minor league training site of the Bengals since 1953. The complex includes multiple ball fields, dormitory, cafeteria, recreation center, enclosed training facilities, and an administration building. (Lakeland Tigers)

Joker Marchant Stadium is the home field for two of the Tigers' Class A minor league teams, the Lakeland Tigers and the Gulf Coast League Tigers. This ballpark has also served as the spring training home of the Detroit Tigers since 1966. (Lakeland Tigers)

Detroit's minor league relationship with Toledo dates back to the 1930s when infielder Fred Haney managed the Mud Hens. The team's present affiliation began in 1990. The Tigers' Triple A ball club plays in the International League. Their home park, Fifth Third Field, is located downtown a short distance from the Maumee River. (Toledo Mud Hens)

team's history at the time; Sparky Anderson, destined to join the Hall of Fame and the third winningest manager in the history of the game; and a venerable old ballpark that had staged more than ninety years of Tiger baseball.

The Tigers were putting on a new face and moving toward a new chapter of their winning tradition. Although the Florida Marlins' success in 1997 suggested a quicker route to glory, the Detroit Tigers were trying to develop a competitive team in a more conventional way. Management believed the foundation had been established. Its farm system seemed to be producing a steady stream of prospects. Ownership and management remained committed to a vision based on player development and patience.

The 1999 season promised to be memorable, being the last to ever be played in Tiger Stadium. Clearly the owner and his management cadre sought to field a competitive team and take advantage of the uplift expected from the 2000 season when the Tigers occupied their new home at Comerica Park. The team locked in two of its core players, Bobby Higginson and Damion Easley, by signing them to multiple-year contracts. GM Randy Smith lured big run producer and free agent Dean Palmer and signed him to a five-year deal. Smith also picked up Gregg Jefferies via free agency, claiming the Tigers would finally have an effective number two hitter in the lineup. On that same day late in December 1998, Smith accommodated Luis Gonzalez's desire to be traded to a team where he could play regularly for an unproven yet once highly sought prize, Karim Garcia. In January 1999, Smith reacquired Brad Asmus, slated to be Detroit's first-string catcher. The team also added gate attraction and cachet in bringing back Alan Trammell as hitting coach.

Despite *Baseball Weekly*'s rating the Tigers' odds of making the playoffs 1 in 250,000, the optimists were led by Smith: "We had to start acquiring some of the pieces we felt necessary to compete." Free agent signings and contract extensions had elevated the team's payroll by $12 million to a new high of $35 million.

Going into spring training, Tiger officials remained confident that hitting would be solid. Although they were more cautious about their pitching, manager Larry Parrish had Justin Thompson, Brian Moehler, Willie Blair, and Seth Greisinger slated for his starting rotation. But before leaving camp Greisinger went on the disabled list and his replacement was a player to be named later. Opinions are free and *Baseball Weekly* columnist Paul White

picked the Tigers to finish second in the Central Division and make the playoffs as the wild card: "The Detroit offense is loaded, we think. . . . The Tigers have reason to be concerned about their pitching inconsistencies, for sure."

The club opened the season in Texas flashing an impressive hitting attack that scored 11 runs but then shifted into a lower gear, losing the next six games in which they were shut out three times. Bright sunny weather provided a perfect atmosphere for the Tigers final home opener on April 12, the start of the team's 104th season at the corner of Michigan and Trumbull. With a full house of 47,449 excited fans, the home team battled the Minnesota Twins for 12 innings before falling 1–0 in an old-fashioned pitcher's duel. The participants on and off the field were full of reflection on this day as most spoke of the cherished history of this hallowed ground. By April 27 the team worked its way back to respectability with a record of 10–10 but unfortunately would never reach the .500 level again in the

Jerry Uht Park in Erie, Pennsylvania, opened in 1995 and became an affiliate of the Detroit Tigers in 2001. The ballpark has a very inviting left-field fence just 312 feet away from the batter. The Sea Wolves play in the AA Eastern League. (Erie Sea Wolves)

Fifth Third Park in Grand Rapids is home to the West Michigan Whitecaps. Blessed with strong fan support, this ballpark has a capacity of over 11,000 and has experienced three expansions since it opened in 1994. The Whitecaps became a Tiger farm team in 1997 and have since won three Midwest League championships. (West Michigan Whitecaps)

season. After a spurt of strong pitching that spurred this early comeback, the staff remained in a state of disarray. While starter Bryce Florie joined Greisinger on the DL, Smith negotiated a trade with the Dodgers that brought over Dave Mlicki, who soon became the Bengals' best hurler. Needing help, the team reached down to its AA Jacksonville club and brought up rookie Jeff Weaver to plug a hole in the starting rotation. Early in May, Moehler was ejected for allegedly using a small piece of sandpaper on his thumb to scuff up the ball. He drew a ten-day suspension. Sean Runyan, a mainstay in the bullpen the previous season, developed a sore arm, landing yet another pitcher on the disabled list. After pitching poorly, former number one pick Matt Anderson was relegated to Toledo. "He's fried mentally," said man-

ager Parrish. "When you're a stud horse and you have your ears pinned back for the first time, it's a blow to your ego."

Detroit played .357 winning percentage baseball in May and continued to struggle in all aspects of the game. As frustration mounted, Parrish held closed-door meetings and dressed his team down. On one occasion while accusing the hitters of a lack of work ethic, he said, "The way they are hitting, they should be out there taking batting practice until their hands bleed, not getting into the shower and out of here so fast." Later he appointed tri-captains, hoping to improve communications. By the All-Star Game break Detroit had accumulated a record of 34–49 and were 20 1/2 games behind the division-leading Cleveland Indians.

The Oneonta Tigers played their home games at Damasche Field, which had a facelift in 2007. The town and its ball team are located just 20 miles from Cooperstown, New York. This Class A ball club is a member of the short season New York–Penn League. (Oneonta Tigers)

The construction of Comerica Park progresses (August 21, 1999) a short distance away from the Tigers' former home at the corner of Michigan and Trumbull. (Mark Cunningham)

During the second half of the season the team continued to perform below expectations, setting up the manager for increasing criticism. When the Tigers lost to Baltimore on August 5 it represented still another low point in the season, its ninth consecutive defeat and 24 games below .500. Surprisingly, second line pitcher C. J. Nitkowski spoke extensively to the press about Parrish's shortcomings as the Tiger manager. Although Tony Clark and Damion Easley finally got on track, Bobby Higginson suffered through a miserable season of inept hitting and was hobbled by an injured toe. By late August Justin Thompson was gone from the rotation, needing surgery on his ailing arm. Among the position players only new acquisition Dean Palmer consistently performed at a high level.

The fortunes of chance smiled on this storied franchise as the curtain was drawn on venerable old Tiger Stadium on October 2, 1999. Just as all of the Tiger faithful wanted it to happen, Detroit rallied in the ninth when rookie Robert Fick hit a dramatic grand slam home run off the right-field roof to power his team to a 4–3 victory over Kansas City. Turnstiles clicked as fans hurried to capture one more memory of the old ballpark and season attendance reached 2,026,441, best since 1988. The final game festivities

To symbolize the transition, three players expected to be part of the new future pose at the construction site of Comerica Park. *Left to right:* Seth Greisinger, Juan Encarnacion, Matt Anderson. The prophecy was not fulfilled. (Mark Cunningham)

The finishing touches are still being applied in this early 2000 photograph of Comerica Park during the beginning of its inaugural season. (Mark Cunningham)

included a homecoming for 65 players whose careers represented special moments in the club's history. Over and over they were asked to reminisce about their first impressions of Tiger Stadium. Al Kaline's memory spoke for many when he said, "When I got to the ballpark, I walked right behind home plate and it was absolutely the most beautiful place I'd ever seen in my life. All the seats were dark green. The grass was as green as I had ever seen. Boy, that had a lasting impression on me when I first saw it." Management had been unable, however, to position its ball club as a legitimate competitor for the opening of Comerica Park the next season. Detroit fin-

ished third in the Central Division with a 69 and 92 record 27 1/2 games back of the Tribe. In winning 14 games, Dave Mlicki had become the ace of a weak pitching staff. Third baseman Dean Palmer paid major dividends on the Tigers' investment, hitting a team-leading 38 home runs, 100 runs batted in, and 92 runs scored.

Club president John McHale remained philosophical: "What happened with our team overshadowed some things, but not everything. What has happened as the stadium has closed has been a great, great experience. I think we can all sense this franchise's great tradition."

When Pudge Rodriguez signed with Detroit, his presence signaled that the franchise was serious about building a winner and that he wanted to be part of the rebirth. A future Hall of Famer, Rodriguez has made the American League All-Star team in each of his four seasons with the Tigers. He had a blockbuster year in 2004, his first with Detroit, finishing with a .334 batting average, 86 runs batted in, and 19 home runs. (Mike Litaker)

12
A New Beginning
2000–2007

Going into the new century, the Tigers had a set outfield of Higginson, Encarnacion, and Hunter, but by early May they had given up on their centerfielder, trading Hunter to Houston. That led to the recall of Gabe Kapler, the previous year's minor league player of the year according to *Baseball Weekly*. Centerfield was unfamiliar territory for the alleged phenom, though he did manage to hit 18 home runs along with a disappointing .245 batting average. Late in the season Randy Smith forecasted the need for a starting pitching and a big bat in the middle of the lineup while manager Parrish criticized the play of his outfield. Hindsight is easy, yet looking back on the Gonzalez for Garcia swap must be considered one of the worst trades in franchise history. Garcia remained an unfulfilled prospect and was soon shipped on to another team willing to buy forecasted potential. Gonzalez, on the other hand, hit .336 and 26 home runs, drove in 111 runs, and scored 112 with his new club. He went on to be one of the National League's premier hitters, including a season when he hit 57 home runs.

As expected, Detroit fired manager Larry Parrish and then in very short order hired Phil Garner, who had just been dismissed by the Milwaukee Braves after seven losing seasons. Commissioner Bud Selig was furious, claiming the club had failed to consider minority candidates and threatened to impose a $250,000 fine. Garner became the third new Tiger manager in three years.

Acquired from Minnesota in a trade, left-hander Mark Redmond had a short 32-game career with Detroit. In his only full season (2002) and on a bad ball club, he had an 8–15 record. (Mike Litaker)

After that excitement settled down, GM Smith evoked another level of attention with the acquisition of two-time MVP and slugging outfielder Juan Gonzalez. The Tigers sent what appeared to be a rich package of talent including Gabe Kapler, Justin Thompson, Francisco Cordero, Bill Haselman, Frank Catalanotto, and minor leaguer Alan Webb for Gonzalez, relief pitcher Danny Patterson, and back-up catcher Gregg Zaun. On paper it looked as though Smith had landed the big run producer he coveted, but Comerica's deep left-field power alley promised to reduce the impact of a hitter like Gonzalez and he had already spoken disparagingly about the dimensions of the park. And, Smith and company would need to sign Gonzalez to a new contract or lose him to free agency and the players they had swapped to Texas. Clearly Smith thought he had the star to light up the new ballpark for the 2000 season.

The new season represented a watershed moment in Tiger history, leaving behind the historic real estate of Bennett Park, Navin Field, and Tiger Stadium and its enshrined memories as the team moved a short distance to a new home field devoid of heritage or a storied past. Both owner Mike Ilitch and his top brass hoped to unveil Comerica Park with a strong team and take advantage of the excitement that would surely be generated by the new ballpark. They had geared up by acquiring a marquee player and a more experienced manager, but the pieces were not all in place to win consistently. With typical new season optimism, General Manager Smith said, "I think those two are worth a lot of wins for us. I think we are significantly better." There was reason to hope that reliefer Danny Patterson would strengthen the bullpen, as he had compiled a 4.26 ERA in 170 games with Texas, all in relief. Smith also signed an experienced free agent starting pitcher in Hideo Nomo. The former National League Rookie of the Year had won 61 games for the

Nate Cornejo was a Tiger farmhand promoted to the major league team short on pitching. Over four seasons hampered by arm trouble, Cornejo won 12 games, all as a starting pitcher. (Mike Litaker)

Los Angeles Dodgers, including a no-hitter in 1996.

Like his boss, Garner expressed confidence: "Cleveland's vulnerable this year. We're going to be better." The ball club continued to search for a dependable cadre of starting pitchers. C. J. Nitkowski, who had been impressive during his short stint as a starter at the end of season, was being mentioned as the fifth starter in the rotation. Surely he didn't help his cause when he again spoke critically to the press, this time being upset with the way his contract was settled through arbitration: "I'm so disappointed in my employer that winning a couple of hundred extra

grand [$300,000] hardly seems worth it." With much higher stakes, the club offered Gonzalez a seven-year contract worth $122 million but he didn't respond.

At last, the long-awaited day arrived and the Detroit Tigers inaugurated their new home at Comerica Park on April 11, defeating the Oakland Athletics, 5–2, behind Brian Moehler. Distinctively different in so many ways, the new park is spacious, designed to favor pitchers and line-drive hitters who spray the ball around. Its many features include a lower profile, allowing a panoramic view of the city's landscape, a giant scoreboard, a water feature in centerfield, wide concourses with museum exhibits and easy access to concession stands and restroom facilities, a Ferris wheel, a carousel, and a series of five stainless steel statues honoring Tiger greats Ty Cobb, Charlie Gehringer, Hank Greenberg, Al Kaline, and Hal Newhouser. Gone are the obstructed-view seats and the intimacy of the enclosed old stadium where these Tiger greats built a cherished heritage.

Juan Gonzalez brought credentials that portended the stature of a future Hall of Fame inductee: a .294 batting average over nine-plus seasons, 340 career home runs, five seasons in which he hit 40 or more round-trippers, and seven seasons when he drove in more than 100 runs. At his peak he had slugged 47 home runs in a season and in another year knocked in 157 runs. At 30 years of age, he had been on the disabled list six times in his major league career. High expectations and the urgent need to sign him to a multiple-year contract would absorb tons of attention throughout the season. Following an early meeting with his agent, General Manager Smith said, "I think he will finish his career in Detroit." Given that the Tigers had gambled heavily in its acquisition of Gonzalez, when Smith was asked if he was concerned about the risk

Juan Acevedo was a bright spot on a weak team when he saved 28 games for the 2002 Tigers in his only season with the club. (Mike Litaker)

After toiling in the minor leagues for years, Jason Johnson finally got established as a starting pitcher for the Baltimore Orioles, winning a career-best 10 victories. Detroit signed him as a free agent after the 2003 season and he pitched for the Tigers for the next two years winning 16 games and losing 28. (Mike Litaker)

of not signing him, he retorted, "I'll just go out and get another big hitter." When the staff of *Baseball Weekly* made their annual season preview of each team, they included a forecast of the "worst case" scenario. For Detroit they wrote, "Vast Comerica Park reduced the power output of Gonzalez & Co., Garner records his eighth consecutive losing season and Gonzalez bolts via free agency."

Following a pattern that was becoming all too familiar, the Tigers got off to a horrible start in 2000 and by May 10 had racked up a futile record of 9–23, or a winning percentage of .281, matching its worst start in team history. Perhaps with nerves frayed by an inability to win, Detroit fought the Chicago White Sox in a two-round brawl during a 14–6 loss on April 22 in the Windy City. The commissioner's office leveled heavy penalties on both teams and multiple Tigers drew suspensions: Garner 8 games, coach Juan Samuel 15 games, Palmer 8 games, Brocail 4 games, Higginson 4 games, Luis Polonia 3 games, and Karim Garcia 3 games. With the team not playing well despite a $58 million player payroll and with disappointing attendance, team president John McHale spoke candidly: "It's frustrating and disappointing." Frequent injuries and weak hitting forced Garner to juggle his lineup, often filling in with marginal players.

In May and June the team came alive, playing .500 ball during that stretch as both hitting and pitching improved, allowing the club to crawl out of the cellar and advance to the third rung. Concern over Gonzalez—his injuries, lack of hitting, contract extension, and unhappiness over the dimensions of Comerica Park—continued to plague the season. As projected, the spacious confines, 398 in left center and 420 in centerfield, kept many long drives in the ballpark and reduced home run production. Early on, Bobby Higginson referred to the place as "Co-

merica National Park." Speculation increased that the Tigers would try to trade their ailing slugger Gonzalez before the July 31 trading deadline.

By late August the team had pulled even with a 63–63 record and some began to speculate that the surging Tigers had a shot at being the playoff wild-card team. "It's been a long time coming. Practically the whole decade of the 1990s was a downer for Detroit," stated Ernie Harwell. "The fact that the Tigers have at least an outside chance at the wild card . . . has created a lot of interest." With an 18–10 record in August there was reason to be hopeful, and although the Bengals climbed to three games over .500 in early September the momentum could not be maintained as they finished the season with a 79–83 record, 16 games behind the division-winning Chicago White Sox.

Higginson had his career season, batting an even .300 and leading his team with the most hits, home runs, and runs scored, and tied for best in RBIs with Dean Palmer. He also led the majors with 19 assists. Cruz and Encarnacion also enjoyed their best seasons. The often injured Tony Clark played in only 60 games and the Tigers' big star, Juan Gonzalez, had his worst career season, playing in just 115 games, hitting 22 home runs, and driving in 67 runs. Brian Moehler compiled the best record among pitchers, 12–9, while Todd Jones emerged as a big-

Supposedly Pudge Rodriguez helped persuade Tiger management to sign his former teammate with the Florida Marlins. The pick-up proved a good one, for Ugueth Urbina notched 21 saves and averaged more than a strikeout per inning as the closer for the 2004 Tigers. Sadly, his career would end with a criminal conviction and a prison sentence. (Mike Litaker)

time closer with a team record-setting 42 saves.

The new ballpark also established an all-time record with its inaugural season attendance of 2,533,752. All of the anticipated effects of its expansive real estate were also realized—lower team earned run average, higher team batting average, and fewer home runs. Speculation increased as to whether the fences should be moved closer to home plate. The club hit 69 home runs at home and a record 108 on the road. Gonzalez had 8 at Comerica and 14 at other parks.

Gonzalez's experience with a Grand Canyon outfield and unappreciative fans made his decision easy; he wanted to exit Detroit and soon signed a one-year deal with Cleveland, leaving the high-stakes gambler Randy Smith holding the bag. In December he completed another multiple player transaction with Houston, sending Brad Ausmus, Doug Brocail, and Nelson Cruz over to the National League for outfielder Roger Cedeno, pitcher Chris Holt, and catcher Mitch Meluskey. The deal on paper seemed favorable to Detroit for Cedeno, a flier, had the potential to be an outstanding lead-off man, Holt represented a starting pitcher, though without any significant record of success, and Meluskey, a youngster, had shown the previous year that he could hit. Both of the position players were being counted on to be quality everyday players and pitcher Holt was slated to join the starting rotation.

Predicting the fortunes of a ball club before the season begins is great sport in baseball. Opinions are free and it's only when one has some authority that people remember what was said. Following its usual drill, *Baseball Weekly* issued its editorial opinion. Using a scenario approach, the writers suggested a best case: "The team was three games over .500 last Sept. 5. If Phil Garner can pull that off again, everybody should be ecstatic." They represented the other extreme as well: "People come to the ballpark to ride the Ferris wheel, not to see the club." An even more prophetic statement came from Garner at the end of spring training: "I felt like we were going to move in another direction this year."

The Tigers continued their consistent pattern of digging a hole in April and then struggling through much of the remaining season. They finally snapped a seven-game losing streak by beating Baltimore on April 26 and Garner quipped, "We're hot. We have a one-game streak now." His club finished the month with an 8–15 record.

When a team has notable weaknesses and plays in a tough division, injuries are especially cruel. Casualties occurred early when Meluskey's ailing right shoulder required surgery, knocking the expected starting catcher out for the season. That loss elevated minor leaguer Brandon Inge into a starting role with Garner announcing, "He's going to be our catcher unless he gets overwhelmed as a hitter." The team's best pitcher, Brian Moehler, went eight innings in the second game of the season but would not pitch another inning as a result of a prolonged sore arm.

Meanwhile, Juan Gonzalez was happy in Cleveland and hitting like he had with Texas before playing for Detroit the previous year. He returned to the Motor City for an early season series and he was not welcomed. And recently jettisoned Hideo Nomo pitched a no-hitter on April 4 for his new team, the Boston Red Sox. The Tiger faithful were not happy with him either.

May brought warmer weather and a rejuvenated team that started winning; by mid-month they pulled even with a 17–17 record and flirted with a .500 record for the rest of May. May and July were the two high points of the season as the team won one more game than it lost in each month. Overall, Detroit began sliding backward and the descent quickened in August and September.

Team president John McHale, who had been hired to oversee the development of a new ballpark, moved on in late May to take a position as chief operating officer of the Tampa Bay Devil Rays. Owner Mike Ilitch became the new president and he appointed a five-member committee to advise him.

A very marginal pitching staff struggled most of the season. Todd Jones started slowly and by June

Fleet-footed Roger Cedeno was acquired by the Tigers in an off-season trade with Houston. Detroit needed to shore up centerfield and Cedeno held lots of promise. His tenure in the Motor City became shortened, however, when he found himself locked in manager Phil Garner's doghouse despite hitting .293 and swiping 56 bases in 2001. (Mike Litaker)

had lost his closer role to Matt Anderson. The young flamethrower began strong, converting 15 relief opportunities into saves. In late July Smith traded Jones to Minnesota for starting pitcher Mark Redman. Redman had debuted in 2000 but had been on the DL since May with a sore arm. Dave Mlicki, the team's best pitcher in 1999, was traded to Houston in June and Detroit reacquired pitcher Jose Lima.

Various hurlers were summoned from the farm but none emerged with immediate success. The dismal experience of Heath Murray (1–7 with 6.54 ERA) illustrated the reality of very thin ranks.

This second season at Comerica Park was riven with strife as the emotions of frustration and futility cropped up with regularity. After an 11–3 loss in May marked by sloppy play, Garner ordered a pregame workout the next day for the first time in his 10-year managerial career: "We weren't ready to play. I'm embarrassed by that. It reflects on me. I take it personal." Higginson, the regular who had been on the team the longest, was particularly outspoken,

calling for the need to make some changes. Shane Halter, a career utility man who became a one-season regular on a mediocre team, also aired his frustration: "We're not competing. It's almost like we're not even trying." Garner at one point expressed his disgust, saying, "It's awful." At midseason, a headline on the sports page of the *Grand Rapids Press* asked, "Why do the Tigers stink?" The fact that another utility infielder played centerfield part of the season portrayed the talent level of this squad. During one week in August they scored just one run in each of five consecutive games.

But the rancor didn't stop. On August 10, the Royals decided that Weaver was throwing at one of their players and a brawl exploded, resulting in suspensions and fines. When Weaver complained about a lack of support from some of his teammates after he was knocked down by Mike Sweeney, Garner called a clubhouse meeting to restore some team cohesiveness.

Then on September 11 the nation was stunned like almost never before by the terrorists' attacks and a soon growing recognition that life would never be quite the same again. All professional baseball games were suspended for days. Play resumed on September 17. Like many other teams, Detroit held intrasquad games and workouts.

Garner, in a sour mood, criticized his squad for their lack of effort in past games. New outfielder Roger Cedeno was in the manager's doghouse, and Garner benched him for the last month of the season despite a team-leading .293 batting average and 55 stolen bases. Cedeno, who would be a free agent at the end of the season, said, "I wouldn't stay if they offered me $200 million. I don't want to be here another day. I can't wait to get out of here."

Given the suspension of games, the season ended later, on October 7. Although not having the

Eric Munson was a highly regarded prospect when Detroit drafted him in 1999. He began as a catcher and then switched to third base but never became very accomplished defensively. In two seasons with Detroit he flashed some power, hitting a season-high 19 homers in 2004. (Mike Litaker)

Knuckleballer Steve Sparks emerged as the ace of the staff in 2001 winning 14 games with a fine 3.65 ERA but he won only eight games over his final two seasons with Detroit. (Mike Litaker)

work. On the downside, Easley, Encarnacion, Palmer, and Cruz all experienced disappointing seasons.

The Tigers did not wait until the next year to begin righting a troubled ship. The big off-season trade with Houston didn't pan out. Roger Cedeno elected free agency, Mitch Meluskey would continue on the DL and only play in a total of eight games in his two seasons for the Tigers, and Chris Holt was released following the season. Tony Clark, once believed to be a fixture, was lost on waivers to Boston and Devi Cruz was released outright.

But the hiring of highly regarded baseball executive Dave Dombrowski in November represented the big change in the Tiger organization. In signing Dombrowski to a five-year contract as president and

worst record in its division, Detroit finished a miserable season with 66 wins against 96 losses and a distant 25 games behind the perennial powerhouse Cleveland Indians. Weak catching didn't help an inferior pitching corps; the team set a single season record for passed balls, eclipsing a record set in 1912. Even in a dismal season, however, there are always a few bright spots. Steve Sparks, a pitcher signed as a minor league free agent in 2000, had a breakout year, leading the staff with 14 victories and a fine ERA of 3.65. Utility infielder Shane Halter played regularly and enjoyed a career year, batting .284 in 136 games, and rookie Robert Fick demonstrated he could hit big league pitching, belting a team best 19 home runs. Jeff Weaver continued to show promise, winning 13 games and contributing 229 innings of

Randall Simon had his best season in 2002 with Detroit-hitting a team best .301. With other first base candidates, Detroit did not retain Simon. (Mike Litaker)

Jeff Weaver seemed to have all of the tools to become a quality pitcher when Detroit rushed him to the big leagues in 1999 after just six outings with three minor league teams. His top mark with Detroit came in 2001 when he recorded 13 wins to go along with 16 defeats. The following season they traded Weaver, their most sought-after player, for three prospects. (Mike Litaker)

Detroit? When Dombrowski assumed his new challenge, he inherited a floundering team with one of the lowest payrolls in baseball. "You can be competitive without a top payroll," claimed the new team president.

Changes were inevitable and needed and the new boss executed a number of them that would help in the transformation of the Detroit Tigers. Organizationally, the owner's committee was disbanded and there were changes made in the coaching staff. Dombrowski and Smith, who was retained as GM, swapped Juan Encarnacion to Cincinnati in exchange for Dmitri Young. They bolstered the bullpen in the short term, signing minor league free agent Juan Acevedo and free agent Craig Paquette, and claiming Craig Monroe off waivers from Texas. Paquette had enjoyed his best season in 2001 while playing for the St. Louis Cardinals and demonstrated an ability to play well in both the infield and outfield.

Although Dombrowski's presence gave reason for hope, it would take some magic from him to alter the course as the Tigers headed into the 2002 campaign. Moehler was out of commission following shoulder surgery, and Palmer had undergone his second surgery over the winter and his future remained questionable. The starting rotation included Jeff Weaver, Nate Cornejo, Mark Redman, Steve Sparks, and Jose Lima. Weaver and Sparks were the two mainstays, racking up a combined 27 victories in 2001 while the other three starters managed a grand total of 12 wins. Only Higginson could be considered a consistent quality performer among the position players; Jose Macias and Robert Fick would join him in completing the outfield. Utility infielder Macias would attempt to play centerfield and Garner, searching for a suitable position for Fick, would try him in right field.

Weaver, Anderson, and newly acquired Dmitri Young, considered the nucleus to build upon, were all signed to multiple-year contracts. Writers believed that with set-up man Patterson and Anderson as closer, Detroit had a potent bullpen combination.

chief executive officer, owner Mike Ilitch knew he had landed one of baseball's best administrative leaders. "I wanted to go out and find the best baseball person I could find to help turn this thing around, and I think I've found him," said Ilitch. Dombrowski had had a significant role in building a world champion team in Miami from a new franchise in just five years. Would the owner be willing to spend the money necessary to construct a winner in

But before heading north the list of walking
wounded grew: Meluskey remained tentative,
Palmer was not responding to his shoulder repair,
and pitchers Anderson, Patterson, Bill Simas, and
Adam Pettyjohn were all hurting. With the ranks
thinning, management picked up a backup infielder
and catcher, anticipating the need to plug holes. Although Dombrowski had more concerns than any
new top executive deserved, the cover of *Baseball
Weekly* featured a photograph of Matt Anderson,
Dmitri Young, and Jeff Weaver with the banner
"New Tune in Motown: Tigers' Clubhouse Ensem-
ble Tries to Create More Hits and Harmony" and included a story on the team's new direction. Garner
and a number of his players were interviewed and all
of them were smoking spring flowers and sunshine
optimism. "It's definitely exciting to be a player in
this organization and to be a fan of the Detroit
Tigers, because we're doing things the right way,"
assured Higginson. Although recognizing that the
team had suffered through years of defeat, Weaver,
too, saw a new and promising future: "I guess the
worst part [of being in Detroit] is how long we've
struggled and had a bad record. The fans haven't
been able to see a good product in a lot of years. I
really think that's changed and there could be a
quick turnaround with the core guys we have signed
up here for a few years." Managers and players are
supposed to say positive things to the media, but an
experienced executive is bound to be a little more
reserved in predicting the turnaround of a team in
shambles, knowing its failure to play competitive
baseball will ultimately land in his lap. "I do know
that what you try to do is to come in and make good,
sound decisions on a daily basis," said Dombrowski.
"When you've won 66 games the previous year and
you've lost (something like) 10 straight years, you're

not going to snap your fingers and have one thing
happen that makes all the difference. So you try to
change the approach, change the attitude."

The Bengals opened the season in Florida and
were swept in a three-game series by lowly Tampa
Bay. Always game, Tiger manager Phil Garner
stated, "Stick with us. We're going to give you a lot
to be cheering about." The bloodletting continued
as the team came back to Detroit for its home
opener and proceeded to lose three straight to the
Cleveland Indians. Dombrowski acted quickly and

At a time when Detroit only signed second- and third-tier free agents, they
acquired starting pitcher Hideo Nomo. He won only eight games in 2000 and
though the Tigers had an option for the following year, they did not exercise it.
After leaving Detroit he returned to form, winning 16 games in successive seasons with the Los Angeles Dodgers. (Mike Litaker)

Much had been expected of Juan Encarnacion, and when he failed to become an excellent player he was swapped to Cincinnati for Dmitri Young, a perennial .300 hitter. Young had his best season in his five-year stay with Detroit in 2003 when he made the All-Star team and hit .297 with a career-high 29 home runs. (Mike Litaker)

team staged a brief comeback following its pathetic 0–11 start to play slightly better than .500 ball over the next 33 games.

That encouraging surge masked reality as the Tigers then began a season-long tailspin that buried them in the cellar. They lost nine of ten games in one stretch during June and suffered losing streaks of six during June, July, and August, although they played respectably in July. Earlier in the season Jeff Weaver had expressed his take on the Tigers' woes: "There's no easy explanation for what's going wrong. One day it's our pitching, the next day it's our defense, then the next day it's our offense—and sometimes it's all of those things." Searching for a better combination, management moved players in and out. When they recalled rookie Ramon Santiago to replace their slumping shortstop, Shane Halter harshly criticized the decision: "I definitely want out. I wouldn't mind being a utility player on another team. I don't think I should be a utility player on the Tigers, with the personnel we have here."

Dave Dombrowski had accepted the challenge of turning this franchise around and that required making more changes in the major league team. Given their overall lack of talent and the presence of too many veterans with big contracts, it was difficult to attract much interest in most of what he undoubtedly shopped around. The uncertainty of an unsettled union contract with the players further complicated what Dombrowski tried to achieve. In early July he used his most salable property to effect a major trade involving both the New York Yankees and the Oakland Athletics. The three-cornered swap sent Jeff Weaver to Oakland, which forwarded him on to the Yankees, and Detroit acquired highly regarded rookie first baseman Carlos Pena, fireballing reliever and prospect Franklyn German, and a player

decisively—General Manager Randy Smith and field boss Phil Garner were fired as the wheels of change gained momentum. The team's president and CEO now took on the role of general manager and he promoted bench coach Luis Pujols to interim manager, a title soon adjusted by dropping the interim.

The losses piled up: 11 straight setbacks, the fifth worst start to begin a season in major league history. The 11th consecutive loss was particularly brutal when the Tigers led the Twins, 7–5, in the eighth only to be crushed by an eight-run Minnesota rally in that fatal inning. April ended like all others with a losing record of 8 wins and 17 losses. The

Hitting coach Alan Trammell helps Rob Fick work on a hitting technique. (Lloyd Wallace)

to be named later. That anonymous player turned out to be another prized rookie—Jeremy Bonderman. Tiger beat writer Tom Gage called the transaction a "daring move" by Dombrowski while Higginson and Fick spoke critically to the press. Most fans were equally upset. "I've made numerous deals like this throughout my career," related the Tiger CEO. "Any time you trade a known player for unknown players, it's not popular. . . . We need to get better, not just here, but within our system."

With ailing reliever Matt Anderson limited to 12 games and his sidekick Patterson only able to make six appearances, the bullpen underwent a makeover. Fortunately off-season acquisition Juan Acevedo emerged to lead the staff with 28 saves. In addition to Weaver's departure, the Tigers released starter Jose Lima and traded Brian Moehler.

In all, the team utilized 30 pitchers and 27 different position players. Things got worse in the last two months of the season as the team just couldn't score many runs. They compiled a 10–19 record in August while hitting .227 as a team and went 5–21 in September with a team batting average of .220. Their final stretch nearly mirrored the beginning of the season as the Tigers lost 10 of their last 11 contests to finish dead last with a record of 55 victories and 106 losses, the team's worst showing in its history and tied with Tampa Bay for the poorest performance in major league baseball.

Mark Redman, 8–15, and Steve Sparks, 8–16, led the team in victories. Pitching was bad but the offense performed at an even lower level, hitting just .248. The team scored just 575 runs, the lowest total in a non-strike season in 17 years. They were deficient in every key aspect of the game including the inability to catch the ball and ranking last in the American League. Reflecting on the situation he had assumed nearly a year previously, Dave Dombrowski admitted, "I didn't expect it to be this bad." The only rays of sunshine in the offense were the team's leading hitter, Randall Simon, who had a mark of .301, and the continuing development of Robert Fick.

As expected the Tigers fired Luis Pujols soon after the season ended. Among the several candidates under consideration, former star shortstop Alan Trammell emerged as the team's choice to begin a new day of winning baseball in Motown. Though recognizing his immense popularity, Dombrowski insisted that the hiring of Trammell was influenced by other, stronger considerations. Trammell came with minimal managerial experience, having served one season as a coach for San Diego. "I'm not worried about that," said Dombrowski, "because he's managed in his head in every game he's been part of. He's ready for this." Kaline claimed that Trammell had a quality that made others want to follow him. Former manager Sparky Anderson worried about Trammell in this role, believing he was too nice. "I've grown," stated Trammell. "It's just the right time for me to come back to this organization and get it turned around."

Fans reacted with great enthusiasm that only got stronger when he announced his coaching staff with the headliners being Lance Parrish and Kirk Gibson. Naturally Gibson being Gibson would be pursued for his comments: "I want to see Tram succeed and I want to see the Tigers succeed. But it's one heck of a challenge. We're talking about playing good, hard-nosed baseball. It's not like nobody else has tried, but it's a matter of getting these guys to buy into the program and seeing it through." All new managers want their handpicked staff of coaches and Trammell announced a stronger team-management approach than many field bosses would subscribe to: "As an inexperienced manager, I want guys around me I'm comfortable with. We're going to interact more than most staffs. Everybody will have more input than normal. Because of our relationship, we're going to be very open with each other."

The depth of the left-centerfield alley had been an issue debated since Comerica Park opened, and in December the Tigers announced that the fence would be moved in from 395 feet to 370 feet. The home run production at home in 2001 had been considerably less (58) than on the road (81). Yet in 2002 the numbers were practically the same (61 vs. 63). However, that may have been influenced by a lineup that didn't have much power. "Our goal is to create an exciting environment that gives the hitter an opportunity to hit the long ball," stated Dave Dombrowski. Although the left-centerfield confines would become a little friendlier to right-handed power hitters, Comerica would retain its original intent of favoring pitchers.

Coming off yet another losing season, Tiger management found themselves in a big hole—a farm system that wasn't producing, a big league club with major deficiencies, and some big contracts being paid to veterans who were not producing. For some hard-to-understand reasons, Dombrowski did not resign Juan Acevedo, traded Randall Simon, and released Robert Fick, leaving many fans scratching their heads. In Simon's case, he was strictly a first baseman, the team had too many first sackers, and Dmitri Young had groused about being shifted to a secondary position. Although the press reported that Fick had been released as a cost-cutting move, his free-spirited and sometimes quirky behavior were probably the real reasons the Tigers jettisoned him. One way to strengthen a team is to trade an established player for a package of potential contributors, and that is what the president did by shipping starting pitcher Mark Redmond and a minor league pitcher to the Florida Marlins. In return, Detroit acquired three pitchers, Gary Knotts, who had some big league experience, and two promising rookies, Nate Robertson and Rob Henkel. The Tigers also claimed left-handed pitching prospect Wilfred Ledezma in the Rule 5 Draft from Boston.

With an emphasis on youth, Trammell would become a teaching manager. He frequently spoke of the need for professionalism, playing the game the right way, and cutting down on errors. Dave Dombrowski sounded a very supporting refrain, saying, "Tram has a great love for the game and wants to see it played the way it should be played. We think that will translate well to our players." With his great trademark attitude, Trammell sought the counseling

Signed to a two-year contract, Fernando Vina is credited with giving the lowly Tigers creditability and prompting a chain of free agents to sign with the team. However, his role on the playing field was short and expensive; he played in only 29 games and experienced a career-ending injury. (Mike Litaker)

of his mentor Sparky Anderson, who spent time with him during spring training. "I want him to be a consultant to critique me, the coaching staff, and our players," said Trammell. "Whatever he wants to pass on to us, I'll use."

Seemingly everywhere Trammell looked there was a challenge. Pitching, particularly his starting rotation, represented a major concern. It was hoped that newly acquired relief pitcher Gary Knotts could be converted to a starting role. Steve Avery, who had not pitched for two years, represented another candidate along with untested rookies.

The always philosophical and loquacious Sparky Anderson remained concerned for his former star player: "I never wanted him to manage. . . . I never wanted to see him abused. He will be abused." Then with a father's understanding and pride, he

Detroit signed the much-traveled Rondell White as a free agent prior to the 2004 season. Although he was nearing the end of a fine career, White played for the Tigers for two years, making his best contribution in 2004 with a .270 batting average and driving 19 balls over the fence. (Mike Litaker)

said, "But after talking with him two times, he has to do it. It's there. That's him. You can talk to him, and you know he must do this. And the one thing I like about Tram is he's not afraid of failure. . . . I wish players could be that way, never be afraid to lose."

Detroit opened at home on March 31 playing Minnesota with a starting lineup featuring six very inexperienced and undistinguished position players, a former third baseman so infirmed he could only DH, an over-the-hill right fielder, a starting pitcher with a 6–10 record in his first year in the majors, and a career .296 hitter and unhappy left fielder. Fans would need a scorecard to know the names of this mainly unknown bunch of wannabees: Gene Kingsdale, cf; Omar Infante, ss; Dmitri Young, lf; Bobby Higginson, rf; Dean Palmer, dh; Carlos Pena, 1b; Eric Munson, 3b; Brandon Inge, c; Ramon Santiago, 2b; and Mike Maroth, p. They managed only four hits that day and an inept offense delivered just six runs in the team's first six games, all losing efforts.

Detroit lost its first nine games, got their first win at the expense of the White Sox on April 12, and then dropped the next eight in succession. By April 22 they were already mired in last place with a 1–17 record. The toothless Tigers finished the month with only three victories and a whopping total of 21 defeats. An almost total lack of run production accounted for most of the team's woes; the squad sported a .182 team batting average at this point in the season.

Surprisingly, their young corps of pitchers, Mike Maroth, Jeremy Bonderman, Adam Bernero, Nat Cornijo, and Gary Knotts, performed better than expected and were remarkably durable as the rotation stayed intact through June. The losses continued to pile up, 18 in May and 22 in June, with no reason to expect a turn in fortune. Soon the focus seemed to be a goal of avoiding setting the worst record in baseball history, and their number one competitor became the 1962 New York Mets, who lost 120 games. Although players were shuffled back and forth between Detroit and Toledo, the Mud Hens' roster was not well stocked either. In a minor transaction, the Bengals acquired centerfielder and speedster Alex Sanchez from Milwaukee. He provided a little spark, though something much bigger was needed. Trammell maintained his professionalism and good nature throughout it all. "This team is frustrated and it's a challenge for me and our staff to keep these guys above water—if we are above water now. . . . Our players are pressing. We've got to find a way as a staff to keep them going," said Trammell.

With so many team losses, two young starting pitchers, Maroth and Bonderman, were on course to absorb 20-loss seasons, an unwelcome confidence burden for the future. On August 30 Maroth lost his 19th game while the team matched the hapless 1962 Mets, the only previous team to lose 100 games before the first of September. Two weeks later, Detroit set a franchise mark by recording its 110th loss of

the season. Just when it appeared likely they would go into the record book with the worst season in baseball history, the sleeping Tigers came to life and won five of their last six games to finish a terrible season with 43 wins and 119 losses, one short of tying the New York Mets and a place in infamy.

There were no surprises in this season except that it was much worse than anyone expected. As a team, the Tigers hit .240 for the season while their opponents batted .286 against them. Opponents compiled a 3.29 ERA while Tiger pitchers recorded a generous 5.30 ERA versus the opposition. These biting statistics tell most of the story for this regrettable season. Maroth lost 21 games and Bonderman 19 contests. Franklyn German had the most saves with a puny five in a season with very few opportunities. Only Dmitri Young enjoyed a strong season,

Dave Dombrowski announces the signing of All-Star free agent Pudge Rodriguez, February 2, 2004. With this mutual decision, owner Mike Ilitch signaled his willingness to invest heavily in the acquisition of high-quality free agent players. "We needed to do something," said Ilitch. "We think Rodriguez can help us because we think he has a lot of baseball left in him. We really wanted him, and ultimately, he wanted to be here." (Mark Cunningham)

Claimed on waivers, Craig Monroe became the Tigers' regular left fielder in 2004. A free swinger with power, Monroe delivered some key clutch hits in his brief career. His 92 RBIs and 28 homers in 2006 represent career highs. (Mike Litaker)

year veteran, had a career ERA under 4.00, Vina had twice been awarded a Gold Glove and had hit .300 or better three times, Johnson had won 10 games for Baltimore the previous season, the well-traveled White had consistently hit for a high average and over .300 in several seasons, and in Rodriguez, the Tigers acquired a true star player. Rodriguez had been selected to the All-Star team 10 times and had won the Gold Glove Award in 10 seasons. While playing for Texas he batted .300 or better in eight consecutive seasons. The Tigers with their record of futility, including 17 consecutive losing seasons, were a tough sell to quality free agents regardless of the contract offer. They had been rebuffed by marquee players the likes of Miguel Tejada. "I think signing the first player is important," stated Dombrowski. "A lot of players are hesitant to be that first player." In December 2003, he signed first Vina and then White on the same day. Vina came with impressive credentials, carrying a .284 career batting average. His decision clearly influenced others and exhibited confidence in a better future for the Tigers. A pleased Rodriguez said, "We're going to see this organization, this Detroit Tigers team, in the playoffs very soon." Early in January, Dombrowski engineered a trade with Seattle giving up infielder Santiago and a minor league outfielder for shortstop Carlos Guillen, who would soon be a major factor in the team's future success.

Then just before that season kicked off, Detroit signed free agent Ugueth Urbina. This seasoned closer had recorded as many as 41 saves in a season and had notched a career total of 111. In all, the team had invested over $63 million in free agents and Dombrowski stated that all of their acquisition goals had been fulfilled. Ticket sales soared with the signing of Pudge Rodriguez, who in addition to his star credentials was expected to have a significant influence on the team's cadre of young hurlers.

Enthusiasm reigned supreme as the 2004 season started with a bang when pitcher Jason Johnson and the newly constituted Tigers won the opener in convincing style, 7–0, over the Toronto Blue Jays. Off

hitting .297 and leading his teammates in nine offensive categories. Youngsters Monroe and Pena showed some pop, hitting 23 and 18 home runs, respectively.

The 2003–4 off-season was a transformational time in the franchise's history as the owner and senior management made major moves for the future. Detroit signed several free agents: right-handed pitcher Al Levine, infielder Fernando Vina, starting pitcher Jason Johnson, and outfielder Rondell White, and then, amazingly, they landed perennial All-Star catcher Ivan Rodriguez. Levine, a reliever and eight-

After having his playing time limited to just 39 games due to injury in 2006, Gary Sheffield, a 38-year-old outfielder from the Yankees, was acquired by Detroit, hoping he would be the big bat and clutch hitter that was needed in the heart of the lineup. After a slow start in April, Sheffield came on like gangbusters, leading his team in home runs with 21 and runs scored at the All-Star break. Batting third in the Tigers' potent lineup, Sheffield has done even more than the team had expected. (Mike Litaker)

Like Pudge Rodriguez, Magglio Ordonez came to the club with some physical problems but the Tigers were willing to take the risk and offer a long-term contract. Like Rodriguez, Ordonez has proven to be a great investment, returning to his past level of high performance and beyond. In 2006 he hit .298 and drove in 104 runs. Voted onto the 2007 All-Star team, Ordonez was the leading hitter in all of major league baseball with a .370 average. (Mike Litaker)

and running, Detroit won five of its first six contests, giving them the best start in 19 years. Optimism flowed freely as players were eager to express their confidence in the future. "We're looking to go from worst to first," proclaimed an excited Craig Monroe. New shortstop Carlos Guillen chimed in, stating, "Some teams are not worried about us, but they better start worrying." Detroit finished the month of April winning 12 and losing 11, the first winning record in April in 11 years.

Lacking consistency, the team struggled in May,

winning just 11 games and finishing the month with a five-game losing streak before reeling off six straight victories. Near the end of the month the offense tied a team record set in 1928 with 27 hits, while belting the Royals, 17–7. A few days later on June 1, the Tigers hit five home runs in their home park, and for the first time, four cleared the fences. All teams have to play through injuries and the Bengals' list of incapacitated grew as Young, Vina, and Cornejo were all on the disabled list together.

Rodriguez caught fire early in the season and he kept getting hotter, hitting a torrid .500 during the

Not a typical lead-off man, Curtis Granderson does not take a lot of walks but has shown considerable power in his young career. In his first full season with the big club, Granderson hit 19 home runs and scored a team second best 90 runs. Though not a base stealer, he can get to third base in a hurry when he hits a ball in the gap. A fine centerfielder, management believes he is a star in the making. (Mike Litaker)

month of June as his batting average grew to .373 and members of the media began speculating on his chances of winning a batting title. In storybook fashion, these Bengals won three back-to-back games in dramatic style when Munson, Pena, and Young hit walk-off home runs to close out the month of June.

At the midpoint in the season, the team stood at 42 and 45, much better than the recent past but not what they had hoped to achieve. "We've come a long way," said Trammell. "But if there's one thing that describes our play this season, it's that we're consistently inconsistent." Although there were plenty of bright moments in the season, the Tigers couldn't quite get over the hump and become a winning team. Except for April and June, they had losing records in every month. Yet they had made progress and were competitive much of the time. "It's a completely different atmosphere in this place," said Minnesota manager Ron Gardenhire. "You used to come in here expecting to win, and now every game is a fight."

August and September represented the worst of the season, not the way a rebuilding team wants to finish. Pitching slumped as the hurlers allowed over five earned runs a game—the Tigers won 22 and lost 34 during this disappointing finish. Despite the letdown, the season taken as a whole represented real improvement with a gain of 29 wins. Reflecting on the psychological hole Detroit had climbed out of, Dmitri Young said, "The record really was an important [motivational] factor. Every time you turned on the TV, everywhere you went, that's all we heard. It was like Gilligan trying to get off the island. The whole crew kept screwing it up over and over."

Rodriguez and Guillen had banner years: the team's All-Star catcher hit a sizzling .334 to go with 19 home runs and 86 runs batted in, and the new Tiger shortstop had a career season, sporting a .318 batting average, driving in 97 runs, and scoring a like number. He also belted 20 balls over the fences. Monroe and Inge both had breakout seasons. Although youngsters Pena and Munson demonstrated some power, neither hit for a very respectable average and former mainstay Bobby Higginson continued to fade. Robertson, Bonderman, and Maroth led the way among the starters, winning a total of 34 victories among the threesome.

Although newly acquired Alex Sanchez could fly and hit an impressive .322, he collected only 14 extra-base hits and his fielding was a liability. Thus GM Dombrowski revealed that the club was looking for a centerfielder. The team's off-season acquisition activity was relatively quiet compared with that of the previous year but they did acquire another star caliber player by signing free agent Magglio Ordonez in February 2005. A career .307 hitter, Ordonez hit 38 home runs and drove in 135 runs for the White Sox in 2002. A four-time All-Star, he had driven in over 100 runs in four consecutive seasons. Yet in 2004 a serious knee injury limited him to just 52 games. As with the earlier signing of Rodriguez, he was considered a high-risk deal. At the time, *Detroit Free Press* columnist Drew Sharp wrote, "The Tigers' motto in free-agent sweepstakes is pretty clear: Bring us your tired, your poor, your shaky vertebrae, your weakened meniscus." Owner Mike Ilitch's aggressive leadership proved a critical factor. "After our disastrous season [2003], I made up my mind, we've got to build a championship team," said Ilitch. "I can't wait around. The city doesn't want to wait around, either. I've got to do everything in my power—I have to extend myself, and keep extending myself." That strong commitment had decisive influence on Ordonez's decision and Dombrowski signed the All-Star outfielder to a seven-year deal worth $105 million.

Aiming to shore up the pen, the Tigers acquired free agent closer Troy Percival, who had logged 324 career saves, and hard-throwing right-hander Kyle Farnsworth by trading three prospects to the Chicago Cubs. For good reason, many believed the Tigers were ready to compete in the Central Division. "In two years, they've come a long way," claimed Yankee manager Joe Torre. A cautious Alan Trammell agreed: "Without question, we have more

Enjoying a great season in 2007, Placido Polanco was voted to the All-Star team, his first selection. Considered an ultimate team player, Polanco performs at a high level both offensively and defensively yet most observers consistently speak of the critical intangibles he contributes. In his first full season with Detroit (2006), he hit a very respectable .295 and when he was out with an injury in August, the team greatly missed his quiet impact. (Mike Litaker)

talent, but it is not all about talent. We have to be more efficient in all areas and do the little things better, and if we do, we can contend in our division." Pudge Rodriguez also added his expression of confidence: "I see a much better team here, with more veterans who are ready to bring respect back to the Detroit Tigers." Despite the very positive signs, the team's holes were exposed as spring training

Most trades are designed to help both clubs involved in the player transaction. When Detroit acquired Carlos Guillen from Seattle, Tiger president Dave Dombrowski could have been arrested for larceny. This fine shortstop has had career seasons after arriving in the Motor City, sporting a four-year batting average of .312 and hitting with power. In 2004 he scored 97 runs and drove in an identical number. (Mike Litaker)

sore arm, limiting him to only 25 appearances for the season. The 2005 Tigers were a streaky ball club, winning and losing with consistency yet for the most part hanging around the .500 winning percentage mark. After Bonderman pitched a five-hitter in beating the Minnesota Twins 7–2 on June 20, a realistic Trammell said, "Sometimes when we play like this, we look pretty good. We just haven't been able to sustain it." Earlier in the month, GM Dombrowski made one of his best deals in acquiring second baseman Placido Polanco from the Phillies. Polanco brought a variety of assets to the team—he was a consistent .300 hitter, a slick fielder, and a clubhouse leader. Dissatisfied with his team's hitting, Trammell convinced the forthright Kirk Gibson to become the hitting coach.

Jeremy Bonderman emerged as the ace of the staff, racking up his 13th victory in late July as Detroit pulled even with 49 wins and 49 defeats while winning 12 of its last 18 games. "If he [Bonderman] stays healthy, he's going to be one of the best ever," predicted outfielder Rondell White. The team continued its tendency to win about as many as it lost through most of August but then it went into a deep funk, finishing the season with its worst performance, notching an 8–24 record in September and the closing days in October.

In a disappointing season, Detroit slid backward, finishing with 71 wins and 91 losses and way behind the division champions. Spotty hitting with too many big guns out of action due to a variety of injuries really slowed down the offense. Ordonez played in 82 games, Guillen in 87, and White in 97. Craig Monroe had a solid season, hitting 20 home runs and knocking in 89 runs. Youngsters Chris Shelton and Curtis Granderson flashed signs of promise,

drew to a close. Detroit released centerfielder Sanchez, unable to afford his sloppy fielding, and the concern over an unstable starting rotation reemerged.

They continued to reverse a longstanding trend of digging a hole in April by playing .500 ball at month's end with the offense hitting a highly respectable .284. Ordonez and Percival, from whom much was expected, went down earlier. Ordonez missed much of the first half of the season with a hernia and the Tigers' new closer suffered with a

and Polanco immediately began paying dividends. Among the starters, Bonderman and Maroth each won 14 games, career bests, but Johnson and Robertson provided a combined record of 15 victories and 29 losses.

As expected, Alan Trammell was fired immediately after the close of the season and Dombrowski brought back another former Tiger, Jim Leyland. First signed as a player in 1963, Leyland went on to manage in Detroit's minor league system before being hired as a coach by the White Sox. He had his big league managerial debut with the Pirates in 1986

Although Omar Infante has not achieved the success some predicted for him earlier, he became a valuable utility man and sometimes potent hitter. In November 2007, the Tigers swapped Infante for Cubs outfielder Jacque Jones. (Mike Litaker)

The Tigers acquired Chris Shelton as a Rule 5 Draftee and kept him on the big team, believing he could hit major league pitching. He performed well, hitting 18 home runs in a partial season in 2005, and then had a spectacular start in April 2006 and was named Tiger of the Month largely as a result of his 10 home runs. But then reality struck and Shelton dropped into a prolonged slump, earning him a trip back to Toledo where he had yet to recover his stroke. Following the 2007 season, Shelton was traded to Texas. (Mike Litaker)

and subsequently managed the Marlins and Rockies before resigning amid his 14th campaign. The *Sporting News* had recognized him as manager of the year on three occasions. As so often happens, Tiger brass sought to compensate for a perceived leadership weakness by replacing a junior manager with a veteran field boss.

In his never-ending pursuit of reinforcements, Dave Dombrowski sought to shore up the pitching staff and signed two older free agent hurlers in December, starter Kenny Rogers and closer Todd Jones. At 42, Rogers brought a record of 190 victories to Detroit and was coming off a suspension-marred sea-

returning to the Motor City.

The new season started in Kansas City and Detroit carried a squad made up primarily of players from the previous year along with their two major free agent signees. A couple of hard-throwing rookie pitchers also made the team—Justin Verlander and Joel Zumaya.

The Tigers expected to improve in 2006 but few if any expected the results to be so dramatic. They left the starting gate like a champion, winning

When Shelton stopped hitting, Detroit needed another bat playing first base. It acquired Sean Casey, who was known as a slick-fielding and consistent line-drive hitter, from Pittsburgh. He got into 58 games with Detroit in 2006 and though he hit way below his normal .300 average, he had his moments, particularly in the postseason, hitting .529 in the World Series. (Mike Litaker)

Jim Leyland tells that his brother kept touting a long ball hitter named Marcus Thames who played for the Toledo Mud Hens, urging him to bring him up to the big league club. Used primarily as a designated hitter and part-time outfielder, Thames demonstrated he could swing a thunder stick at a higher level, whacking 20 home runs in just 348 times at bat during the 2006 season. (Mike Litaker)

son in which he won 14 games for the Texas Rangers. Among his many pitching feats none stood out brighter than a perfect game hurled against California in 1994. Jones, the younger at 38, had been an effective closer for the Florida Marlins in 2005 with 40 saves among his career total of 226. He had pitched for the Tigers from 1997 to 2001 and chalked up a career-high 42 saves in the 2000 season. Since departing, he had pitched for six clubs before

Brandon Inge along with Curtis Granderson are the two everyday players produced by the farm system. Inge began his big league career as a catcher, showing strong defensive skills but a weak bat. After he was switched to third base in 2004, his career began to flourish. Inge is considered an outstanding fielder with a rifle arm. "Those of us on this team who get to watch him every day know how much he means defensively," said Sean Casey. "We see how invaluable he is." He is an unusually productive number nine hitter. (Mike Litaker)

their first five contests. Strong hitting combined with effective pitching produced a 16–9 start in a magical season. Detroit bombarded Texas in the third game of the season by hitting seven home runs, and during most of April youngster Chris Shelton hit the long ball with unexpected frequency. Manager Jim Leyland immediately established a rapport with his new team. All-Star catcher Rodriguez was one of the first to speak openly about the new skipper: "He's good. Everybody respects him. We are going to play hard for him." Following their initial five-game winning streak, the team lost seven of their next nine games, and then after the Tigers were hammered 10–2 by the Indians, Leyland blew up. Though not a speech maker, the manager held a closed-door meeting and unleashed his anger: "We stunk. The whole ball of wax was lackluster. It's been going on here before." Throughout the season, Leyland remained dedicated to earning the respect of the fans and always recognizing how important it was to present a good product to their deserving supporters. A record crowd of 44,179 attended the home opener on April 10.

They opened the month of May with an impressive sweep of Minnesota, winning games by the scores of 9–0, 18–1, and 6–0. On May 14, the Bengals swept the Indians, the first time in Cleveland since 1990, to run its record to 24–13, second best in baseball. "The difference is obviously their pitching," said Tribe manager Eric Wedge. "That's been the separator." The facts bore out the accuracy of his statement. Both the team ERA of 3.25 and the rotation's ERA of 3.26 were the best in all of baseball. The bullpen had achieved an ERA of 3.23—the best in the American League and second best in the majors. With an eight-game winning streak Detroit raced out to a division-leading record of 34–14 and finished the month with 35 games in the win column.

After a slow start in June, the Tigers got red-hot, winning 17 of 19 games to close out the month. On the 16th they won their 43rd game, matching Detroit's season total for 2003 and demonstrating how far they had advanced. Three days later Kenny Rogers won his 200th career game and the Tigers celebrated by hitting eight home runs. This victory marked his 10th of the season and Leyland said of him, "You can't say enough for what he has done for us." After Detroit shut out Houston, nullifying a fine pitching performance by Roger Clemens, Astros manager Phil Garner said, "He couldn't have

Jeremy Bonderman was the player to be named later in the big trade that sent Jeff Weaver to Oakland and spawned sharp criticism from many of the Tiger faithful. Now in his sixth season with Detroit, Bonderman is considered one of the best young hurlers in the American League. He won 14 games in two previous seasons and with 10 wins by mid-July 2007, he was poised to have his biggest year to date, but his effectiveness dropped off sharply as a result of a sore arm. Bonderman throws in the mid-nineties and his slider is often described as nasty by opposing hitters. (Mike Litaker)

pitched any better playing against the hottest team on the planet."

Rodriguez, Ordonez, and Rogers made the American League All-Star team with the Tigers' 10-game winner getting the start. The team cooled off a bit in July, winning 15 of 25 while the pitching staff suffered its only slump of the season. After Detroit absorbed a 7–3 loss on the last day of July, Leyland was disgusted. "Write this down," he told the press. "There was a manager, six coaches, and 25 people in Tiger uniform tonight. Thirty-two total. And we all stunk. And that's all I got for you." The following day Dave Dombrowski announced the acquisition of first baseman Sean Casey in a trade with Pittsburgh. On August 2, Guillen hit for the cycle, Verlander became baseball's first 14-game winner, and Detroit won its 71st game, matching its victory total for the previous year. Five days later Detroit reached its regular season high-water mark, stretching its record to 76–36, 40 games over .500 with a division lead of 10 games. Yet their fortunes took a sudden turn beginning with the next game and continued for the rest of the month as the club won only seven of its next 22 games. Following a 10–0 shellacking by the Chicago White Sox, the ever-candid Leyland stated, "They look like they were having fun, and we looked tired. When you have a real ugly game, it's usually a combination of bad pitching, hitting, managing, and defense—we had all of that." During the month, the Tigers lost Placido Polanco after he injured his shoulder making a spectacular play and they soon learned how much he meant to the team.

As remarkable as 2006 would become, Detroit continued to slide during the last two months of the season, playing below .500 in August and September. Yet as their division lead dwindled, they mounted a three-game sweep of the Royals and by winning their 94th game clinched the American League wild-card spot in postseason play. A thrilled Mike Ilitch said, "This is one of the greatest moments in my life." With the division championship theirs to win, Detroit floundered badly, closing the season with five consecutive losses, the last three to

◀ Selected by the Tigers as the second overall pick in the 2005 draft, the highly rated Justin Verlander moved quickly onto the big league stage. After only 20 games in the minors, Verlander earned a place in the starting rotation, winning 17 games and Rookie of the Year honors. Frequently hitting 100 miles per hour on the radar gun, Verlander has the tools of an ace veteran hurler armed with a sharp breaking curve ball and an excellent off-speed pitch. Selected for the 2007 All-Star team, he pitched a no-hitter on June 12 and registered his 10th victory in early July. (Mike Litaker)

Left-hander Nate Robertson came into his own in 2004 when he led the staff with 12 victories. He posted a career-best 13 wins in 2006. (Mike Litaker)

the hapless Kansas City Royals, a team they had mauled throughout the year. Detroit had occupied the catbird seat in the division starting on May 16 and surrendered its reign to the Minnesota Twins on the last day of the season.

Its loss meant the Bengals would enter the American League postseason competition as an underdog and have to face the mighty New York Yankees. The first game of the opening round began in the Bronx and the Yankees played like Yankees, easily handling the Tigers by a score of 8–4. The Tigers evened the series with a 4–3 win in game two, scoring the winning run on a Granderson triple. Kenny Rogers pitched a jewel in the next game, shutting out New York as Detroit won 6–0, putting them one game away from eliminating the Yankees. In the next game played in Detroit, Bonderman opened with five perfect innings while pitching his mates to a stunning 8–3 victory and winning the American League Division Series. This huge feat evoked lots of printed words. *Detroit Free Press* columnist Mitch Albom asked rhetorically, "Who are these guys in the Detroit uniforms?" The Yankee lineup was considered awesome. Albom reported that Leyland lay awake thinking about the challenge of facing all of their big bats. But the fearsome Tigers prevailed and on that happy night members of the team circled the stands spraying exuberant fans with champagne.

Next it was on to Oakland to determine the American League pennant winner. The now favored Tigers took the opener 5–1 behind the strong pitching of Nate Robertson and the long ball hitting of Pudge Rodriguez and Brandon Inge. In game two

Kenny Rogers rejuvenated his new team and his career with a sparkling 17-win season in 2006. Rogers was sick when he notched his seventh victory. "I give him a lot of credit for going out there and giving us that performance," said Leyland. "It says a lot about Kenny Rogers, and that's why we signed him." Having never won a postseason game in his 18-year career, Rogers pitched brilliantly, winning all three of his starts in October and allowing no earned runs in 23 innings. (Mike Litaker)

Verlander allowed four runs but his teammates scored eight to post an 8–4 victory. In a rare moment of glory, the usually light-hitting Alex Gomez filled in as the designated hitter and drove in four runs with a home run and a single. The American League Championship Series then moved to Detroit, where on October 13 Rogers pitched another masterpiece, shutting down the Oakland attack and limiting them to just two hits as the Tigers won their third straight, 3–0. On the following night, Magglio Ordonez supplied the heroics. With two out and two on in the ninth and the score tied 3–3, he launched a tremendous home run into the left-field seats. Comerica Park erupted with joy. "You can't hear anything; everyone [is] yelling at [the] top of their voices," related Inge. Members of the Tigers' bullpen were the quieter heroes of this American League pennant, posting a collective ERA of 0.84 for this ALCS. Placido Polanco received the series' Most Valuable Player award on the strength of a .529 batting average. Coach Andy Van Slyke said of him, "To me, baseball's not about the big things. It's the little things that add up. Moving a guy over. Getting a base hit with two outs and man on first. He's the consummate professional. I never saw him give away an at bat this whole year."

Because the Tigers dispatched Oakland so quickly and the St. Louis Cardinals and New York Mets series went the full seven games, Detroit would have a long seven-day break before beginning World Series play. Although Jim Leyland insisted his team would not lose its edge, opinion in hindsight may differ. It certainly gave his team a needed rest and the opportunity for both Zumaya's and Casey's injuries to heal. Detroit was heavily favored and the Tigers played host to the Cardinals in the opener.

The pitching matchup of 17-game winner Verlander opposing Anthony Reyes with a 5–7 record seemed to clearly give Detroit the edge. But the Tiger ace faltered and his adversary pitched like an All-Star, holding the Bengals to just four safeties and notching an easy 7–2 win. Detroit rebounded in game two with old reliable Kenny Rogers again in command as his team managed a 3–1 victory. Rogers was the center of controversy over an undetermined substance on his pitching hand. According to Rogers, "It was a big clump of dirt and I whipped it off." According to Cards' manager Tony LaRussa, "It didn't look like dirt." Game three was played in St. Louis and starter

Chris Carpenter handcuffed Tigers' batsmen with a three hitter in a 5–0 win. Through the first three games, the first three hitters in the Tigers' lineup were hitless with a combined 0 for 34. Detroit got off to an early 3–1 lead in game four but the Cardinals pecked away, tying the game in the eighth and then pushing over the winning tally in the ninth for a 5–4 victory. Detroit was now just one game away from elimination. In the deciding contest, former Tiger Jeff Weaver overmatched the Bengals as the bats were quieted again and Detroit bowed to the world champion St. Louis Cardinals, 4–2. Two factors contributed most to the Tigers' disappointing defeat: terrible defense by the pitching staff, who committed five costly errors, one in each game, and terrible hitting, combining for a batting average of .199. Clearly the Tigers were flat, causing one to speculate that the long layoff contributed to their poor showing. Pudge Rodriguez summed up the difference succinctly: "We lost because St. Louis played better."

In perspective, 2006 was a magical season. Detroit played in the postseason for the first time in 19 years. The club won 95 games and drew 2,595,937 spectators. It held first place in its division for 138 consecutive days, ultimately winning the American League pennant. The team won seven straight postseason games. They had the best pitching staff in baseball with a 3.84 ERA while their opponents had a combined ERA of 4.73. Detroit hit a combined .274 and scored 822 runs; their opponents hit .257 and scored 675 runs.

The bullpen turned in a superb 3.51 ERA with Joel Zumaya registering a stingy 1.94 earned run average and Todd Jones garnering 37 saves. Kenny Rogers and Justin Verlander each won 17 games, Jeremy Bonderman recorded 14 victories, and Nate Robertson won a career high 13. Carlos Guillen had the highest individual batting average at .320 and he

scored a team-leading 100 runs. Magglio Ordonez hit .298 with 24 home runs and a team-leading 104 RBIs, Pudge Rodriguez had a .300 batting average, and Placido Polanco hit .295. Craig Monroe led with 28 home runs and was also a big RBI man with 92. The bottom two hitters in the lineup had amazing punch: the combination of Marcus Thames and Brandon Inge whacked 53 home runs. Jim Leyland was named American League Manager of the Year and Justin Verlander earned recognition as American League Rookie of the Year.

Mike Maroth got to the big leagues full-time in 2004 and suffered through a 21-loss season. He rebounded with 11 victories and a much-improved ERA the following season and achieved even greater respectability, winning 14 games in 2005. (Mike Litaker)

After an extended minor league career interspersed with two stints pitching for Kansas City, Jamie Walker became a fixture among the Bengals' relief corps in 2002. Frequently used against left-handed hitters, this southpaw had an excellent walk-to-strikeout ratio. (Mike Litaker)

After four impressive years in the minors, Joel Zumaya made the team, heading north from Lakeland in 2006 and bursting on the big league scene with brilliance. Converted from a starting role, Zumaya became the consummate set-up man in the Tiger bullpen. Throwing a blazing fastball, he won six games with a 1.94 ERA and struck out 97 in 83 innings. (Mike Litaker)

Coming off a remarkable season that had laid the foundation for a winning tradition at Comerica Park, the Tiger organization and its loyal supporters were primed for another pennant run in 2007. Hopes were high and management made a major investment in arming the team for victory in the new year. Following the World Series, the Tigers acquired a premier hitter in Gary Sheffield, trading three minor league pitchers to the New York Yankees. Although 38 and coming off an injury-plagued season, Sheffield was a legitimate candidate for Baseball's Hall of Fame. The nine-time All-Star had a lifetime batting average of .297 and 455 career home runs. The Tiger management believed another clutch hit-

ter was needed in the heart of the lineup and was excited about acquiring a star performer. "I was a pretty happy camper when I got my pad out and wrote that name into the lineup," stated Tiger skipper Jim Leyland. Sheffield was also pleased—glad to rejoin two baseball leaders he respected. "I'm more than happy to rejoin to be [re]united with guys I'm familiar with," reported Sheffield. "I remember going to the Florida Marlins in 1993 and Dave Dombrowski saying, 'Just be patient. We're going to get the players to win.'"

As the calendar turned over everything seemed to be in place though Detroit elected not to re-sign left-hander Jamie Walker, an important cog in what had been a highly effective bullpen during the prior season. Though not a port-sider, Dombrowski signed veteran reliever Jose Mesa to help shore up the hole left by Walker's departure to the Baltimore Orioles. Yet the much bigger blow came early in the spring when the team announced that ace hurler Kenny Rogers had been diagnosed with a blood clot in his left shoulder that required surgery and an absence

Fernando Rodney came up through the Tiger farm system where he had pitched in 162 games, compiling a sterling 2.52 earned run average. He had a breakout year in 2006 as a member of an outstanding Detroit bullpen crew. As a short man he averaged nearly a strikeout per inning and has an exceptional changeup. (Mike Litaker)

from the mound until at least July 1. With great faith in a bevy of promising young pitchers, the team tightened its belt and made ready to compete for the flag.

With a nearly set roster, spring training focused on getting ready for the games that count with a small amount of adjustment. Curtis Granderson set a personal goal to cut down on his number of strike-outs while Marcus Thames was learning how to play first as an added dimension and to give him more at bats with Sheffield being a lock as the designated hitter. After a horrendous display of poor fielding by pitchers in the World Series, the hurlers received some extra attention on their defensive skills. Todd Jones, who is known for his sense of humor, said, "If you're going to make five errors in the World Series, you've got to be able to accept the knock-knock jokes. 'How many Detroit Tiger pitchers does it take to screw up a World Series? 11.'"

In its "Baseball Season Preview," *USA Today* concluded, "The Central [Division] is loaded, but the Tigers are primed to repeat as AL champions." An in-house poll of *Detroit Free Press* sports writers produced the same prediction: although all five writers believed the Bengals would win their division, only one believed the team would win the World Series. "It's a good time to be a Tiger," claimed skipper Jim Leyland. "We're a team that's talked about. We've got some respect, obviously. I like the fact that people are expecting us to do something. . . . I don't know how we're going to do, but this is good pressure." Jacked-up Tiger fans were also anticipating a great season, purchasing 1,800,000 tickets before the season began, nearly a million more than at the same time in 2006.

A record opening day crowd of 44,297 whooped it up as their Tigers rallied from a three-run deficit to send the contest into extra innings only to lose to the Blue Jays, 5–3, in the tenth inning. Players and fans alike got to bask in their newborn pride as Brandon Inge and longtime franchise employee Audrey Zielinski unfurled their 2006 AL pennant flag. The celebration of the glorious 2006 season continued on

When Mike Maroth went down with a serious arm injury early in the 2006 season, Detroit needed another starter. They promoted Zach Monroe from their AAA farm team and he immediately started winning, racking up seven big wins. (Mike Litaker)

the second playing day of the season with players receiving their championship rings and the ball club managing a 10–9 victory amid swirling winds and temperatures only slightly above 40 degrees.

The Tigers weren't hitting and the team got off to a sluggish start. After absorbing an error-filled 7–5 loss to the White Sox, Leyland was exercised: "There was some stuff that went on today that was embarrassing. . . . If all of us aren't embarrassed, we should be. I'm talking about myself, the coaches, and everybody else." Detroit finished the month with a record of 14–11, slipping to second place behind Cleveland on the last day as the first four teams were closely bunched. Several concerns were developing, including a bullpen crew with a losing record and an earned run average over 5.00.

There were some tense moments in Detroit's 8–4 victory over the Orioles on April 30. Assuming that Baltimore pitcher Daniel Cabrera was throwing at him, Sheffield became angry and a non-physical confrontation ensued in which Leyland also entered the emotional fray. Oriole manager Sam Perlozzo credited the dispute to his pitcher's wildness and said, "I have the utmost respect for Gary, and if I was going to pick someone to get angry [with], it wouldn't be him." That Sheffield will not give ground was a well-known fact throughout major league baseball. "He's fearless," claimed Boston manager Terry Francona. "If you throw a ball at his neck, on the next pitch he's not going anywhere. He's going to swing that ferocious swing and put the bat on the ball." After hitting .119 through the first 17 games of the season, Sheffield got untracked and heated up. Seemingly the bench-clearing incident in the Baltimore game ignited an even higher level of determination. Oriole pitcher Steve Trachsel was sorry they had unleashed the Tiger: "You're sup-

posed to let sleeping dogs lie, and we didn't do that."

With Sheffield on a terror, the Tigers put together their longest winning streak of the season, stretching it out to eight games with a win over Seattle on May 8. But in the midst of building momentum, the Bengals were dealt another severe blow when Joel Zumaya suffered a ruptured tendon in the middle finger of his pitching hand, requiring surgery and the prospect of a 12-week stay on the disabled list. Despite the growing casualty list, the Tigers continued to rack up victories in the month of May. But by the end of the month fortunes had turned when the Indians inflicted four losses and Detroit dropped six of seven to close out May. Following a 12–11 fifth straight loss to Cleveland, Sheffield was

Jason Grilli had a watershed season pitching for Toledo in 2005. In his eighth minor league year he pitched well as a starter, earning a late-season call up to Detroit. Grilli became a valuable member of the bullpen, pitching in 51 games, most often in middle relief. (Mike Litaker)

suspended for three games after he allegedly threw a piece of a broken bat in the direction of the home plate umpire.

With a third of the season over and the team perched in second place just a hot series behind the Indians, their "pulse" was being taken. The hitters had established their presence but pitching continued to be disappointing. "Once we get our pitching straightened out, we'll be fine. . . . So far this year it's been our weak suit," said Leyland. Brandon Inge, always ready to accommodate an interview, chimed in, saying, "Everything went perfectly last year and it's not this year." The Tigers cut free agent reliever Jose Mesa after he piled up a 12.34 ERA.

Tiger bats continued to boom with multiple high-scoring wins including 8–7 and 15–7 victories over the Mets that left Leyland concerned about scores similar to those of slow-pitch softball games. The Bengals number four hitter, Magglio Ordonez, led the majors, hitting .367 with a very strong supporting cast surrounding him. "Quietly, he's the best player in baseball this season," claimed first sacker Sean Casey.

On a magical night, June 12, another forever memory was made at Comerica Park as Justin Verlander hurled a no-hitter against the Milwaukee Brewers. With all of his pitches working, Verlander struck out a career-high 12 batters en route to his masterpiece. Perhaps none was more impressed than the Brewers' hitters and several shared their feelings. "He's got electric stuff. It won't be his only no-hitter," stated Bill Hall. "There's nobody in the National League like him, not with the control and power he has." Verlander's gem was the first at the home park since Virgil Trucks threw a no-hitter in 1952.

◄ Jim Leyland brought 25 years of managerial experience, 14 at the big league level, when he signed on with the Detroit Tigers on October 4, 2005. A former Tiger farmhand, he was thrilled to be back with the team. Leyland came with rich credentials, having taken the Pittsburgh Pirates into postseason play several times, and won the World Series as manager of the Florida Marlins in 1997. He had also been named manager of the year twice by the Baseball Writers Association. A man with a dry sense of humor, he deliberately minimizes his personality in favor of the players. (Mike Litaker)

With the Tigers continuing to pound the ball, their offensive production drew raves from many of the victims. After sweeping the Washington Nationals including a 15–1 beating, Nationals' manager Manny Acta said, "That's the best hitting team in

the world." Pitching changes continued to be made with highly regarded prospect Andrew Miller inserted into the starting rotation, and Wil Ledezma and Mike Maroth were traded. Hopes were raised by the return of Kenny Rogers, who won his first start in convincing fashion. The Tigers stepped out in front of the Indians momentarily as the month wound down. June proved to be the best month of play in the 2007 season: Detroit compiled a .615 winning percentage with 16 wins and 10 losses, leaving them one game behind the league-leading Cleveland Indians.

At the All-Star break and after sweeping the Red Sox, Detroit regained the division lead, posting a record of 52–34, good for a one-game margin over the tough Cleveland Indians. Leyland knew that the Indians were not going away. "They play like we do. They pitch. They whack it. And they're very good at it. I just think we're two similar teams that are going to slug it out with each other. Whoever pitches best is going to win." The Tigers had the highest-scoring offense in baseball and with Rogers back, the starting rotation seemed to be solidifying. The 2007 All-Star Game played in San Francisco featured five Tiger players—Carlos Guillen, Magglio Ordonez, Placido Polanco, Pudge Rodriguez, and Justin Verlander—and the American League All-Stars were managed by Jim Leyland. Although the AL won by a score of 5–4, it was not a particularly productive night for the Tigers' contingent as its position players went one for seven with Rodriguez getting the only base rap. Verlander didn't shine either, allowing a run on two hits in his one inning of work.

On July 23, the Tigers reached their season's high-water mark when, after defeating the White Sox, their record stood at 59–38, 21 games over .500, earning them a two-game lead over the Tribe. But just when the season looked the brightest, fate

Needing a closer, the Tigers reacquired Todd Jones in December 2005. He recorded 37 saves in his first year back with the team, ranking fourth in the American League, and during the season became the all-time save leader in Detroit history. (Mike Litaker)

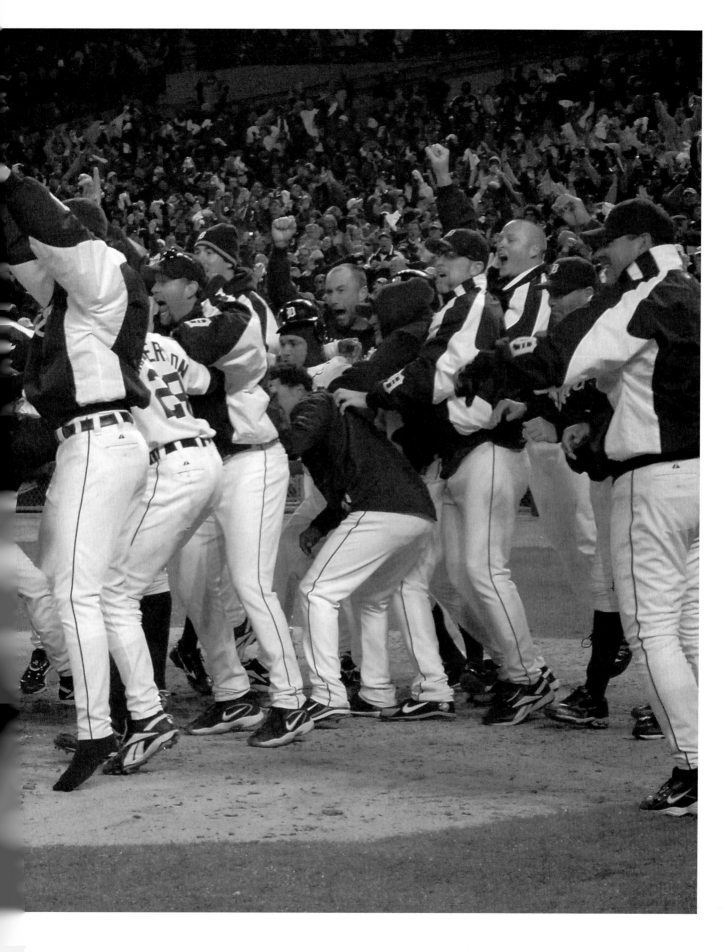

◀ Magglio Ordonez stamped his own mark on Tiger memory with a climatic home run to win game four of the American League Championship Series, giving Detroit its first pennant since 1984. His teammates explode with joy awaiting his arrival at home plate. (Mark Cunningham)

The transformation of the Detroit Baseball Club began when owner Mike Ilitch hired Dave Dombrowski as the team's new president and CEO in November 2001. Most recently, Dombrowski had served as president of the Florida Marlins and was credited with building an expansion team into a world champion in very short order. Although there must be some luck involved, Dombrowski has made a string of remarkable decisions in player acquisitions: trading to acquire Jeremy Bonderman, Carlos Guillen, Placido Polanco, Nate Robertson, Gary Sheffield, Edgar Renteria, Jacque Jones, Miguel Cabrera, and Dontrelle Willis; signing free agents Todd Jones, Magglio Ordonez, Kenny Rogers, and Ivan Rodriguez; drafting Curtis Granderson, Andrew Miller, Marcus Thames, Justin Verlander, and Joel Zumaya; and claiming Craig Monroe off waivers. He also signed manager Jim Leyland. (Detroit Tigers)

turned and a disastrous slide began with seven losses in nine games at the end of July.

And August only got worse. With the starting pitchers winning only once in the previous 22 contests, the Tampa Bay Devil Rays bedeviled Jeremy Bonderman and the Tigers, 8–1, on August 10. A concerned Jim Leyland said, "The little extra spark we had last year is not here. We better find it. . . . We're playing like it doesn't mean enough to us." Though the team was reeling, there were bright moments for some of the players. On the 12th, Ordonez made Tiger history by belting two home runs in the second inning of a victory over Oakland to match Al Kaline's feat in 1955. The next night second baseman Placido Polanco established a new major league record by playing 144 consecutive errorless games.

Fortunately the Indians were also in a funk, allowing the Tigers to stay close at hand in the division race. During the third week of August, Joel Zumaya came off the disabled list and Tiger management traded Craig Monroe, convinced the team needed more production from its left fielder. The awful month of August finally ended with Detroit winning only 11 games out of 29 played and opening up a four-and-a-half-game gap between the second place Tigers and the front-running Indians. Leyland's statement after his squad had been whitewashed by the Royals sounded like a benediction unless the Tigers staged a remarkable run in September: "This is a big man's game. These guys know what they need to do. Nobody's on, we get a hit. We get somebody on and we can't get a hit. Two days ago we scored 16 runs. It's a tough game to explain."

Although Detroit was not eliminated from postseason play until the last week in September, they were overmatched by a Cleveland club that was on fire (the Indians finished the season 31–13) and couldn't overcome the Bronx Bombers, who refused to bend in the wild-card race. Detroit won a very respectable 16 games in September, matching its best victory total for any month, but it wasn't enough. Yet

Dave Dombrowski (*left*) and Jim Leyland converse in the dugout before a 2006 postseason game. (Mark Cunningham)

it was a season of high achievement capped off with a thumping of the Chicago White Sox in the final game and a grand statement of pride as so many Tigers rung up personal records. Magglio Ordonez won his first batting title with an average of .363; Placido Polanco reached the 200 season hit plateau along with a third best league batting average of .341 and played the entire year without making an error; Curtis Granderson finished with a flourish to hike his batting average to the coveted mark of a .300 hitter; Carlos Guillen with a great day at the plate set career records with 21 home runs and 102 RBIs; and back-up catcher Mike Rabello struck his first big league home run.

But it was much more than the last game feats; a host of Tigers enjoyed a stellar season and aging veterans pushed their career records into elite company. Of Ordonez's incredible year Leyland said, "It's probably the best single-season performance a player I've managed has ever had." Ordonez ranked among the league leaders in nine categories, including first in batting average and doubles, and second in total bases, runs batted in, on-base percentage, and hits. Rising star Curtis Granderson had a breakout season in only his second campaign at the major league level. In early September he became the third player in major league history to have 20 doubles, 20 triples, 20 home runs, and 20 stolen bases in the

The loquacious Sparky Anderson is offering some free advice to Tiger skipper Jim Leyland during the 2006 World Series. (Mark Cunningham)

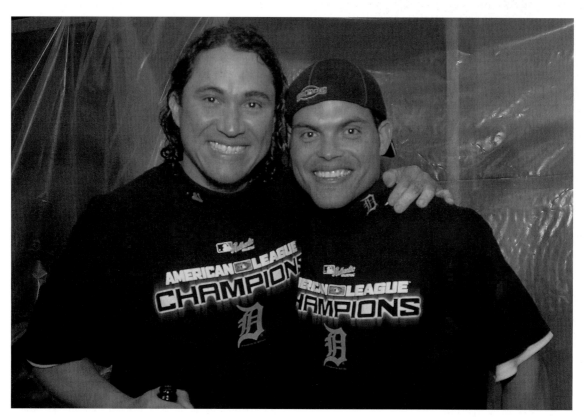

Champagne flowed freely in the post-ALCS celebration and among the champions, Magglio Ordonez and Pudge Rodriguez were readily available to share their exuberance. (Mark Cunningham)

same season. Verlander defied the sophomore jinx by racking up 18 victories and a fine 3.66 ERA to rank among the league leaders in these two measures of excellence. Todd Jones reached a career milestone, surpassing 300 saves, the first in Tiger history. And Hall-of-Famer-in-waiting Pudge Rodriguez caught his 2,061st game with only two others ahead of him in the annals of baseball.

Tiger ace Kenny Rogers gets ready to deal in game two of the 2006 World Series at Comerica Park. As in his two previous postseason starts, Rogers pitched brilliantly, besting the Cardinals by a score of 3–1 while permitting just two hits in eight innings of work. (Mark Cunningham)

The team finished second with 88 wins, eight games behind the champion Cleveland Indians. This was a strong team needing so little more to carry it into the postseason competition. Undoubtedly disappointed that his 2007 Tigers couldn't find that little extra, Leyland was still very proud of his ball club: "I just think this team is a special team. In a lot of ways, I'm prouder of this team than I was last year, because everything that went right for us last year went wrong this year." It is always easy to look back and identify the blown opportunities that could have resulted in victories, but the real difference between playing in October and going home is very evident. Though Leyland never dwelled on the player injuries Detroit suffered, they were a critical factor in the season's result. Kenny Rogers lost 149 days of the season, Joel Zumaya 111, and Fernando Rodney 58. After Sheffield warmed up in early May, he drove the Tiger offensive in front of Ordonez, but when his production dropped off dramatically with an injured shoulder, the negative impact was profound. The Tigers had won the American League pennant in 2006 with an outstanding combination of starters and relievers who registered a team ERA of 3.84. In 2007, the number of quality starts diminished (88 in 2006 versus 71 in 2007), the bullpen was inconsistent, and the team ERA escalated to 4.57.

All associated directly and emotionally with the team had hoped for more in 2007. That well-placed confidence remains strong as the future is anticipated. Tiger fans poured through the turnstiles in record numbers, totaling more than 3,000,000 for the first time in franchise history.

Important decisions were quickly being made: Gary Sheffield underwent surgery on his right shoulder and the Tigers extended Jim Leyland's contract through 2009 and picked up the option on Pudge Rodriguez's contract for 2008. But no one could possibly anticipate how masterfully and dramatically Detroit would reload its arsenal for the 2008 season. With Rodriguez secured, Dave Dombrowski re-signed two important cogs in the pitching staff as both free agents Todd Jones and Kenny Rogers inked contracts for the upcoming campaign. With the overall free agent pool not particularly strong, the Tiger CEO sought to bolster key positions via trades. His first big acquisition was five-time All-Star shortstop Edgar Renteria in a trade with Atlanta, giving up promising rookie pitcher Jair Jurrjens and a minor league outfielder. Renteria, a 12-year veteran, sports a .291 lifetime batting average playing for the Florida Marlins, St. Louis Cardinals, and the Braves. In 2003 he drove in 100 runs while batting .330.

His next pickup came via trade with the Chicago Cubs, acquiring veteran outfielder Jacque Jones in exchange for infielder Omar Infante. Jones helps shore up left field and gives the team another left-handed batter. He also brings postseason experi-

ence, having played with the Minnesota Twins for a number of years. Although his power numbers were down in 2007, he has hit as many as 27 home runs in a couple of seasons. And then came the winter meetings of major league baseball in Atlanta. As reported to the press, Dombrowski and company went to this annual meeting feeling pretty good about the team they had assembled and did not expect to make any more significant moves. But before leaving, Tiger leadership rocked the baseball world with what most called a blockbuster deal that sent six young players including the team's two top prospects, Cameron Maybin and Andrew Miller, to the Florida Marlins for All-Star third baseman Miguel Cabrera and two-time All-Star pitcher Dontrelle Willis. Although only

The Detroit Tigers, Inc., began a new chapter of its history at 1:18 P.M. on April 11, 2000, when the first pitch was thrown by Brian Moehler at Comerica Park, located at 2100 Woodward Avenue, with a record attendance of 44,179 on hand. Its semi-classical architecture fits the mold of the most appealing modern ballparks and provides an impressive view of the Detroit skyline. A number of features add entertainment value to the park. (Mark Cunningham)

This beautiful night view of Comerica Park was captured from the roof of the Detroit Athletic Club. (Mark Cunningham)

24, Cabrera has made the All-Star team each of the last four years and carries a career .313 batting average and has already hit 119 home runs in just 720 games. Recognizing that the Tigers had given up some great talent, Jim Leyland said, "We don't think 24-year-old superstars come along very often. You can wait a lifetime to get a player like Cabrera." In Willis, the Tigers acquired another quality hurler who significantly strengthens the starting rotation. Willis is capable of pitching a lot of innings and has already recorded a 22-win season in his young career.

The John Smoltz for Doyle Alexander trade made in 1987 has haunted the Tiger faithful for a long time and it is surely on the minds of many as they witness these postseason player transactions. Most baseball executives would contend that a franchise trades its future only when it has a strong chance to win big. The Detroit Tigers future is now. They have become an elite team with what will be a feared lineup loaded with prime-time talent and a starting rotation better than most. Let the games begin is the battle cry in Michigan.

Like Verlander, young Andrew Miller followed a fast track to the show. After just five innings of work at Lakeland, Miller wore a Tiger uniform and pitched out of the Tiger bullpen in eight games during the 2006 season. Sent to the minors to gain more seasoning in 2007, he was soon summoned to the big club and became the fifth starter. (Mike Litaker)

Great things are predicted for 21-year-old Cameron Maybin. The tall, rangy outfielder is a four-dimension player who hit .304 for both West Michigan and Lakeland in his first two seasons as a professional. Promoted to AA Erie late in the season, he hit a sizzling .400 with four home runs in eight games and quickly joined the big club in Detroit. Although he hit a home run off Roger Clemens, he wasn't yet ready for the majors.

A Detroit Tigers
Hall of Fame

The fascination with baseball is felt and experienced in so many ways, yet perhaps none is more compelling than reflecting on the feats of past heroes. Their accomplishments are embellished by time and affection as our idols of the past take on superhuman dimensions. Most fans think they know more about baseball and possess better judgment than umpires, managers, directors of player development, and, for sure, general managers. All fans have an opinion about almost anything concerning their team; it's a big part of the special interest that baseball commands.

Wouldn't it be great if fans like you and me, the experts, would elect the greatest players for induction into a Detroit Tigers Hall of Fame? One thing is certain: many would challenge the decisions just as adamantly as the choices made for the National Baseball Hall of Fame.

This photographic history of the team concludes with a presentation of the 35 players I think should be selected if a Detroit Tigers Hall of Fame were inaugurated. This fantasy shrine includes the 10 greatest pitchers, outfielders, and infielders, and the five greatest catchers. Each player's record while an active member of the Detroit Tigers was the foremost consideration. In each category there were numerous easy choices, but the decisions became more difficult when selecting the last few. The impact of the player's performance on the team and the league and the length of his Tiger career were all factors. Only when necessary to "break a tie" was a player's record with other teams considered.

So, from among the more than 1,400 players who have worn a Tiger uniform, here are the best, those whom I believe should be inducted into a Detroit Tigers Hall of Fame. Only the player's record while a member of the Tiger organization is presented.

T E N B E S T P I T C H E R S

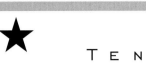

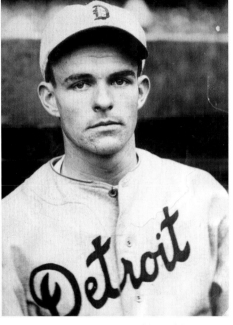

(William M. Anderson)

Tommy Bridges

	W	L	PCT	ERA	G	GS	CG	IP	H	BB	SO	ShO
1930	3	2	.600	4.06	8	5	2	37.2	28	23	17	0
1931	8	16	.333	4.99	35	23	15	173	182	108	105	2
1932	14	12	.538	3.36	34	26	10	201	174	119	108	4
1933	14	12	.538	3.09	33	28	17	233	192	110	120	2
1934	22	11	.667	3.67	36	35	23	275	249	104	151	3
1935	21	10	.677	3.51	36	34	23	274.1	277	113	163	4
1936	23	11	.676	3.60	39	38	26	294.2	289	115	175	5
1937	15	12	.556	4.07	34	31	18	245.1	267	91	138	3
1938	13	9	.591	4.59	25	20	13	151	171	58	101	0
1939	17	7	.708	3.50	29	26	16	198	186	61	129	2
1940	12	9	.571	3.37	29	28	12	197.2	171	88	133	2
1941	9	12	.429	3.41	25	22	10	147.2	128	70	90	1
1942	9	7	.563	2.74	23	22	11	174	164	61	97	2
1943	12	7	.632	2.39	25	22	11	191.2	159	61	124	3
1945	1	0	1.000	3.27	4	1	0	11	14	2	6	0
1946	1	1	.500	5.91	9	1	0	21.1	24	8	17	0
16 years	**194**	**138**	**.584**	**3.57**	**424**	**362**	**207**	**2826.1**	**2675**	**1192**	**1674**	**33**

(Detroit News Archives)

Jim Bunning

	W	L	PCT	ERA	G	GS	CG	IP	H	BB	SO	ShO
1955	3	5	.375	6.35	15	8	0	51	59	32	37	0
1956	5	1	.833	3.71	15	3	0	53.1	55	28	34	0
1957	20	8	.714	2.69	45	30	14	267.1	214	72	182	1
1958	14	12	.538	3.52	35	34	10	219.2	188	79	177	3
1959	17	13	.567	3.89	40	35	14	249.2	220	75	201	1
1960	11	14	.440	2.79	36	34	10	252	217	64	201	3
1961	17	11	.607	3.19	38	37	12	268	232	71	194	4
1962	19	10	.655	3.59	41	35	12	258	262	74	184	2
1963	12	13	.480	3.88	39	35	6	248.1	245	69	196	2
9 years	**118**	**87**	**0.576**	**3.45**	**304**	**251**	**78**	**1867.1**	**1692**	**564**	**1406**	**16**

TEN BEST PITCHERS

(Courtesy of the Burton Historical Collection
of the Detroit Public Library)

George "Hooks" Dauss

	W	L	PCT	ERA	G	GS	CG	IP	H	BB	SO	ShO
1912	1	1	.500	3.18	2	2	2	17	11	9	7	0
1913	13	12	.520	2.68	33	29	22	225	188	82	107	2
1914	18	15	.545	2.86	45	35	22	302	286	87	150	3
1915	24	13	.649	2.5	46	35	27	309.2	261	112	132	1
1916	19	12	.613	3.21	39	29	18	238.2	220	90	95	1
1917	17	14	.548	2.43	37	31	22	270.2	243	87	102	6
1918	12	16	.429	2.99	33	26	21	249.2	262	58	73	1
1919	21	9	.700	3.55	34	32	22	256.1	308	63	73	2
1920	13	21	.382	3.56	38	32	18	270.1	275	84	82	0
1921	10	15	.400	4.33	32	28	16	233	245	81	68	0
1922	13	13	.500	4.20	39	25	12	218.2	251	59	78	1
1923	21	13	.618	3.62	50	39	22	316	331	78	105	4
1924	12	11	.522	4.59	40	10	5	131.1	155	40	44	0
1925	16	11	.593	3.16	35	30	16	228	238	85	58	1
1926	11	7	.611	4.20	35	5	0	124.1	135	49	27	0
15 years	**221**	**183**	**.547**	**3.32**	**538**	**388**	**245**	**3390.2**	**3407**	**1064**	**1201**	**22**

TEN BEST PITCHERS

(William M. Anderson)

William "Wild Bill" Donovan

	W	L	PCT	ERA	G	GS	CG	IP	H	BB	SO	ShO
1903	17	16	.515	2.29	35	34	34	307	247	95	187	4
1904	17	16	.515	2.46	34	34	30	293	251	94	137	3
1905	18	15	.545	2.6	34	32	27	280.2	236	101	135	5
1906	9	15	.375	3.15	25	25	22	211.2	221	72	85	0
1907	25	4	.862	2.19	32	28	27	271	222	82	123	3
1908	18	7	.720	2.08	29	28	25	242.2	210	53	141	6
1909	8	7	.533	2.31	21	17	13	140.1	121	60	76	4
1910	17	7	.708	2.42	26	23	20	208.2	184	61	107	3
1911	10	9	.526	3.31	20	19	15	168.1	160	64	81	1
1912	1	0	1	0.9	3	1	0	10	5	2	6	0
1918	1	0	1	1.5	2	1	0	6	5	1	1	0
11 years	**141**	**96**	**0.595**	**2.49**	**261**	**242**	**213**	**2139.1**	**1862**	**685**	**1079**	**29**

(William M. Anderson)

Mickey Lolich

	W	L	PCT	ERA	G	GS	CG	IP	H	BB	SO	ShO	W	L	SV
1963	5	9	.357	3.55	33	18	4	144.1	145	56	103	0	0	2	0
1964	18	9	.667	3.26	44	33	12	232	196	64	192	6	2	1	2
1965	15	9	.625	3.44	43	37	7	243.2	216	72	226	3	1	0	3
1966	14	14	.500	4.77	40	33	5	203.2	204	83	173	1	0	1	3
1967	14	13	.519	3.04	31	30	11	204	165	56	174	6	0	0	0
1968	17	9	.654	3.19	39	32	8	220	178	65	197	4	4	0	1
1969	19	11	.633	3.14	37	36	15	280.2	214	122	271	1	0	0	1
1970	14	19	.424	3.79	40	39	13	273	272	109	230	3	0	0	0
1971	25	14	.641	2.92	45	45	29	376	336	92	308	4	0	0	0
1972	22	14	.611	2.50	41	41	23	327	282	74	250	4	0	0	0
1973	16	15	.516	3.82	42	42	17	309	315	79	214	3	0	0	0
1974	16	21	.432	4.15	41	41	27	308	310	78	202	3	0	0	0
1975	12	18	.400	3.78	32	32	19	240.2	260	64	139	1	0	0	0
13 years	207	175	0.542	3.45	508	459	190	3362	3093	1014	2679	39	7	4	10

TEN BEST PITCHERS

(Dianne Chapman)

Jack Morris

	W	L	PCT	ERA	G	GS	CG	IP	H	BB	SO	ShO
1977	1	1	.500	3.72	7	6	1	46	38	23	28	0
1978	3	5	.375	4.33	28	7	0	106	107	49	48	0
1979	17	7	.708	3.27	27	27	9	198	179	59	113	1
1980	16	15	.516	4.18	36	36	11	250	252	87	112	2
1981	14	7	.667	3.05	25	25	15	198	153	78	97	1
1982	17	16	.515	4.06	37	37	17	266.1	247	96	135	3
1983	20	13	.606	3.34	37	37	20	293.2	257	83	232	1
1984	19	11	.633	3.65	35	35	9	241.1	224	87	149	1
1985	16	11	.593	3.33	35	35	13	257	212	110	191	4
1986	21	8	.724	3.27	35	35	15	267	229	82	223	6
1987	18	11	.621	3.38	34	34	13	266	227	93	208	0
1988	15	13	.536	3.94	34	34	10	235	225	83	168	2
1989	6	14	.300	4.86	24	24	10	170.1	189	59	115	0
1990	15	18	.455	4.51	36	36	11	249.2	231	97	162	3
14 years	198	150	0.569	3.73	430	408	154	3043.1	2767	1086	2047	24

(Detroit News Archives)

George Mullin

	W	L	PCT	ERA	G	GS	CG	IP	H	BB	SO	ShO
1902	13	16	.448	3.67	35	30	25	260	282	95	78	0
1903	19	15	.559	2.25	41	36	31	320.2	284	106	170	6
1904	17	23	.425	2.40	45	44	42	382.1	345	131	161	7
1905	21	21	.500	2.51	44	41	35	347.2	303	138	168	1
1906	21	18	.538	2.78	40	40	35	330	315	108	123	2
1907	20	20	.500	2.59	46	42	35	357.1	346	106	146	5
1908	17	13	.567	3.10	39	30	26	290.2	301	71	121	1
1909	29	8	.784	2.22	40	35	29	303.2	258	78	124	3
1910	21	12	.636	2.87	38	32	27	289	260	102	98	5
1911	18	10	.643	3.07	30	29	25	234.1	245	61	87	2
1912	12	17	.414	3.54	30	29	22	226	214	92	88	2
1913	1	6	.143	2.75	7	7	4	52.1	53	18	16	0
12 years	**209**	**179**	**0.539**	**2.76**	**435**	**395**	**336**	**3394**	**3206**	**1106**	**1380**	**34**

(William M. Anderson)

Hal Newhouser

	W	L	PCT	ERA	G	GS	CG	IP	H	BB	SO	ShO
1939	0	1	.000	5.40	1	1	1	5	3	4	4	0
1940	9	9	.500	4.86	28	20	7	133.1	149	76	89	0
1941	9	11	.450	4.79	33	27	5	173	166	137	106	1
1942	8	14	.364	2.45	38	23	11	183.2	137	114	103	1
1943	8	17	.320	3.04	37	25	10	195.2	163	111	144	1
1944	29	9	.763	2.22	47	34	25	312.1	264	102	187	6
1945	25	9	.735	1.81	40	36	29	313.1	239	110	212	8
1946	26	9	.743	1.94	37	34	29	292.1	215	98	275	6
1947	17	17	.500	2.87	40	36	24	285	268	110	176	3
1948	21	12	.636	3.01	39	35	19	272.1	249	99	143	2
1949	18	11	.621	3.36	38	35	22	292	277	111	144	3
1950	15	13	.536	4.34	35	30	15	213.2	232	81	87	1
1951	6	6	.500	3.92	15	14	7	96.1	98	19	37	1
1952	9	9	.500	3.74	25	19	8	154	148	47	57	0
1953	0	1	.000	7.06	7	4	0	21.2	31	8	6	0
15 years	**200**	**148**	**0.575**	**3.07**	**460**	**373**	**212**	**2943.2**	**2639**	**1227**	**1770**	**33**

TEN BEST PITCHERS

(William M. Anderson)

Paul "Dizzy" Trout

	W	L	PCT	ERA	G	GS	CG	IP	H	BB	SO	ShO
1939	9	10	.474	3.61	33	22	6	162	168	74	72	0
1940	3	7	.300	4.47	33	10	1	100.2	125	54	64	0
1941	9	9	.500	3.74	37	18	6	151.2	144	84	88	1
1942	12	18	.400	3.43	35	29	13	223	214	89	91	1
1943	20	12	.625	2.48	44	30	18	246.2	204	101	111	5
1944	27	14	.659	2.12	49	40	33	352.1	314	83	144	7
1945	18	15	.545	3.14	41	31	18	246.1	252	79	97	4
1946	17	13	.567	2.34	38	32	23	276.1	244	97	151	5
1947	10	11	.476	3.48	32	26	9	186.1	186	65	74	2
1948	10	14	.417	3.43	32	23	11	183.2	193	73	91	2
1949	3	6	.333	4.40	33	0	0	59.1	68	21	19	0
1950	13	5	.722	3.75	34	20	11	184.2	190	64	88	1
1951	9	14	.391	4.04	42	22	7	191.2	172	75	89	0
1952	1	5	.167	5.33	10	2	0	27	30	19	20	0
14 years	161	153	0.513	3.20	493	305	156	2591.2	2504	978	1199	28

TEN BEST PITCHERS

(Detroit News Archives)

Earl Whitehill

	W	L	PCT	ERA	G	GS	CG	IP	H	BB	SO	ShO
1923	2	0	1.000	2.73	8	3	2	33	22	15	19	1
1924	17	9	.654	3.86	35	32	16	233	260	79	65	2
1925	11	11	.500	4.66	35	33	15	239.1	267	88	83	1
1926	16	13	.552	3.99	36	34	13	252.1	271	79	109	0
1927	16	14	.533	3.36	41	31	17	236	238	105	95	3
1928	11	16	.407	4.31	31	30	12	196.1	214	78	93	1
1929	14	15	.483	4.62	38	28	18	245.1	267	96	103	1
1930	17	13	.567	4.24	34	31	16	220.2	248	80	109	0
1931	13	16	.448	4.06	34	34	22	272.1	287	118	81	0
1932	16	12	.571	4.54	33	31	17	244	255	93	81	3
10 years	**133**	**119**	**0.528**	**4.16**	**325**	**287**	**148**	**2172.1**	**2329**	**831**	**838**	**12**

T E N   B E S T   O U T F I E L D E R S

(Library of Congress)

Ty Cobb

	G	AB	H	2B	3B	HR	HR%	R	RBI	BB	SO	SB	BA	SA
1905	41	150	36	6	0	1	0.7	19	15	10	–	2	.240	.300
1906	98	350	112	13	7	1	0.3	45	41	19	–	23	.320	.406
1907	150	605	212	29	15	5	0.8	97	116	24	–	49	.350	.473
1908	150	581	188	36	20	4	0.7	88	108	34	–	39	.324	.475
1909	156	573	216	33	10	9	1.6	116	107	48	–	76	.377	.517
1910	140	509	196	36	13	8	1.6	106	91	64	–	65	.385	.554
1911	146	591	248	47	24	8	1.4	147	144	44	–	83	.420	.621
1912	140	553	227	30	23	7	1.3	119	90	43	–	61	.410	.586
1913	122	428	167	18	16	4	0.9	70	67	58	31	52	.390	.535
1914	97	345	127	22	11	2	0.6	69	57	57	22	35	.368	.513
1915	156	563	208	31	13	3	0.5	144	99	118	43	96	.369	.487
1916	145	542	201	31	10	5	0.9	113	68	78	39	68	.371	.493
1917	152	588	225	44	23	7	1.2	107	102	61	34	55	.383	.571
1918	111	421	161	19	14	3	0.7	83	64	41	21	34	.382	.515
1919	124	497	191	36	13	1	0.2	92	70	38	22	28	.384	.515
1920	112	428	143	28	8	2	0.5	86	63	58	28	14	.334	.451
1921	128	507	197	37	16	12	2.4	124	101	56	19	22	.389	.596
1922	137	526	211	42	16	4	0.8	99	99	55	24	9	.401	.565
1923	145	556	189	40	7	6	1.1	103	88	66	14	9	.340	.469
1924	155	625	211	38	10	4	0.6	115	74	85	18	23	.338	.450
1925	121	415	157	31	12	12	2.9	97	102	65	12	13	.378	.598
1926	79	233	79	18	5	4	1.7	48	62	26	2	9	.339	.511
22 years	**2805**	**10586**	**3902**	**665**	**286**	**112**	**1.1**	**2087**	**1828**	**1148**	**329**	**865**	**.369**	**.517**

TEN BEST OUTFIELDERS

(Courtesy of the Burton Historical Collection
of the Detroit Public Library)

Sam Crawford

	G	AB	H	2B	3B	HR	HR%	R	RBI	BB	SO	SB	BA	SA
1903	137	550	184	23	25	4	.7	88	89	25	–	18	.335	.489
1904	150	571	143	21	17	2	0.4	49	73	44	–	20	.250	.357
1905	154	575	171	40	10	6	1.0	73	75	50	–	22	.297	.433
1906	145	563	166	25	16	2	0.4	65	72	38	–	24	.295	.407
1907	144	582	188	34	17	4	0.7	102	81	37	–	18	.323	.460
1908	152	591	184	33	16	7	1.2	102	80	37	–	15	.311	.457
1909	156	589	185	35	14	6	1.0	83	97	47	–	30	.314	.452
1910	154	588	170	26	19	5	0.9	83	120	37	–	20	.289	.423
1911	146	574	217	36	14	7	1.2	109	115	61	–	37	.378	.526
1912	149	581	189	30	21	4	0.7	81	109	42	–	41	.325	.470
1913	153	610	193	32	23	9	1.5	78	83	52	28	13	.316	.489
1914	157	582	183	22	26	8	1.4	74	104	69	31	25	.314	.483
1915	156	612	183	31	19	4	0.7	81	112	66	29	24	.299	.431
1916	100	322	92	11	13	0	0.0	41	42	37	10	10	.286	.401
1917	61	104	18	4	0	2	1.9	6	12	4	6	0	.173	.269
15 years	**2114**	**7994**	**2466**	**403**	**250**	**70**	**0.9**	**1115**	**1264**	**646**	**104**	**317**	**.308**	**.448**

TEN BEST OUTFIELDERS

(William M. Anderson)

Bob Fothergill

	G	AB	H	2B	3B	HR	HR%	R	RBI	BB	SO	SB	BA	SA
1922	42	152	49	12	4	0	0.0	20	29	8	9	1	.322	.454
1923	101	241	76	18	2	1	0.4	34	49	12	19	4	.315	.419
1924	54	166	50	8	3	0	0.0	28	15	5	13	2	.301	.386
1925	71	204	72	14	0	2	1.0	38	28	6	3	2	.353	.451
1926	110	387	142	31	7	3	0.8	63	73	33	23	4	.367	.506
1927	143	527	189	38	9	9	1.7	93	114	47	31	9	.359	.516
1928	111	347	110	28	10	3	0.9	49	63	24	19	8	.317	.481
1929	115	277	98	24	9	6	2.2	42	62	11	11	3	.354	.570
1930	55	143	37	9	3	2	1.4	14	14	6	10	1	.259	.406
9 years	**802**	**2444**	**823**	**182**	**47**	**26**	**1.1**	**381**	**447**	**152**	**138**	**34**	**.337**	**.482**

TEN BEST OUTFIELDERS

(William M. Anderson)

Ervin "Pete" Fox

	G	AB	H	2B	3B	HR	HR%	R	RBI	BB	SO	SB	BA	SA
1933	128	535	154	26	13	7	1.3	82	57	23	38	9	.288	.424
1934	128	516	147	31	2	2	0.4	101	45	49	53	25	.285	.364
1935	131	517	166	38	8	15	2.9	116	73	45	52	14	.321	.513
1936	73	220	67	12	1	4	1.8	46	26	34	23	1	.305	.423
1937	148	628	208	39	8	12	1.9	116	82	41	43	12	.331	.476
1938	155	634	186	35	10	7	1.1	91	96	31	39	16	.293	.413
1939	141	519	153	24	6	7	1.3	69	66	35	41	23	.295	.405
1940	93	350	101	17	4	5	1.4	49	48	21	30	7	.289	.403
8 years	997	3919	1182	222	52	59	1.5	670	493	279	319	107	.302	.430

TEN BEST OUTFIELDERS

(Library of Congress)

Harry Heilmann

	G	AB	H	2B	3B	HR	HR%	R	RBI	BB	SO	SB	BA	SA
1914	67	182	41	8	1	2	1.1	25	22	22	29	1	.225	.313
1916	136	451	127	30	11	2	0.4	57	76	42	40	9	.282	.410
1917	150	556	156	22	11	5	0.9	57	86	41	54	11	.281	.387
1918	79	286	79	10	6	5	1.7	34	44	35	10	13	.276	.406
1919	140	537	172	30	15	8	1.5	74	95	37	41	7	.320	.477
1920	145	543	168	28	5	9	1.7	66	89	39	32	3	.309	.429
1921	149	602	237	43	14	19	3.2	114	139	53	37	2	.394	.606
1922	118	455	162	27	10	21	4.6	92	92	58	28	8	.356	.598
1923	144	524	211	44	11	18	3.4	121	115	74	40	8	.403	.632
1924	153	570	197	45	16	10	1.8	107	113	78	41	13	.346	.533
1925	150	573	225	40	11	13	2.3	97	133	67	27	6	.393	.569
1926	141	502	184	41	8	9	1.8	90	103	67	19	6	.367	.534
1927	141	505	201	50	9	14	2.8	106	120	72	16	11	.398	.616
1928	151	558	183	38	10	14	2.5	83	107	57	45	7	.328	.507
1929	125	453	156	41	7	15	3.3	86	120	50	39	5	.344	.565
15 years	**1989**	**7297**	**2499**	**497**	**145**	**164**	**2.2**	**1209**	**1454**	**792**	**498**	**110**	**.342**	**.518**

T E N   B E S T   O U T F I E L D E R S

(Mel Bailey)

Willie Horton

	G	AB	H	2B	3B	HR	HR%	R	RBI	BB	SO	SB	BA	SA
1963	15	43	14	2	1	1	2.3	6	4	0	8	2	.326	.488
1964	25	80	13	1	3	1	1.3	6	10	11	20	0	.163	.288
1965	143	512	140	20	2	29	5.7	69	104	48	101	5	.273	.490
1966	146	526	138	22	6	27	5.1	72	100	44	103	1	.262	.481
1967	122	401	110	20	3	19	4.7	47	67	36	80	0	.274	.481
1968	143	512	146	20	2	36	7.0	68	85	49	110	0	.285	.543
1969	141	508	133	17	1	28	5.5	66	91	52	93	3	.262	.465
1970	96	371	113	18	2	17	4.6	53	69	28	43	0	.305	.501
1971	119	450	130	25	1	22	4.9	64	72	37	75	1	.289	.496
1972	108	333	77	9	5	11	3.3	44	36	27	47	0	.231	.387
1973	111	411	130	19	3	17	4.1	42	53	23	57	1	.316	.501
1974	72	238	71	8	1	15	6.3	32	47	21	36	0	.298	.529
1975	159	615	169	13	1	25	4.1	62	92	44	109	1	.275	.421
1976	114	401	105	17	0	14	3.5	40	56	49	63	0	.262	.409
1977	1	4	1	0	0	0	0.0	0	0	0	0	0	.250	.250
15 years	**1515**	**5405**	**1490**	**211**	**31**	**262**	**4.8**	**671**	**886**	**469**	**945**	**14**	**.276**	**.472**

TEN BEST OUTFIELDERS

(Grand Rapids History and Special Collections,
Grand Rapids Public Library)

Al Kaline

	G	AB	H	2B	3B	HR	HR%	R	RBI	BB	SO	SB	BA	SA
1953	30	28	7	0	0	1	3.6	9	2	1	5	1	.250	.357
1954	138	504	139	18	3	4	0.8	42	43	22	45	9	.276	.347
1955	152	588	200	24	8	27	4.6	121	102	82	57	6	.340	.546
1956	153	617	194	32	10	27	4.4	96	128	70	55	7	.314	.530
1957	149	577	170	29	4	23	4.0	83	90	43	38	11	.295	.478
1958	146	543	170	34	7	16	2.9	84	85	54	47	7	.313	.490
1959	136	511	167	19	2	27	5.3	86	94	72	42	10	.327	.530
1960	147	551	153	29	4	15	2.7	77	68	65	47	19	.278	.426
1961	153	586	190	41	7	19	3.2	116	82	66	42	14	.324	.515
1962	100	398	121	16	6	29	7.3	78	94	47	39	4	.304	.593
1963	145	551	172	24	3	27	4.9	89	101	54	48	6	.312	.514
1964	146	525	154	31	5	17	3.2	77	68	75	51	4	.293	.469
1965	125	399	112	18	2	18	4.5	72	72	72	49	6	.281	.471
1966	142	479	138	29	1	29	6.1	85	88	81	66	5	.288	.534
1967	131	458	141	28	2	25	5.5	94	78	83	47	8	.308	.541
1968	102	327	94	14	1	10	3.1	49	53	55	39	6	.287	.428
1969	131	456	124	17	0	21	4.6	74	69	54	61	1	.272	.447
1970	131	467	130	24	4	16	3.4	64	71	77	49	2	.278	.450
1971	133	405	119	19	2	15	3.7	69	54	82	57	4	.294	.462
1972	106	278	87	11	2	10	3.6	46	32	28	33	1	.313	.475
1973	91	310	79	13	0	10	3.2	40	45	29	28	4	.255	.394
1974	147	558	146	28	2	13	2.3	71	64	65	75	2	.262	.389
22 years	2834	10116	3007	498	75	399	3.9	1622	1583	1277	1020	137	.297	.480

T E N   B E S T   O U T F I E L D E R S

(Ray Billbrough)

Henry "Heinie" Manush

	G	AB	H	2B	3B	HR	HR%	R	RBI	BB	SO	SB	BA	SA
1923	109	308	103	20	5	4	1.3	59	54	20	21	3	.334	.471
1924	120	422	122	24	8	9	2.1	83	68	27	30	14	.289	.448
1925	99	277	84	14	3	5	1.8	46	47	24	21	8	.303	.430
1926	136	498	188	35	8	14	2.8	95	86	31	28	11	.378	.564
1927	152	593	177	31	18	6	1.0	102	80	47	29	12	.298	.442
5 years	616	2098	674	124	42	38	1.8	385	335	149	129	48	.321	.475

TEN BEST OUTFIELDERS

(William M. Anderson)

Bobby Veach

	G	AB	H	2B	3B	HR	HR%	R	RBI	BB	SO	SB	BA	SA
1912	23	79	27	5	1	0	0.0	8	15	5	–	2	.342	.430
1913	138	494	133	22	10	0	0.0	54	64	53	31	22	.269	.354
1914	149	531	146	19	14	1	0.2	56	72	50	29	20	.275	.369
1915	152	569	178	40	10	3	0.5	81	112	68	43	16	.313	.434
1916	150	566	173	33	15	3	0.5	92	91	52	41	24	.306	.433
1917	154	571	182	31	12	8	1.4	79	103	61	44	21	.319	.457
1918	127	499	139	21	13	3	0.6	59	78	35	23	21	.279	.391
1919	139	538	191	45	17	3	0.6	87	101	33	33	19	.355	.519
1920	154	612	188	39	15	11	1.8	92	113	36	22	11	.307	.474
1921	150	612	207	43	13	16	2.6	110	128	48	31	14	.338	.529
1922	155	618	202	34	13	9	1.5	96	126	42	27	9	.327	.468
1923	114	293	94	13	3	2	0.7	45	39	29	21	10	.321	.406
12 years	1605	5982	1860	345	136	59	1.0	859	1042	512	345	189	.311	.444

(William M. Anderson)

Gerald "Gee" Walker

	G	AB	H	2B	3B	HR	HR%	R	RBI	BB	SO	SB	BA	SA
1931	59	189	56	17	2	1	0.5	20	28	14	21	10	.296	.423
1932	126	480	155	32	6	8	1.7	71	78	13	38	30	.323	.465
1933	127	483	135	29	7	9	1.9	68	64	15	49	26	.280	.424
1934	98	347	104	19	2	6	1.7	54	39	19	20	20	.300	.418
1935	98	362	109	22	6	7	1.9	52	53	15	21	6	.301	.453
1936	134	550	194	55	5	12	2.2	105	93	23	30	17	.353	.536
1937	151	635	213	42	4	18	2.8	105	113	41	74	23	.335	.499
7 years	793	3046	966	216	32	61	2.0	475	468	140	253	132	.317	.469

TEN BEST INFIELDERS

(William M. Anderson)

Owen "Donie" Bush

	G	AB	H	2B	3B	HR	HR%	R	RBI	BB	SO	SB	BA	SA
1908	20	68	20	1	1	0	0.0	13	4	7	–	2	.294	.338
1909	157	532	145	18	2	0	0.0	114	33	88	–	53	.273	.314
1910	142	496	130	13	4	3	0.6	90	34	78	–	49	.262	.323
1911	150	561	130	18	5	1	0.2	126	36	98	–	40	.232	.287
1912	144	511	118	14	8	2	0.4	107	38	117	–	35	.231	.301
1913	153	593	149	19	10	1	0.2	98	40	80	32	44	.251	.322
1914	157	596	150	18	4	0	0.0	97	32	112	54	35	.252	.295
1915	155	561	128	12	8	1	0.2	99	44	118	44	35	.228	.283
1916	145	550	124	5	9	0	0.0	73	34	75	42	19	.225	.267
1917	147	581	163	18	3	0	0.0	112	24	80	40	34	.281	.322
1918	128	500	117	10	3	0	0.0	74	22	79	31	9	.234	.266
1919	129	509	124	11	6	0	0.0	82	26	75	36	22	.244	.289
1920	141	506	133	18	5	1	0.2	85	33	73	32	15	.263	.324
1921	104	402	113	6	5	0	0.0	72	27	45	23	8	.281	.321
14 years	1872	6966	1744	181	73	9	0.1	1242	427	1125	334	400	.250	.301

T E N   B E S T   I N F I E L D E R S

(Mel Bailey)

Norm Cash

	G	AB	H	2B	3B	HR	HR%	R	RBI	BB	SO	SB	BA	SA
1960	121	353	101	16	3	18	5.1	64	63	65	58	4	.286	.501
1961	159	535	193	22	8	41	7.7	119	132	124	85	11	.361	.662
1962	148	507	123	16	2	39	7.7	94	89	104	82	6	.243	.513
1963	147	493	133	19	1	26	5.3	67	79	89	76	2	.270	.471
1964	144	479	123	15	5	23	4.8	63	83	70	66	2	.257	.453
1965	142	467	124	23	1	30	6.4	79	82	77	62	6	.266	.512
1966	160	603	168	18	3	32	5.3	98	93	66	91	2	.279	.478
1967	152	488	118	16	5	22	4.5	64	72	81	100	3	.242	.430
1968	127	411	108	15	1	25	6.1	50	63	39	70	1	.263	.487
1969	142	483	135	15	4	22	4.6	81	74	63	80	2	.280	.464
1970	130	370	96	18	2	15	4.1	58	53	72	58	0	.259	.441
1971	135	452	128	10	3	32	7.1	72	91	59	86	1	.283	.531
1972	137	440	114	16	0	22	5.0	51	61	50	64	0	.259	.445
1973	121	363	95	19	0	19	5.2	51	40	47	73	1	.262	.471
1974	53	149	34	3	2	7	4.7	17	12	19	30	1	.228	.416
15 years	**2018**	**6593**	**1793**	**241**	**40**	**373**	**5.7**	**1028**	**1087**	**1025**	**1081**	**42**	**.272**	**.490**

TEN BEST INFIELDERS

(William M. Anderson)

Charlie Gehringer

	G	AB	H	2B	3B	HR	HR%	R	RBI	BB	SO	SB	BA	SA
1924	5	13	6	0	0	0	0.0	2	1	0	2	1	.462	.462
1925	8	18	3	0	0	0	0.0	3	0	2	0	0	.167	.167
1926	123	459	127	19	17	1	0.2	62	48	30	42	9	.277	.399
1927	133	508	161	29	11	4	0.8	110	61	52	31	17	.317	.441
1928	154	603	193	29	16	6	1.0	108	74	69	22	15	.320	.451
1929	155	634	215	45	19	13	2.1	131	106	64	19	28	.339	.532
1930	154	610	201	47	15	16	2.6	144	98	69	17	19	.330	.534
1931	101	383	119	24	5	4	1.0	67	53	29	15	13	.311	.431
1932	152	618	184	44	11	19	3.1	112	107	68	34	9	.298	.497
1933	155	628	204	42	6	12	1.9	103	105	68	27	5	.325	.468
1934	154	601	214	50	7	11	1.8	134	127	99	25	11	.356	.517
1935	150	610	201	32	8	19	3.1	123	108	79	16	11	.330	.502
1936	154	641	227	60	12	15	2.3	144	116	83	13	4	.354	.555
1937	144	564	209	40	1	14	2.5	133	96	90	25	11	.371	.520
1938	152	568	174	32	5	20	3.5	133	107	112	21	14	.306	.486
1939	118	406	132	29	6	16	3.9	86	86	68	16	4	.325	.544
1940	139	515	161	33	3	10	1.9	108	81	101	17	10	.313	.447
1941	127	436	96	19	4	3	0.7	65	46	95	26	1	.220	.303
1942	45	45	12	0	0	1	2.2	6	7	7	4	0	.267	.333
19 years	**2323**	**8860**	**2839**	**574**	**146**	**184**	**2.1**	**1774**	**1427**	**1185**	**372**	**182**	**.320**	**.480**

T E N   B E S T   I N F I E L D E R S

(William M. Anderson)

Hank Greenberg

	G	AB	H	2B	3B	HR	HR%	R	RBI	BB	SO	SB	BA	SA
1930	1	1	0	0	0	0	0	0	0	0	0	0	.000	.000
1933	117	449	135	33	3	12	2.7	59	87	46	78	6	.301	.468
1934	153	593	201	63	7	26	4.4	118	139	63	93	9	.339	.600
1935	152	619	203	46	16	36	5.8	121	170	87	91	4	.328	.628
1936	12	46	16	6	2	1	2.2	10	16	9	6	1	.348	.630
1937	154	594	200	49	14	40	6.7	137	183	102	101	8	.337	.668
1938	155	556	175	23	4	58	10.4	144	146	119	92	7	.315	.683
1939	138	500	156	42	7	33	6.6	112	112	91	95	8	.312	.622
1940	148	573	195	50	8	41	7.2	129	150	93	75	6	.340	.670
1941	19	67	18	5	1	2	3.0	12	12	16	12	1	.269	.463
1945	78	270	84	20	2	13	4.8	47	60	42	40	3	.311	.544
1946	142	523	145	29	5	44	8.4	91	127	80	88	5	.277	.604
12 years	1269	4791	1528	366	69	306	6.4	980	1202	748	771	58	.319	.616

TEN BEST INFIELDERS

(Grand Rapids History and Special Collections,
Grand Rapids Public Library)

George Kell

	G	AB	H	2B	3B	HR	HR%	R	RBI	BB	SO	SB	BA	SA
1946	105	434	142	19	9	4	0.9	67	41	30	14	3	.327	.440
1947	152	588	188	29	5	5	0.9	75	93	61	16	9	.320	.412
1948	92	368	112	24	3	2	0.5	47	44	33	15	2	.304	.402
1949	134	522	179	38	9	3	0.6	97	59	71	13	7	.343	.467
1950	157	641	218	56	6	8	1.2	114	101	66	18	3	.340	.484
1951	147	598	191	36	3	2	0.3	92	59	61	18	10	.319	.400
1952	39	152	45	8	0	1	0.7	11	17	14	13	0	.296	.368
7 years	826	3303	1075	210	35	25	0.8	503	414	336	107	34	.325	.433

(William M. Anderson)

Harvey Kuenn

	G	AB	H	2B	3B	HR	HR%	R	RBI	BB	SO	SB	BA	SA
1952	19	80	26	2	2	0	0	2	8	2	1	2	.325	.400
1953	155	679	209	33	7	2	0.3	94	48	50	31	6	.308	.386
1954	155	656	201	28	6	5	0.8	81	48	29	13	9	.306	.390
1955	145	620	190	38	5	8	1.3	101	62	40	27	8	.306	.423
1956	146	591	196	32	7	12	2.0	96	88	55	34	9	.332	.470
1957	151	624	173	30	6	9	1.4	74	44	47	28	5	.277	.388
1958	139	561	179	39	3	8	1.4	73	54	51	34	5	.319	.442
1959	139	561	198	42	7	9	1.6	99	71	48	37	7	.353	.501
8 years	1049	4372	1372	244	43	53	1.2	620	423	322	205	51	.314	.426

(William M. Anderson)

Dick McAuliffe

	G	AB	H	2B	3B	HR	HR%	R	RBI	BB	SO	SB	BA	SA
1960	8	27	7	0	1	0	0.0	2	1	2	6	0	.259	.333
1961	80	285	73	12	4	6	2.1	36	33	24	39	2	.256	.389
1962	139	471	124	20	5	12	2.5	50	63	64	76	4	.263	.403
1963	150	568	149	18	6	13	2.3	77	61	64	75	11	.262	.384
1964	162	557	134	18	7	24	4.3	85	66	77	96	8	.241	.427
1965	113	404	105	13	6	15	3.7	61	54	49	62	6	.260	.433
1966	124	430	118	16	8	23	5.3	83	56	66	80	5	.274	.509
1967	153	557	133	16	7	22	3.9	92	65	105	118	6	.239	.411
1968	151	570	142	24	10	16	2.8	95	56	82	99	8	.249	.411
1969	74	271	71	10	5	11	4.1	49	33	47	41	2	.262	.458
1970	146	530	124	21	1	12	2.3	73	50	101	62	5	.234	.345
1971	128	477	99	16	6	18	3.8	67	57	53	67	4	.208	.379
1972	122	408	98	16	3	8	2.0	47	30	59	59	0	.240	.353
1973	106	343	94	18	1	12	3.5	39	47	49	52	0	.274	.437
14 years	**1656**	**5898**	**1471**	**218**	**70**	**192**	**3.3**	**856**	**672**	**842**	**932**	**61**	**.249**	**.408**

TEN BEST INFIELDERS

(Mike Litaker)

Alan Trammell

	G	AB	H	2B	3B	HR	HR%	R	RBI	BB	SO	SB	BA	SA
1977	19	43	8	0	0	0	0.0	6	0	4	12	0	.186	.186
1978	139	448	120	14	6	2	0.4	49	34	45	56	3	.268	.339
1979	142	460	127	11	4	6	1.3	68	50	43	55	17	.276	.357
1980	146	560	168	21	5	9	1.6	107	65	69	63	12	.300	.404
1981	105	392	101	15	3	2	0.5	52	31	49	31	10	.258	.327
1982	157	489	126	34	3	9	1.8	66	57	52	47	19	.258	.395
1983	142	505	161	31	2	14	2.8	83	66	57	64	30	.319	.471
1984	139	555	174	34	5	14	2.5	85	69	60	63	19	.314	.468
1985	149	605	156	21	7	13	2.1	79	57	50	71	14	.258	.380
1986	151	574	159	33	7	21	3.7	107	75	59	57	25	.277	.469
1987	151	597	205	34	3	28	4.7	109	105	60	47	21	.343	.551
1988	128	466	145	24	1	15	3.2	73	69	46	46	7	.311	.464
1989	121	449	109	20	3	5	1.1	54	43	45	45	10	.243	.334
1990	146	559	170	37	1	14	2.5	71	89	68	55	12	.304	.449
1991	101	375	93	20	0	9	2.4	57	55	37	39	11	.248	.373
1992	29	102	28	7	1	1	0.9	11	11	15	4	2	.275	.392
1993	112	401	132	25	3	12	2.9	72	60	38	38	12	.329	.496
1994	76	292	78	17	1	8	2.7	38	28	16	35	3	.267	.414
1995	60	223	60	12	0	2	0.8	28	23	27	19	3	.269	.350
1996	66	193	45	2	0	1	0.5	16	16	10	27	6	.233	.259
20 years	**2279**	**8288**	**2365**	**412**	**55**	**185**	**2.2**	**1231**	**1003**	**850**	**874**	**236**	**.285**	**.415**

TEN BEST INFIELDERS

(Lloyd Wallace)

Lou Whitaker

	G	AB	H	2B	3B	HR	HR%	R	RBI	BB	SO	SB	BA	SA
1977	11	32	8	1	0	0	0	5	2	4	6	2	.250	.281
1978	139	484	138	12	7	3	0.6	71	58	61	65	7	.285	.357
1979	127	423	121	14	8	3	0.7	75	42	78	66	20	.286	.378
1980	145	477	111	19	1	1	0.2	68	45	73	79	8	.233	.283
1981	109	335	88	14	4	5	1.5	48	36	40	42	5	.263	.373
1982	152	560	160	22	8	15	2.7	76	65	48	58	11	.286	.434
1983	161	643	206	40	6	12	1.9	94	72	67	70	17	.320	.457
1984	143	558	161	25	1	13	2.3	90	56	62	63	6	.289	.407
1985	152	609	170	29	8	21	3.4	102	73	80	56	6	.279	.456
1986	144	584	157	26	6	20	3.4	95	73	63	70	13	.269	.437
1987	149	604	160	38	6	16	2.6	110	59	71	108	13	.265	.427
1988	115	403	111	18	2	12	3.0	54	55	66	61	2	.275	.419
1989	148	509	128	21	1	28	5.5	77	85	89	59	6	.251	.462
1990	132	472	112	22	2	18	3.8	75	60	74	71	8	.237	.407
1991	138	470	131	26	2	23	4.8	94	78	90	45	4	.279	.447
1992	130	453	126	26	0	19	4.2	77	71	81	46	6	.278	.461
1993	119	383	111	32	1	9	2.3	72	67	78	46	3	.290	.449
1994	92	322	97	21	2	12	3.7	67	43	41	47	3	.301	.491
1995	63	249	73	14	0	14	5.6	36	44	31	41	4	.293	.518
19 years	**2369**	**8570**	**2369**	**420**	**65**	**244**	**2.8**	**1386**	**1084**	**1197**	**1049**	**144**	**.276**	**.426**

TEN BEST INFIELDERS

(William M. Anderson)

Rudy York

	G	AB	H	2B	3B	HR	HR%	R	RBI	BB	SO	SB	BA	SA
1934	3	6	1	0	0	0	0.0	0	0	1	3	0	.167	.167
1937	104	375	115	18	3	35	9.3	72	103	41	52	3	.307	.651
1938	135	463	138	27	2	33	7.1	85	127	92	74	1	.298	.579
1939	102	329	101	16	1	20	6.1	66	68	41	50	5	.307	.544
1940	155	588	186	46	6	33	5.6	105	134	89	88	3	.316	.583
1941	155	590	153	29	3	27	4.6	91	111	92	88	3	.259	.456
1942	153	577	150	26	4	21	3.6	81	90	73	71	3	.260	.428
1943	155	571	155	22	11	34	6.0	90	118	84	88	5	.271	.527
1944	151	583	161	27	7	18	3.1	77	98	68	73	5	.276	.439
1945	155	595	157	25	5	18	3.0	71	87	59	85	6	.264	.413
10 years	1268	4677	1317	236	42	239	5.1	738	936	640	672	34	.282	.503

FIVE BEST CATCHERS

(William M. Anderson)

Johnny Bassler

	G	AB	H	2B	3B	HR	HR%	R	RBI	BB	SO	SB	BA	SA
1921	119	388	119	18	5	0	0.0	37	56	58	16	2	.307	.379
1922	121	372	120	14	0	0	0.0	41	41	62	12	2	.323	.360
1923	135	383	114	12	3	0	0.0	45	49	76	13	2	.298	.345
1924	124	379	131	20	3	1	0.3	43	68	62	11	2	.346	.422
1925	121	344	96	19	3	0	0.0	40	52	74	6	1	.279	.352
1926	66	174	53	8	1	0	0.0	20	22	45	6	0	.305	.362
1927	81	200	57	7	0	0	0.0	19	24	45	9	1	.285	.320
7 years	767	2240	690	98	15	1	0.0	245	312	422	73	10	.308	.367

FIVE BEST CATCHERS

(Mel Bailey)

Bill Freehan

	G	AB	H	2B	3B	HR	HR%	R	RBI	BB	SO	SB	BA	SA
1961	4	10	4	0	0	0	0.0	1	4	1	0	0	.400	.400
1963	100	300	73	12	2	9	3.0	37	36	39	56	2	.243	.387
1964	144	520	156	14	8	18	3.5	69	80	36	68	5	.300	.462
1965	130	431	101	15	0	10	2.3	45	43	39	63	4	.234	.339
1966	136	492	115	22	0	12	2.4	47	46	40	72	5	.234	.352
1967	155	517	146	23	1	20	3.9	66	74	73	71	1	.282	.447
1968	155	540	142	24	2	25	4.6	73	84	65	64	0	.263	.454
1969	143	489	128	16	3	16	3.3	61	49	53	55	1	.262	.405
1970	117	395	95	17	3	16	4.1	44	52	52	48	0	.241	.420
1971	148	516	143	26	4	21	4.1	57	71	54	48	2	.277	.465
1972	111	374	98	18	2	10	2.7	51	56	48	51	0	.262	.401
1973	110	380	89	10	1	6	1.6	33	29	40	30	0	.234	.313
1974	130	445	132	17	5	18	4.0	58	60	42	44	2	.297	.479
1975	120	427	105	17	3	14	3.3	42	47	32	56	2	.246	.398
1976	71	237	64	10	1	5	2.1	22	27	12	27	0	.270	.384
15 years	**1774**	**6073**	**1591**	**241**	**35**	**200**	**3.3**	**706**	**758**	**626**	**753**	**24**	**.262**	**.412**

FIVE BEST CATCHERS

(Mel Bailey)

Lance Parrish

	G	AB	H	2B	3B	HR	HR%	R	RBI	BB	SO	SB	BA	SA
1977	12	46	9	2	0	3	6.5	10	7	5	12	0	.196	.435
1978	85	288	63	11	3	14	4.9	37	41	11	71	0	.219	.424
1979	143	493	136	26	3	19	3.9	65	65	49	105	6	.276	.456
1980	144	553	158	34	6	24	4.3	79	82	31	109	6	.286	.499
1981	96	348	85	18	2	10	2.9	39	46	34	52	2	.244	.394
1982	133	486	138	19	2	32	6.6	75	87	40	99	3	.284	.529
1983	155	605	163	42	3	27	4.5	80	114	44	106	1	.269	.483
1984	147	578	137	16	2	33	5.7	75	98	41	120	2	.237	.443
1985	140	549	150	27	1	28	5.1	64	98	41	90	2	.273	.479
1986	91	327	84	6	1	22	6.7	53	62	38	83	0	.257	.483
10 years	1146	4273	1123	202	23	212	5.0	577	700	334	847	22	.263	.469

F I V E   B E S T   C A T C H E R S

(Mike Litaker)

Ivan Rodriguez

	G	AB	H	2B	3B	HR	HR%	R	RBI	BB	SO	SB	BA	SA
2004	135	527	176	32	2	19	3.6	72	86	41	91	7	.510	.334
2005	129	504	139	33	5	14	2.7	71	50	11	93	7	.444	.276
2006	136	547	164	28	4	13	2.3	74	69	26	86	8	.437	.300
2007	129	502	141	31	3	11	2.2	50	63	9	96	2	.420	.281
5 years	529	2080	620	124	14	57	2.7	267	268	87	366	24	.298	.450

FIVE BEST CATCHERS

(William M. Anderson)

George "Birdie" Tebbetts

	G	AB	H	2B	3B	HR	HR%	R	RBI	BB	SO	SB	BA	SA
1936	10	33	10	1	2	1	3	7	4	5	3	0	.303	.545
1937	50	162	31	4	3	2	1.2	15	16	10	13	0	.191	.290
1938	53	143	42	6	2	1	0.7	16	25	12	13	1	.294	.385
1939	106	341	89	22	2	4	1.2	37	53	25	20	2	.261	.372
1940	111	379	112	24	4	4	1.1	46	46	35	14	4	.296	.412
1941	110	359	102	19	4	2	0.6	28	47	38	29	1	.284	.376
1942	99	308	76	11	0	1	0.3	24	27	39	17	4	.247	.292
1946	87	280	68	11	2	1	0.4	20	34	28	23	1	.243	.307
1947	20	53	5	1	0	0	0.0	1	2	3	2	0	.094	.113
9 years	646	2058	535	99	19	16	0.8	194	254	195	135	13	.260	.350

Index